Universal's
Concise Commentary
on

The Specific Relief Act, 1963

(47 of 1963)

with

Exhaustive Case Law

First Edition 2015
Reprint September 2015

Universal's
Concise Commentary
on
The Specific Relief Act, 1963

(47 of 1963)

with

Exhaustive Case Law

Universal Law Publishing

an imprint of LexisNexis

LexisNexis®

This book is a publication of **LexisNexis®**
(A Division of Reed Elsevier India (Pvt) Ltd)
14th floor, Building No 10, Tower–B, DLF Cyber City, Phase-II,
Gurgaon–122002, Haryana, India.
Tel : + 91 124 4774444 Fax: + 91 124 4774100
Website : www.lexisnexis.co.in / E-mail : help.in@lexisnexis.com

---

Universal's Concise Commentary - *The Specific Relief Act, 1963,* Reprint 2015

ISBN: 978-93-5035-544-2

Printed by: Deepak Printers, Delhi

Printed and bound in India.

THE SPECIFIC RELIEF ACT, 1963

CONTENTS

CHAPTER V
CANCELLATION OF INSTRUMENTS

CHAPTER VI
DECLARATORY DECREES

TABLE OF CASES

S

THE SPECIFIC RELIEF ACT, 1963

INTRODUCTION

A mature legal system endeavours to provide not merely a remedy for every right infringed, but also an adequate remedy. It was in this process of a search for effective remedial action that Specific Relief emanated from the Equity Courts in England. The principles built up by successive Chancellors of England in this branch of law have been borrowed by the Indian Courts and have served to enrich the Indian Law. This fertilisation of Indian Law by the Equity Jurisprudence of England produced wider course of the Specific Relief Act of 1877. It was modelled on the draft New York Civil Code of 1862 and embodied in it the relevant doctrines evolved by the Courts of Equity in England. The Act of 1877 was not exhaustive. The jurisdiction of Courts in India to grant specific performance of contracts, for instance, existed independently of the Specific Relief Act. In localities to which that Act had no application, cases were governed by the ordinary rules of justice, equity and good conscience. For decades this Act was subjected to judicial interpretations which revealed many deficiencies and lacunae. Accumulated mass of case-law required a thorough overhaul of the provisions of the Act. The Law Commission appointed by the President of India after the advent of the new Constitution addressed itself to this task at its very first meeting. The recommendations of the Commission were embodied in its Ninth Report which was forwarded to the Government of India on 19th July, 1958. On the recommendations of the Law Commission a Bill was introduced in the Parliament on 23rd December, 1960 which lapsed on its dissolution. Again in 1962 the Specific Relief Bill, 1962 was introduced in the Parliament.

STATEMENT OF OBJECTS AND REASONS

This Bill seeks to implement the recommendations of the Law Commission contained in its Ninth Report on the Specific Relief Act, 1877, except, in regard to section 42 which is being retained as it now stands. An earlier Bill on the subject introduced in the Lok Sabha on the 23rd December, 1960, lapsed on its dissolution. The notes on clauses, extracted from the report of the Law Commission explain the changes made in the existing Act.

ACT 47 OF 1963

The Specific Relief Bill having been passed by both the Houses of Parliament received the assent of the President on 13th December, 1963. It came on the Statute Book as THE SPECIFIC RELIEF ACT, 1963 (47 of 1963).

LIST OF AMENDING ACTS

1. The Repealing and Amending Act, 1964 (52 of 1964) (w.e.f. 29-12-1964).
2. The Repealing and Amending Act, 1974 (56 of 1974) (w.e.f. 20-12-1974).

THE SPECIFIC RELIEF ACT, 1963

(47 of 1963)

[*13th December, 1963*]

An Act to define and amend the law relating to certain kinds of specific relief.

BE it enacted by Parliament in the Fourteenth Year of the Republic of India as follows:—

PART I
PRELIMINARY

1. Short title, extent and commencement.—(1) This Act may be called the Specific Relief Act, 1963.

(2) It extends to the whole of India except the State of Jammu and Kashmir.

(3) It shall come into force on such date[1] as the Central Government may, by notification in the Official Gazette, appoint.

2. Definitions.—In this Act, unless the context otherwise requires,—

(a) "obligation" includes every duty enforceable by law;

(b) "settlement" means an instrument [other than a will or codicil as defined by the Indian Succession Act, 1925 (39 of 1925)] whereby the destination or devolution of successive interests movable or immovable property is disposed of or is agreed to be disposed of;

(c) "trust" has the same meaning as in section 3 of the Indian Trusts Act, 1882 (2 of 1882), and includes an obligation in the nature of a trust within the meaning of Chapter IX of that Act;

(d) "trustee" includes every person holding property in trust;

(e) all other words and expressions used herein but not defined, and defined in the Indian Contract Act, 1872 (9 of 1872), have the meanings respectively assigned to them in that Act.

3. Savings.—Except as otherwise provided herein, nothing in this Act shall be deemed—

(a) to deprive any person of any right to relief, other than specific performance, which he may have under any contract; or

(b) to affect the operation of the Indian Registration Act, 1908, on documents.

4. Specific relief to be granted only for enforcing individual civil rights and not for enforcing penal laws.—Specific relief can be granted only for the purpose of enforcing individual civil rights and not for the mere purpose of enforcing a penal law.

1. Came into force on 1-3-1964, *vide* S.O. 189, dated 13th January, 1964, published in the Gazette of India, Pt. II, Sec. 3(ii), p. 214.

PART II

SPECIFIC RELIEF

CHAPTER I

RECOVERING POSSESSION OF PROPERTY

5. Recovery of specific immovable property.—A person entitled to the possession of specific immovable property may recover it in the manner provided by the Code of Civil Procedure, 1908 (5 of 1908).

SYNOPSIS

1. Auction-Purchaser – Law on
2. Cause of Action – Law on
3. Legislative Intent – Law on
4. Limitation – Law on
5. Possession
6. Immovable Property
7. Recovery of Possession of Immovable Property
8. Relief of Recovery of Possession as a Matter of Right and not Discretion
9. Entitled to Possession
10. Manner Provided by the Code of Civil Procedure
11. Defence

COMMENTS

1. Auction-Purchaser – Law on – Once an order was made under Order XXI, rule 92 confirming the sale, the title of the auction-purchaser related back to the date of sale as provided under section 65, C.P.C. The title in the property thereafter vests in the auction-purchaser and not in the judgment-debtor. The issue of sale certificate under Order XXI, rule 94, C.P.C. in favour of the auction-purchaser though mandatory but the granting of certificate is a ministerial act and not judicial; *Sagar Mahila Vidyalaya, Sagar* v. *Pandit Sadashiv Rao Harshe*, AIR 1991 SC 1825: JT 1991 (3) SC 75: 1991 (2) SCALE 32: 1991 (3) SCC 588 **[Hon'ble Judges:** S. Ranganathan, N.M. Kasliwal, S.C. Agrawal].

2. Cause of Action – Law on – A suit based on a plaint which discloses a cause of action is not necessarily to be dismissed on trial solely because it was premature on the date of its institution if by the time the written statement came to be filed or by the time the court is called upon to pass a decree, the plaintiff is found entitled to the relief prayed for in the plaint. Under section 80 of the C.P.C. no suit shall be instituted against the Government or a public officer until the expiration of two months next after service of notice in writing in the manner set out in the provision and if filed before the expiry of said period, the suit is not maintainable because there is clearly a public purpose underlying the provision. The object of the section is the advancement of justice and securing of public good by avoidance of unnecessary litigation; *Vithalbhai Pvt. Ltd.* v. *Union of India*, 2005 (2) SCR 680: AIR 2005 SC 1891: JT 2005 (3) SC 278: 2005 (3) SCALE 132.

3. Legislative Intent – Law on – A reading thereof manifests the legislative intent that if any person is dispossessed from immovable property without his consent otherwise than in due course of law, the person dispossessed or any person claiming through him, is empowered to lay the suit to recover possession thereof, notwithstanding any other title that may be set up in such a suit. But it shall be laid before expiry of six months from the date of dispossession. Such suit shall not lie against the government. The decree or any order passed in that suit shall not be subject to any appeal or review. But it is no bar to any person to sue to establish his title to such property and to recover possession thereof under section 5 in the manner provided in the Code of Civil Procedure, 1908; *East India Hotels Limited* v. *Syndicate Bank*, 1992 (1) Bank Cas 1: 1993 (1) Comp LJ 1: JT 1991 (6) SC 112: 1991 (2) SCALE 638.

4. Limitation – Law on – To be entitled to file a civil suit the plaintiff must be entitled to a relief and the suit must be of a civil nature excepting suits of which cognizance is either expressly or impliedly barred. Section 3 of the Limitation Act, 1963 provides that a suit filed after the prescribed period of limitation, shall be dismissed without regard to the fact whether limitation has been set up as a defence or not. However, there is no such provision which mandates a premature suit being dismissed for this reason. The only relevant provision is the one contained in rule 11 of Order VII of the C.P.C. which provides for a plaint being rejected where it does not disclose a cause of action. Though the plaint is not rejected, yet a suit may be dismissed if the Court on trial holds that the plaintiff was not entitled on the date of the institution of the suit to the relief sought for in the plaint; *Vithalbhai Pvt. Ltd.* v. *Union of India,* 2005 (2) SCR 680: AIR 2005 SC 1891: 2005 (3) SCALE 132: 2005 (4) SCC 315.

5. Possession – Mere occupation or actual user is not necessarily possession; *Bishmambhar Chand* v. *Naina Mal,* 25 IC 35: 14 PR 1915.

Possession consists of not merely physical contact but also a possibility of person dealing with a thing exclusively; *Emperor* v. *Lallu Waghju,* ILR 43 Bom 550: 50 IC 999: 21 Bom LR 251.

Possession implies two elements—(i) *corpus i.e.,* some actual power over the object possessed and apparent control over it; (ii) *animus i.e.,* a will to avail oneself of that power. Where a person in his own right has such control over property that he can exclude others from it and also has the intention of exercising such power of exclusion, he can be said to have possession of that property; *Ramachandra Deb* v. *State of Orissa,* AIR 1957 Ori 80: 23 Cut LT 324.

Possession and ownership are not synonyms. There may be cases where possession of property may be in one person but the ownership in another. But possession is *prima facie* though not by any means, conclusive proof of property. Possession constitutes a limited title to the property in the sense that his title is good against all except the rightful owner. Possession is protected against strangers but not against the true owner or his representative; *Panchabati Ramachandra* v. *Satyabhama Devi,* AIR 1971 Ori 135.

Possession follows title. Where the plaintiff establishes title to the suit property, he is entitled to decree for possession; *L.N. Aswathama* v. *P. Prakash,* (2009) 13 SCC 229 (236).

6. Immovable Property – A person may therefore establish possessory title to tree standing on land and their usufruct and successfully claim on an injunction against wrongful interference; *Pir Bux* v. *Sher Mohammad,* 1969 All LJ 169.

7. Recovery of Possession of Immovable Property – The title of a person who is in possession of the property holds good against the whole world except the true owner; *Kanti Lal* v. *Shanti Devi,* AIR 1997 Raj 230: (1997) 1 Raj LR 476: (1997) 2 Raj LW 1099.

Mere possessory title is good enough to maintain an action under section 5 of the Specific Relief Act, 1963; *Somnath Berman* v. *S.P. Raju,* AIR 1970 SC 846: (1969) 3 SCC 129.

A person who is in possession of lands allegedly for 70 years but is forcibly dispossessed by the defendant and files the suit against the latter for recovery of possession of land, he will succeed because a suit based on prior possession without proof of title, and therefore can eject the latter; *Nair Service Society Ltd.* v. *K.C. Alexander,* AIR 1968 SC 1165: (1968) 3 SCR 163.

In *Prabha Manufacturing Industrial Cooperative Society* v. *Banwari Lal,* AIR 1989 SC 1101: (1989) 2 SCC 69: JT 1989 (1) SC 397 the suit was filed by the society (tenant) for recovery of possession of land. As per concurrent finding of the two courts on facts, the plot of land had been allotted to the society. The Supreme Court, after revaluating evidence, as a special case, agreed with the said finding. It was therefore held that since the plot of land had been allotted to the society as a tenant, the respondent was justified in filing the suit to recover the possession of the property; *Prabha Manufacturing Industrial Co-op. Society* v. *Banwari Lal,* AIR 1989 SC 1101 (1110): (1989) 2 SCC 69: JT 1989 (1) SC 397.

If a plaintiff proves that was dispossessed within 12 years he can maintain his action; *Nair Service Society Ltd.* v. *K.C. Alexander*, AIR 1968 SC 1165: (1968) 3 SCR 163: 1968 SCD 500.

In a suit for recovery of possession along with prayer for partition and separate possession, the court below found that the plaintiffs were never dispossessed but they were entitled to partition and separate possession, the approach of the courts below was held to be not wrong; *Rajedra B. Choudhari* v. *State of Maharashtra*, AIR 2007 (NOC) 418 (Bom): 2007 (1) AIR Bom R 209 (DB).

8. Relief of Recovery of Possession as a Matter of Right and not Discretion – Where the plaintiff has title to the suit property entitling him to the possession of the property he can claim specific relief of possession and the court has no discretion to deny him the Specific Relief and award damages instead on the ground that enforcing of the specific relief would cause hardship to the defendant; *Sheriff Iqbal Hussain Ahmad* v. *Kota Venkata Subbamma*, AIR 1994 AP 164: 1994 (1) APLJ 349: 1994 (1) Andh LT 229: 1994 (3) Civ LJ 224.

9. Entitled to Possession – The expression "entitled to possession" means having right to possession. Where a person is entitled to possession of the immovable property, his possession will prevail unless some title better to him is shown; *Ismail Arif* v. *Mahomed Ghous*, ILR Cal 834 (843) (PC).

Where the plaintiff claimed possessory title on two grounds—(i) permanent settlement; and (ii) title by adverse possession for 60 years, even if he fails to prove his title by adverse possession but is able to establish his title on the ground of permanent settlement, his suit would be maintainable and would be entitled to the declaration asked for; *Haidar Khan* v. *Secretary of State for India in Council*, ILR 36 Cal 1.

Where a plaintiff has been in peaceful possession of the land, and is dispossessed by a trespasser (defendant), he will be entitled to recover the possession of the land by ejecting the defendant; *Satishchandra De* v. *Madanmohan Jati*, AIR 1931 Cal 483 (2): ILR 58 Cal 29.

A person (a tenant) having possessory title can recover possession even from his own landlord who has wrongfully dispossessed him; *Nasib Singh* v. *Bajo Ram*, AIR 1969 J&K 9: 1968 Kash LJ 127 (FB).

Where a person has been partially dispossessed of his land, he can sue to recover partial possession; *Saliapathi Chetti* v. *Subraya Chetti*, (1881) 3 Mad 250.

After the death of *'S'* his three sons succeeded his property. One of his sons *'H'* became 'Sadhu' and went out of village and spent time with Sadhus but he maintained his links with his family. It was not proved that *'H'* had renunciated the world. Held, plaintiffs claiming through other sons of *'S'* cannot challenge inheritance of estate of deceased by *'H'* and his two brothers, moreso, when other sons of *'S'* never assailed inheritance by *'H'*; *Ram Lok* v. *Bogalia*, AIR 2007 (NOC) 2512 (HP).

10. Manner Provided by the Code of Civil Procedure – In a suit for possession of immovable property there cannot be any doubt that all the relevant provisions of the Code of Civil Procedure shall apply; *Dadu Dayalu Mahasabha, Jaipur (Trust)* v. *Mahant Ram Niwas*, (2008) 11 SCC 753 (768): AIR 2008 SC 2187: 2008 AIR SCW 3324: (2008) 7 SCALE 460.

11. Defence – Where a suit for ejectment has been filed, the defendant may take the defence of his enforceable right for specific performance entitling him to continue occupation of land; *Hari Pada Mukherjee* v. *Elokeshi Devi*, AIR 1940 Cal 254: 44 CWN 357: 188 IC 249.

In all suits for recovery of possession of immovable property better title of the defendant is a good defence. Title is a exclusive defence in all suits; *Ganesh* v. *Dasso*, AIR 1927 All 669: 103 IC 428: 25 ALJ 857.

6. Suit by person dispossessed of immovable property.—(1) If any person is dispossessed without his consent of immovable property otherwise than in due course of law, he or any person claiming through him may, by suit, recover possession thereof, notwithstanding any other title that may be set up in such suit.

(2) No suit under this section shall be brought—

(a) after the expiry of six months from the date of dispossession; or

(b) against the Government.

(3) No appeal shall lie from any order or decree passed in any suit instituted under this section, nor shall any review of any such order or decree be allowed.

(4) Nothing in this section shall bar any person from suing to establish his title to such property and to recover possession thereof.

SYNOPSIS

COMMENTS

1. Adverse Possession – Law on – For bringing a suit for possession of immovable property the period of limitation is 12 years when the possession of a defendant becomes adverse to the plaintiff. Once a suit for recovery of possession is instituted against a defendant in adverse possession his adverse possession does not continue thereafter. In other words, the running of time for acquiring title by adverse possession gets arrested; *Babu Khan* v. *Nazim Khan*, AIR 2001 SC 1740: AIR 2001 SCW 1668: 2001 (3) SCALE 363: 2001 (5) SCC 375.

2. Apex Court – Duties of – Article 136 of the Constitution of India does not oblige this Court to fold its hands and become a helpless spectator even when Apex Court perceives that a manifest injustice has been occasioned. If and when the Court is satisfied that great injustice has been done it is not only the 'right' but also the 'duty' of Apex Court to reverse the error and the injustice and to upset the finding notwithstanding the fact that it has been affirmed thrice; *Indira Kaur* v. *Sheo Lal Kapoor*, AIR 1988 SC 1074: JT 1988 (1) SC 652: 1988 (1) SCALE 598: 1988 (2) SCC 488: 1988 (1) UJ 650 (SC).

3. Applicable of Provision in Case of State – Law on – The provisions of section 6 of the Specific Relief Act, 1963 are not applicable in the case of State. Having regard to the fact that the lands cannot be restored back even in a suit filed by the plaintiffs, what would be payable is the amount of compensation to which the plaintiffs may found to be entitled to, but the grant of compensation by no stretch of imagination can be equivalent to the market value of the land in view of the fact that the interest of the assignees in the land was limited. The State while acquiring lands can exercise its power of eminent domain. Solatium is paid only in terms of the provisions of the Land Acquisition Act. There does not exist provisions for payment of solatium if acquisition or requisition of the land is made in terms of the provisions of an Act other than the Land Acquisition Act. It is one thing to say that having regard article 300A of the Constitution of India that no citizen should be deprived of his right to property without payment [of compensation if] the State exercises its power of eminent domain, but, it is another thing to say that they would be entitled to the market value of the land as if they are the full owners thereof despite the fact that they are not. Grant of compensation, therefore, must be determined having regard to the nature of rights and other circumstances attending thereto; *State of Andhra Pradesh* v. *Bondapalli Sanyasi*, 2002 (2) ALD 1: 2002 (1) ALT 543 **[Hon'ble Judges:** S.B. Sinha, Motilal B. Naik, Bilal Nazki, B. Sudershan Reddy, Goda Raghuram].

4. Complete Prohibition of Filing of Further Appeal – Law on – A plain reading of the provision makes it abundantly clear that no further appeal shall lie from the judgment and decree of a single Judge to a Division Bench notwithstanding anything contained in any Letters Patent for any High Court or in any other instrument having the force of law or in any other law for the time being in force. There is a complete prohibition of filing of further appeal against the judgment and decree of a single Judge. It is a legislative declaration. The said legislative declaration prohibits preferring of a further appeal against the judgment and decree of a learned single Judge even if an appeal is provided in any other law for the time being in force. The expression 'in any instrument having the force of law or in any other law for the time being in force' takes into its ambit of the legislations including the special enactments where a right of appeal may have been provided against the judgment and decree of a learned single Judge to a Division Bench. What is prohibited prefers of a further appeal to a Division Bench against the judgment and decree of a single Judge not only under the Letters Patent for any High Court, but also under any special enactments even if an appeal is provided in such special enactments. No provision similar to section 100A of the Code, which prohibits filing of further appeal against the decree and judgment or order of a single Judge to a Division Bench notwithstanding anything contained in Letters Patent, had fallen for consideration in that case. On the other hand, it is implicit in the said judgment that the statutory enactment concerned can always exclude and affect the power flowing from the paramount charter under which an appeal may have been provided against the decree and judgment or order of a learned single Judge; *Gandla Pannala Bhulaxmi* v. *Managing Director, Andhra Pradesh State Road Transport Corporation*, 2003 (3) ACC 289: 2003 ACJ 2004: AIR 2003 AP 458: 2003 (4) ALT 216: 2003 (3) CTC 667.

5. Coparcenary Estate – Law on – It is true that a coparcener takes by birth an interest in the ancestral property, but he is not entitled to separate possession of the coparcenary estate. His rights are not independent of the control of the *karta*. It would be for the *karta* to consider the actual pressure on the joint family estate. It would be for him to foresee the danger to be averted. And it would be for him to examine as to how best the joint family estate could be beneficially put into use to subserve the interests of the family. A coparcener cannot interfere in these acts of management. Apart from that, a father - *karta* in addition to the aforesaid powers of alienation has also the special power to sell or mortgage ancestral property to discharge his antecedent debt which is not tainted with immorality. If there is no such need or benefit, the purchaser takes risk and the right and interest of coparcener will remain unimpaired in the alienated property. No doubt the law confers a right on the coparcener to challenge the alienation made by *karta*, but that right is not inclusive of the right to obstruct alienation. Nor the right to obstruct alienation could be considered as incidental to the right to challenge the alienation. These are two distinct rights. One is the right to claim a share in the joint family estate free from unnecessary and unwanted encumbrance. The other is a right to interfere with the act of management of the joint family affairs. The coparcener cannot claim the latter right and indeed, he is not entitled for it. Therefore, he cannot move the Court to grant relief by injunction restraining the *karta* from alienating the coparcenary property. Those who are of individualistic attitude and separate ownership may find it hard to understand the significance of a Hindu joint family and joint property. But it is there from the ancient time perhaps, as a social necessity. A Hindu joint family consists of male members descended lineally from a common male ancestor, together with their mothers. They are bound together by the fundamental principle of sapindaship or family relationship which is the essential feature of the institution. The cord that knits the members of the family is not property but the relationship of one another. The coparcenary consists of only those persons who have taken by birth an interest in the property of the holder and who can enforce a partition whenever they like. It is a narrower body than joint family. It commences with a common ancestor and includes a holder of joint property and only those males in his male line who are not removed from him by more than three degrees. The reason why coparcenership is so limited is to be found in the tenet of the Hindu religion that only male descendants up to three degrees can offer spiritual ministration to an ancestor. Only males can be coparceners. In a Hindu family, the *Karta* or manager occupies a unique position. It is not as if anybody could become manager of a joint Hindu family. "As a general rule, the father of a family, if alive, and in his absence the senior member of the family, is alone entitled to manage the joint family property." The manager occupies a position superior to other members. He has greater rights and duties. He must look after the family interests. He is entitled to possession of the entire joint estate. He is also entitled to manage the family properties. In other words, the actual possession and management of the joint family property must vest in him. He may consult the members of the family and if necessary take their consent to his action but he is not answerable to every one of them; *Sunil Kumar* v. *Ram Parkash*, AIR 1988 SC 576: JT 1988 (1) SC 387: 1988 (1) SCALE 80: 1988 (2) SCC 77.

6. Delivery of Immovable Property – Law on – Delivery of immovable property from the judgment-debtor should be obtained in execution of the decree under Order XXI, rules 35 and 36 within the period of limitation allowed under article 136 of the Schedule to the Limitation Act, 1963 without the need to file an independent suit for the purpose. It becomes, thereby, clear that after the expiry of the prescribed period, no independent suit for recovery of possession of the property which is the subject-matter of the decree, would lie; *Indian Iron and Steel Company Limited* v. *Chhaganlal Marwari, State of West Bengal*, 1994 (Supp 3) SCC 719.

7. Dispossession – Limitation for – The Limitation Act, before its recent amendment provided a period of twelve years as limitation to recover possession of immovable property when the plaintiff while in possession of the property was dispossessed or had discontinued possession and the period was calculated from the date of dispossession or discontinuance; *Nair Service Society Ltd.* v. *K.C. Alexander*, AIR 1968 SC 1165: 1968 (3) SCR 163 [**Hon'ble Judges:** M. Hidayatullah, S.M. Sikri, K.S. Hegde].

8. Expression 'Lawful Possession' – Law on – Law in general prescribes and insists upon a specified conduct in human relationship or even otherwise. Within the limits of the law, courts strive to take note of the moral fabric of the law. Besides under section 108(q) of the Transfer of Property Act, on the determination of the lease, the lessee is bound to put the lessor into possession of the property. Since the landlord has not assented to the lessee's continuance in possession of the property, the lessee will be liable to *mesne profits* which can again be recovered only in terms of his wrongful possession. Under section 5(1) of the Act, the licensing authority in deciding whether to grant or refuse a licence has regard, amongst others, to the interest of the public generally. Public interest is, therefore, also involved in granting or refusing a licence that being the position. The expression 'lawful possession' in rule 13 of the Tamil Nadu Cinemas (Regulation) Rules, 1957 assumes a peculiar significance of its own in the context of the provisions of the Act. Hence in any view of the matter possession of the respondents on the expiry of the lease is not lawful possession within the meaning of rule 13. The High Court is, therefore, not correct in its interpretation of rule 13 of Tamil Nadu Cinemas (Regulation) Rules, 1957. The Board of Revenue in appeal was, on the other hand, right in interfering with the order of the licensing authority and the learned single Judge of the High Court rightly refused to interfere with the order of the Board under article 226 of the Constitution; *M.C. Chockalingam* v. *V. Manickavasagam*, AIR 1974 SC 104: 1974 (1) SCC 48: 1974 (2) SCR 143.

9. High Court – Powers of – The High Court being the first Court of appeal was fully within its powers to re-examine and re-appreciate the documentary and oral evidence. It could come to a conclusion contrary to the one reached by the trial Court. High Court may be fully justified in taking a contrary view as it did and upsetting the judgment of the trial Court resulting in dismissal of the suit; *Narbada Devi Gupta* v. *Birendra Kumar Jaiswal*, AIR 2004 SC 175: 2003 (9) SCALE 210: 2003 (8) SCC 745: 2003 (7) Supreme 664.

Under article 227 of the Constitution the High Court ought not to have exercised its discretion and interfered with the judgment of the District Judge; *Anima Mallick* v. *Ajoy Kumar Roy*, 2000 (4) SCC 119.

10. Licensee – Right and Meaning of – The legal possession is always with the licensor and it does not create any interest or an estate in the licensee. A licensee is a person, who is neither a servant nor a "rank trespasser", but had come into possession with an authority. A rank trespasser is one who does not stand in any contractual relationship with the owner of the premises. A trespasser is also one who lawfully enters into but unlawfully remains in possession of the property without the consent or acquiescence of the owner. If one goes into possession of the property of another with invitation or permission for instance to a shop or cinema theatre, or marriage hall to celebrate a marriage his initial entry is lawful but if he refuses to leave that place and unlawfully squats on it, he becomes a trespasser of a transient origin with no vestige of right. The initial entry into possession is obviously for short duration with a specified purpose. But if he enters upon the land under a contract and uses the land or premises and does continuous business therein for well over a long period peacefully and uninterruptedly and continues to do the same even after the expiry or termination of licence, the important question arises whether he is a rank trespasser without any protection of law; *East India Hotels Limited* v. *Syndicate Bank*, 1993 (1) Comp LJ 1: JT 1991 (6) SC 112: 1991 (2) SCALE 638: 1992 (Supp 2) SCC 29.

11. Licensee and Trespasser – Law on – The position of licensee is no better than a trespasser and if the true owner comes into possession of the premises without using any force or on account of fire or other act of *vis* major, in my view it would not be in the interest of justice to grant a decree for possession in favour of such licensee under section 6 of the Act; *East India Hotels Limited* v. *Syndicate Bank,* 1993 (1) Comp LJ 1: JT 1991 (6) SC 112: 1991 (2) SCALE 638: 1992 (Supp 2) SCC 29.

12. Limitation Act – Law on – It is, therefore, manifest that the Limitation Act does not extinguish a defence, but only bars the remedy. Since the period of limitation bars a suit for specific performance of a contract, if brought after the period of limitation, it is open to a defendant in a suit for recovery of possession brought by a transferor to take a plea in defence of part performance of the contract to protect his possession, though he may not be able to enforce that right through a suit or action; *S.S. Suryavanshi* v. *P.B. Suryavanshi,* AIR 2002 SC 960: 2002 (2) SCALE 118: 2002 (3) SCC 676: 2002 (1) SCR 393.

13. Necessary Parties – Law on – It is true that a Court may go into a question at any stage if it goes to the root of the matter to decide its validity. Therefore, there is no quarrel on the proposition of law. But the failure to implead the necessary parties does not go to the root of the matter; nor does the execution of the contract in conformity with article 299(1) of the Constitution render the grant of *patta* void; *Beharilal* v. *Bhuri Devi,* AIR 1997 SC 1879: JT 1996 (11) SC 585: 1997 (1) SCALE 6: 1997 (2) SCC 279.

14. No Prayer for Possession – Effect of – Apart from granting a decree for possession as prayed for, the trial Court has granted an additional relief which was not prayed for by him in that the trial Court has directed to remove the construction put up by him including the dismantling of the glass. Such a relief cannot be granted under the provisions of section 6 of the Specific Relief Act, particularly, when there is no prayer therefor in the plaint; *Mahabir Prasad Jain* v. *Ganga Singh,* AIR 1999 SC 3873: 1999 (6) SCALE 370: 1999 (8) SCC 274: 1999 (8) Supreme 454.

15. Order under Section 145 Criminal Procedure Code – Effect of – If there had been an order under section 145, Cr.P.C. based on a compromise, the effect of that would have been that the possession in respect of land would have been restored to the second set of defendants. In that event, there would have been no occasion for the plaintiffs, as successors-in-interest of the second set of defendants, to file a suit for title and possession. Filing of the suit postulates that the possession with regard to the land in question remained with the first set of defendants. This could not have been possible if there had been any valid compromise between the parties resulting in an order passed under section 145, Cr.P.C; *Mst Jiria Devi* v. *Chhatiya Devi,* AIR 2000 SC 3542: AIR 2000 SCW 3388: 2000 (3) ICC 730: JT 2000 (7) SC 333.

16. Law of Jungle – Comments on – If such actions by the mighty or powerful are condoned in a democratic country, nobody would be safe nor can the citizens protect their properties. Law frowns upon such conduct. The Court accords legitimacy and legality only to possession taken in due course of law. If such actions are condoned, the fundamental rights guaranteed under the Constitution of India or the legal rights would be given go bye either by the authority or by rich and influential persons or by muscle men. Law of jungle will prevail and 'might would be right' instead of 'right being might'; *S.R. Ejaz* v. *Tamil Nadu Handloom Weavers Co.-op. Socy. Ltd.,* AIR 2002 SC 1152: 2002 (2) SCALE 304: 2002 (3) SCC 137: 2002 (2) SCR 31.

17. Possession – Law on – Law is well-settled that a person in possession has the right to protect his possession against the entire world, except the true owner and even so far as the true owner is concerned; such person in possession has a right, to be protected against any forcible dispossession by the true owner. Section 6 of the Specific Relief Act clearly protects the possession of a person and if a person is forcibly dispossessed, such person can recover his possession on the basis of his earlier possession if he files a suit within 6 months from the date of forcible dispossession. It is of course true that section 6 of the Specific Relief Act is not applicable against the Government. That however does not mean that the State is authorised to forcibly evict a trespasser from the Government land. Precisely, for the aforesaid purpose, specific provision has been made in the Land Encroachment Act and the Government is expected to follow the law which it has created.

In such a case, mandamus could be issued to the effect that the person should not be forcibly evicted without following the procedure contemplated in law; *Ramaraju S/o N.A. Subbaraja* v. *State of Tamil Nadu, Rep by its Secretary to Government, Revenue Department* [V. Selvaraj, N. Dhilipkumar, T. Lajapathi Roy, P. Srinivas, C. Selvaraj].

18. Possessory Title and Proprietary Title – Law on – Section 6 of the Specific Relief Act, 1963, provides for any person dispossessed without his consent of immovable property otherwise than in due course of law being entitled to claim and successfully sue for recovery of possession thereof, notwithstanding any other title that may be set up in such suit if the suit is brought before the expiry of six months from the date of dispossession except against the Government. Article 64 of Limitation Act, 1963 contemplates a suit for possession of immovable property based on previous possession, and not on title, being brought within twelve years from the date of dispossession. Such a suit is known in law as a suit based on possessory title as distinguished from proprietary title. The law discourages people from taking the law into their own hands, howsoever good and sound their title may be. Possession is nine points in law and law respects peaceful and settled possession. So, the person in possession may not have title to the property yet if he has been inducted into possession by the rightful owner and is in peaceful and settled possession of such property he is entitled in law to protect the possession until dispossessed by due process of law by a person having a title better than what he has. A person in possession of the property cannot be forcibly dispossessed by another rank trespasser and even if the latter does so, the former may be entitled to restoration of possession, because the law respects peaceful possession and frowns upon the person who takes the law in his own hands; *Ramesh Chand Ardawatiya* v. *Anil Panjwani*, AIR 2003 SC 2508: JT 2003 (4) SC 450: 2003 (4) SCALE 652: 2003 (7) SCC 350: 2003 (3) SCR 1149.

19. Provision – Nature of – If decree is passed in a summary suit under section 6 of the Special Relief Act, 1963, this degree would not affect the substantive suit to establish title and for recovery of possession; *Shashi Properties & Industries Ltd.* v. *Sunil Akash Sinha Choudhury*, AIR 2005 SC 1243: 2004 (6) SCALE 580: 2004 (7) SCC 515.

20. Provision Barring an Appeal or Revision – Law on – It is well-settled that any statutory provision barring an appeal or revision cannot cut across the constitutional power of a High Court. Even the power flowing from the paramount charter under which the High Court functions would not get excluded unless the statutory enactment concerned expressly excludes appeals under letters patent. No such bar is discernible from section 6(3) of the Act; *Vanita M. Khanolkar* v. *Pragna M. Pai*, AIR 1998 SC 424: 1997 (7) SCALE 356: 1998 (1) SCC 500: 1997 (10) Supreme 554.

21. Question of Title – Law on – Purpose behind section 6 of the Act is to restrain a person from using force and to dispossess a person without his consent otherwise than in due course of law. The ratio of the decided cases is that the court in trying a suit under section 6 of the Act will not go into the question of title. There cannot be any dispute with this settled proposition. However, in the present case the title of the company as well as the position of the plaintiff bank that its possession was as a licensee is an admitted case. The only prohibition under the provisions of section 6 of the Act is not to use force and not to use any unlawful means for dispossessing a person. Both these circumstances are lacking in the present case. The ratio of the decided cases is that the court in trying a suit under section 6 of the Act will not go into the question of title. There cannot be any dispute with this settled proposition; *East India Hotels Limited* v. *Syndicate Bank*, 1993 (1) Comp LJ 1: JT 1991 (6) SC 112: 1991 (2) SCALE 638: 1992 (Supp 2) SCC 29.

22. Claiming of Possession – Requirements for – The person averring a right to continue in possession shall, as far as possible, give a detailed particularized specific pleading along with documents to support his claim and details of subsequent conduct which establishes his possession. It would be imperative that one who claims possession must give all such details as enumerated hereunder. They are only illustrative and not exhaustive.

(a) Who is or are the owner or owners of the property;

(b) Title of the property;

(c) Who is in possession of the title documents?

(d) Identity of the claimant or claimants to possession;

(e) The date of entry into possession;

(f) How he came into possession, whether he purchased the property or inherited or got the same in gift or by any other method;

(g) In case he purchased the property, what is the consideration; if he has taken it on rent, how much is the rent, license fee or lease amount;

(h) If taken on rent, license fee or lease - then insist on rent deed, license deed or lease deed;

(i) Who are the persons in possession/occupation or otherwise living with him, in what capacity; as family members, friends or servants etc.;

(j) Subsequent conduct, *i.e.,* any event which might have extinguished his entitlement to possession or caused shift therein; and

(k) Basis of his claims that not to deliver possession but continue in possession.

Apart from these pleadings, the Court must insist on documentary proof in support of the pleadings. All those documents would be relevant which come into existence after the transfer of title or possession or the encumbrance as is claimed. While dealing with the civil suits, at the threshold, the Court must carefully and critically examine pleadings and documents. The Court will examine the pleadings for specificity as also the supporting material for sufficiency and then pass appropriate orders. If the pleadings do not give sufficient details, they will not raise an issue, and the Court can reject the claim or pass a decree on admission. On vague pleadings, no issue arises. Only when he so establishes, does the question of framing an issue arise. Framing of issues is an extremely important stage in a civil trial. Judges are expected to carefully examine the pleadings and documents before framing of issues in a given case. In pleadings, whenever a person claims right to continue in possession of another property, it becomes necessary for him to plead with specificity about who was the owner, on what date did he enter into possession, in what capacity and in what manner did he conduct his relationship with the owner over the years till the date of suit. He must also give details on what basis he is claiming a right to continue in possession. Until the pleadings raise a sufficient case, they will not constitute sufficient claim of defence; *Maria Margarida Sequeria Fernandes* v. *Erasmo Jack De Sequeria,* AIR 2012 SC 1727: 2012 (3) SCALE 550: 2012 (5) SCC 370: 2012 (3) SCR 841.

23. Recovery of Possession – Duty of Plaintiff for – In a suit for recovery of possession based on title it is for the plaintiff to prove his title and satisfy the Court that he, in law, is entitled to dispossess the defendant from his possession over the suit property and for the possession to be restored with him; *R.V.E. Venkatachala Gounder* v. *Arulmigu Viswesaraswami and V.P. Temple,* AIR 2003 SC 4548: 2003 (8) SCALE 474: 2003 (8) SCC 752: 2003 (8) Supreme 193.

24. Recovery of Possession – Law on – A landlord by letting out the property to a tenant does not lose possession as he continues to retain the legal possession although actual possession, user and control of that property is with the tenant. By retaining legal possession or in any case constructive possession, the landlord also retains all his legal remedies. As a matter of law, the dispossession of tenant by a third party is dispossession of the landlord. The word "dispossessed" in section 6(1) must be read in this context and not in light of the actual possession alone. If a tenant is thrown out forcibly from the tenanted premises by a trespasser, the landlord has implied right of entry in order to recover possession (for himself and his tenant). Similarly, the expression "any person claiming through him" would bring within its fold the landlord as he continues in legal possession over the tenanted property through his tenant. As a matter of fact, on plain reading of section 6(1), it is clear that besides the person who has been dispossessed, any person claiming through him can also file a suit seeking recovery of possession. Obviously, a landlord who holds the possession through his tenant is competent to maintain suit under section 6 and recover possession from a trespasser who has forcibly dispossessed his tenant. A landlord when he lets out his property to the tenant is not deprived of his possession in the property in law. What is altered is mode in which the landlord held his possession in the property inasmuch as the tenant comes into physical possession while the landlord retains possession through his tenant; *Sadashiv Shyama Sawant (Dead) Through LRs.* v. *Anita Anant Sawant,* 2010 (2) SCALE 530: 2010 (3) SCC 385: 2010 (2) SCR 1070.

25. Recovery of Possession – Requirement for – It is trite to say that section 6 of the Specific Relief Act gives a summary remedy to the plaintiff to seek restoration of possession from the defendant within six months of illegal recovery of possession by the defendant, without referring to the title of the plaintiff and defendant. It is purely a possessory suit wherein status of the party is irrelevant. In such type of suits the plaintiff is not required to prove his title or a superior right to possession as compared to the defendant and has only to show that he was in possession of the suit immovable property and he was illegally dispossessed within a period of six months prior to the date of the suit. Once the plaintiff proves this case, he becomes entitled to succeed and can get status quo ante and restoration of possession of the suit premises through the assistance of the Court; *Mansukhlal Dhanraj Jain* v. *Eknath Vithal Ogale,* AIR 1995 SC 1102: JT 1995 (8) SC 293: 1995 (1) SCALE 513: 1995 (2) SCC 665.

26. Relief for Possession – Law on – There may be circumstances in which a relief for possession cannot be effectively granted to the decree-holder without specifically claiming relief for possession, *viz.,* where the property agreed to be conveyed is jointly held by the defendant with other persons. In such a case the plaintiff in order to obtain complete and effective relief must claim partition of the property and possession over the share of the defendant. It is in such cases that a relief for possession must be specifically pleaded; *Babu Lal* v. *Hazari Lal Kishori Lal,* AIR 1982 SC 818: 1982 GLH 954: 1982 (1) SCALE 79: 1982 (1) SCC 525: 1982 (3) SCR 94.

27. Second Appellate Court – Restriction for – Under section 100, C.P.C. in Second Appeal it was not open to the Second Appellate Court to reappreciate the evidence and reject the evidence accepted by the Courts below on the question of possession; *Tirumala Tirupati Devsthanam* v. *K.M. Krishnaiah,* AIR 1998 SC 1132: 1998 (2) SCALE 119: 1998 (3) SCC 331:1998 (2) Supreme 267.

28. Statutory Functions and Non-Statutory Function – Law on – Statutory Bodies may perform statutory functions and may perform non-statutory function. When Statutory Bodies perform statutory functions their acts will be amenable to judicial review by the Court. When Statutory Bodies perform non-statutory functions their acts may not be amenable to judicial review by the Court. When non-statutory bodies perform non-statutory functions, their acts will not be subject to judicial review by the Court but when they perform statutory functions there is no valid reason why it not be held that their actions will be amenable to judicial review by the Court inasmuch as non-statutory bodies when performing statutory functions will be nothing else than mere instrumentalities acting under the Statute which imposes duties upon it affecting the rights of third persons and parties; *Vaish College (Society) Shamli* v. *Lakshmi Narain,* AIR 1974 All 1 **[Hon'ble Judges:** K.B. Asthana, R.B. Misra, T.S. Misra].

29. Suit for Ejectment – Law on – Where a suit for ejectment is filed on the basis of tenancy and relationship of landlord and tenant, then such suit should not be converted into a title suit based on ownership and the controversy should be decided on the basis of the relationship of landlord and tenant only. There can be no manner of dispute that in a suit for eviction on the basis of tenancy, all that need be gone into is whether there is a contract of tenancy between the parties and if the plaintiff fails to prove such contract of tenancy, then the court is entitled to dismiss such suit. But in a case where the question of title has also been gone into and the parties were at issue on the point of title and the parties had led evidence, it would not be just and proper to direct the plaintiff to file another suit for possession on the basis of title. Law Courts always discourage and abhor the multiplicity of suits; *Pushpa Sharma* v. *Gopal Lal Rawat*, AIR 1986 Raj 187: 1986 Raj LW 618: 1986 RLR 623 **[Hon'ble Judges:** Dwarka Prasad, N.M. Kasliwal, S.N. Bhargava].

30. Suit for Ejection and for Possession – Requirement for – If the plaintiff's suit is for ejection and for possession of the suit property, she must succeed or fail on the title that she establishes. If she cannot succeed in proving her title, the suit must fail notwithstanding that the defendant in possession may or may not have title to the property; *Bajranglal Shivchandrai Ruia* v. *Shashikant N. Ruia*, AIR 2004 SC 2546: 2004 (3) SCALE 580: 2004 (5) SCC 272: 2004 (5) Supreme 711.

31. Suit for Mandatory Injunction – Additional Relief Therein – If the suit is in effect one for possession though couched in the form of a suit for mandatory injunction as what would be given to the plaintiff in case he succeeds in possession of the property to which he may be found to be entitled. Courts are of the opinion that the plaintiff should not be denied relief merely because he had couched the plaint in the form of a suit for mandatory injunction; *Sant Lal Jain* v. *Avtar Singh*, AIR 1985 SC 857: 1985 (1) SCALE 423: 1985 (2) SCC 332: 1985 (3) SCR 184.

32. Suit for Possession – Limitation for – Article 58 of the Limitation Act, 1963, prescribes limitation of three years from the date when the right to sue first accrues to obtain a declaration. Under article 65, the period of limitation prescribed for filing a suit for possession of immovable property or any interest therein based on title is 12 years from the date when possession of the defendants becomes adverse to the plaintiff. It held that the suit for possession would be governed by article 65 of the Limitation Act, 1963. It was further held that a suit is within time even from the date when the possession of the suit property was taken on the execution of the sale deed; *State of Maharashtra* v. *Pravin Jethalal Kamdar*, AIR 2000 SC 1099: 2000 (2) SCALE 239: 2000 (3) SCC 460.

33. Vendor's Obligations under Agreement – Law on – Relief for possession in favour of the successful plaintiff in a suit for specific performance cannot be considered as a separate and distinct one. The same is only an ancillary or consequential one. Accordingly, the said prayer for delivery of possession of the property agreed to be transferred cannot be treated as an additional relief chargeable with court fees under clause (v) of 7 of the West Bengal Court Fees Act, 1970. When an agreement for transfer of an immovable property is enforced by the court upon the plaintiff fulfilling his part of the obligation, the defendant vendor is bound not only to execute necessary documents in favour of the plaintiff vendee and to register the same but also to put the said vendee in possession in discharge of the vendor's obligations under the said agreement. The said obligation of the vendee has been recognised both in section 55(1)(f) and section 108(b) of the Transfer of Property Act; *Jathia Estate Pvt. Ltd.* v. *Dhiraj Bala Karia*, 1982 (1) Cal LT 252 **[Hon'ble Judges:** Ramendra Mohan Datta, Pabitra Kumar Banerjee, Chittatosh Mookerji].

34. Wrongfully Dispossessed from Property Recovering it by Proving Previous Possession – Law on – Section 6 of the Specific Relief Act, 1963 says that if any person is dispossessed without his consent of immovable property otherwise than in due course of law, he or any person claiming through him may, by suit recover possession thereof, notwithstanding any other title that may be set up in such suit. Section 6 is a corresponding provision to section 9 of the Specific Relief Act, 1877. Section 9 of the earlier Act, which has been retained with some changes in the Specific Relief Act, 1963 is based on the principle that even a trespasser is entitled to protect his possession except against a true owner and purports to protect a person in possession from being dispossessed except in due course of law. Section 6 provides a summary remedy for a person who being in possession of immovable property is ousted therefrom. In such circumstances, it is possible that the person so dispossessed may pursue summary and speedy remedy through the medium of the Civil Court for restoration of possession. This section is a reproduction of provision of the Roman Law under which by an *interdictum de via* person wrongfully dispossessed from property could recover it by proving previous possession, without being required to prove his title. Disputed questions of title are to be decided by due process of law but the peaceful possession is to be protected from a trespasser under section 6 of the Act without regard to the question of the origin of the possession. Such suit can be entertained and decreed, only where both the plaintiff and the defendant have no title to the suit land, but as the plaintiff proves his prior possession, because of that he is entitled to a decree for possession against the defendant who has dispossessed him; *Nagar Palika, Jind* v. *Jagat Singh, Advocate*, AIR 1995 SC 1377: JT 1995 (3) SC 281: 1995 (2) SCALE 512: 1995 (3) SCC 426.

35. Forcible Dispossession – Law on – There are two different sets of principles which have to be borne in mind regarding course to be adopted in case of forcible dispossession. Taking up the first aspect, it is true that where a person is in settled possession of property, even on the assumption that he has no right to remain in property, he cannot be deposed by the owner except by recourse of law. This principle is laid down in section 6 of the Specific Relief Act, 1963. That section says that if any person is dispossessed without his consent from immovable property otherwise than in due course of law, he or any person claiming through him may, by suit, recover possession thereof, notwithstanding any other title that may be set up in such suit. That a person without title but in "settled" possession - as against mere fugitive possession - can get back possession 'if' forcibly dispossessed or rather, if dispossessed otherwise than by due process of law, has been laid down in several cases; *Sopan Sukhdeo Sable* v. *Assistant Charity Commissioner*, 2004 (1) SCR 1004: AIR 2004 SC 1801: 2004 (3) SCC 137: 2004 (3) SRJ 97; *Yashwant Singh* v. *Jagdish Singh,* AIR 1968 SC 620; *Krishna Ram Mohate* v. *Mrs. Shobha Venkata Rao,* 1989 (4) SCC 131 (136); *Ram Rattan* v. *State of Uttar Pradesh*, 1977 (1) SCC 188 and *State of Uttar Pradesh* v. *Maharaja Dharmender Prasad Singh,* 1989 (2) SCC 505. The leading decision quoted in these rulings is the decision of the Bombay High Court in *K.K. Verma* v. *Union of India,* AIR 1954 Bom 358.

36. Relinquishment – Law on – Under Order II, rule 1 of the Code which contains provisions of mandatory nature, the requirement is that the plaintiffs are duty bound to claim the entire relief. The suit has to be so framed as to afford ground for final decision upon the subjects in dispute and to prevent further litigation concerning them. Rule 2 further enjoins on the plaintiff to include the whole of the claim which the plaintiff is entitled to make in respect of the cause of action. If the plaintiff omits to sue or intentionally relinquishes any portion of his claim, it is not permissible for him to sue in respect of the portion so omitted or relinquished afterwards; *Sopan Sukhdeo Sable* v. *Assistant Charity Commissioner*, 2004 (1) SCR 1004: AIR 2004 SC 1801: 2004 (2) SCALE 82: 2004 (2) Supreme 40.

37. Remedy of a Person Unsuccessful in a Suit – Law on – A suit under section 6 of the Act is often called a summary suit inasmuch as the enquiry in the suit under section 6 is confined to finding out the possession and dispossession within a period of six months from the date of the institution of the suit ignoring the question of title. Sub-section (3) of section 6 provides that no appeal shall lie from any order or decree passed in any suit instituted under this section. No review of any such order or decree is permitted. The remedy of a person unsuccessful in a suit under section 6 of the Act is to file a regular suit establishing his title to the suit property and in the event of his succeeding he will be entitled to recover possession of the property notwithstanding the adverse decision under section 6 of the Act. Thus, as against a decision under section 6 of the Act, the remedy of unsuccessful party is to file a suit based on title. The remedy of filing a revision is available but that is only by way of an exception; for the High Court would not interfere with a decree or order under section 6 of the Act except on a case for interference being made out within the well-settled parameters of the exercise of revisional jurisdiction under section 115 of the Code; *Sanjay Kumar Pandey* v. *Gulbahar Sheikh*, AIR 2004 SC 3354: 2004 (4) SCALE 441: 2004 (4) SCC 664: 2004 (3) Supreme 205.

38. Suit for Recovery of Possession – Law on – A person who has been illegally dispossessed of his immovable property may himself or through any person claiming through him recover such possession by filing a suit. In such a suit, the entitlement of the plaintiff to recover possession of property from which he claims to have been illegally dispossessed has to be adjudicated independently of the question of title that may be set up by the defendant in such a suit. In a suit under section 6, the only question that has to be determined by the Court is whether the plaintiff was in possession of the disputed property and he had been illegally dispossessed therefrom on any date within six months prior to the filing of the suit. This is because section 6(2) prescribes a period of six months from the date of dispossession as the outer limit for filing of a suit. As the question of possession and illegal dispossession therefrom is the only issue germane to a suit under section 6, a proceeding thereunder, naturally, would partake the character of a summary proceeding against which the remedy by way of appeal or review has been specifically excluded by sub-section 3 of section 6. Sub- section 4 also makes it clear that an unsuccessful litigant in a suit under section 6 would have the option of filing a fresh suit for recovery of possession on the basis of title, if any. Though section 6(3) of the Act of 1963 bars the remedy of appeal and review, a small window, by way of a revision, was kept open by the legislature possibly to enable the High Court to have a second look in the matter in an exceptional situation; *I.T.C. Limited* v. *Adarsh Co-op. Housing Soc. Ltd.*, 2012 (8) SCALE 11: 2013 (10) SCC 169: 2012 (4) ICC 8.

39. Material 'Facts' and 'Particulars' – Law on – The Order VII, rule 11 does not justify rejection of any particular portion of the plaint; Order VI, rule 16 of the Code is relevant in this regard. It deals with, 'striking out pleadings'. It has three clauses permitting the Court at any stage of the proceeding to strike out or amend any matter in any pleading *i.e.*, (a) which may be unnecessary, scandalous, frivolous or vexatious, or, (b) which may tend to prejudice, embarrass or delay the fair trial of the suit, or (c) which is otherwise an abuse of the process of the Court. Order VI, rule 2(1) of the Code states the basic and cardinal rule of pleadings and declares that the pleading has to state material facts and not the evidence. It mandates that every pleading shall contain, and contain only, a statement in a concise form of the material facts on which the party pleading relies for his claim or defence, as the case may be, but not the evidence by which they are to be proved; *Sopan Sukhdeo Sable* v. *Assistant Charity Commissioner*, 2004 (1) SCR 1004: AIR 2004 SC 1801: 2004 (2) SCALE 82: 2004 (3) SCC 137.

40. Possession – Comments on – The key words in section 6(1) are "dispossessed" and "he or any person claiming through him". A person is said to have been dispossessed when he has been deprived of his possession; such deprivation may be of actual possession or legal possession. Possession in law follows right to possession. The right to possession, though distinct from possession, is treated as equivalent to possession itself for certain purposes; *Sadashiv Shyama Sawant (Dead) Through LRs.* v. *Anita Anant Sawant*, JT 2010 (2) SC 305: 2010 (2) SCALE 530: 2010 (3) SCC 385: 2010 (2) SCR 1070.

41. Provision – Purpose of – A proceeding under section 6 is intended to be a summary proceeding the object of which is to afford an immediate remedy to an aggrieved party to reclaim possession of which he may have been unjustly denied by an illegal act of dispossession. Questions of title or better rights of possession does not arise for adjudication in a suit under section 6 where the only issue required to be decided is as to whether the plaintiff was in possession at any time six months prior to the date of filing of the suit. The legislative concern underlying section 6 is to provide a quick remedy in cases of illegal dispossession so as to discourage litigants from seeking remedies outside the arena of law. The same is evident from the provisions of section 6(3) which bars the remedy of an appeal or even a review against a decree passed in such a suit; *Mohd. Mehtab Khan* v. *Khushnuma Ibrahim,* JT 2013 (2) SC 522: 2013 (1) SCALE 731: AIR 2013 SC 1099: 2013 (9) SCC 221.

42. Provision – Purview of – Plaintiff has not only prayed for grant of a decree for permanent injunction but has also asked for passing a decree for mandatory injunction directing the defendants to handover possession to it. Such prayers would not come within the purview of section 6 of the Specific Relief Act; *H.P. Vedavyasachar* v. *Shivashankara,* 2009 (11) SCALE 31: 2009 (8) SCC 231: 2009 (5) SCJ 254.

43. Recovery of Possession of Immovable Property – Law on – In an action for recovery of possession of immovable property, or for protecting possession thereof, upon the legal title to the property being established, the possession or occupation of the property by a person other than the holder of the legal title will be presumed to have been under and in subordination to the legal title, and it will be for the person resisting a claim for recovery of possession or claiming a right to continue in possession, to establish that he has such a right. To put it differently, wherever pleadings and documents establish title to a particular property and possession is in question, it will be for the person in possession to give sufficiently detailed pleadings, particulars and documents to support his claim in order to continue in possession. Once the title is *prima facie* established, it is for the person who is resisting the title holder's claim to possession to plead with sufficient particularity on the basis of his claim to remain in possession and place before the Court all such documents as in the ordinary course of human affairs are expected to be there. Only if the pleadings are sufficient, would an issue be struck and the matter sent to trial, where the onus will be on him to prove the averred facts and documents; *Maria Margarida Sequeria Fernandes* v. *Erasmo Jack De Sequeria,* AIR 2012 SC 1727: 2012 (3) SCALE 550: 2012 (5) SCC 370: 2012 (3) SCR 841.

44. Term "Due Diligence" – Meaning of – The primary aim of the court is to try the case on its merits and ensure that the rule of justice prevails. For this the need is for the true facts of the case to be placed before the court so that the court has access to all the relevant information in coming to its decision. Therefore, at times it is required to permit parties to amend their plaints. The Court's discretion to grant permission for a party to amend his pleading lies on two conditions, *firstly,* no injustice must be done to the other side and *secondly,* the amendment must be necessary for the purpose of determining the real question in controversy between the parties. Due diligence is the idea that reasonable investigation is necessary before certain kinds of relief are requested. Duly diligent efforts are a requirement for a party seeking to use the adjudicatory mechanism to attain an anticipated relief. An advocate representing someone must engage in due diligence to determine that the representations made are factually accurate and sufficient. The term 'Due diligence' is specifically used in the Code so as to provide a test for determining whether to exercise the discretion in situations of requested amendment after the commencement of trial. A party requesting a relief stemming out of a claim is required to exercise due diligence and is a requirement which cannot be dispensed with. The term "due diligence" determines the scope of a party's constructive knowledge, claim and is very critical to the outcome of the suit; *J. Samuel* v. *Gattu Mahesh,* 2012 (1) SCALE 330: 2012 (2) SCC 300: AIR 2012 SC 811: 2012 (1) SCR 295.

7. Recovery of specific movable property.—A person entitled to the possession of specific movable property may recover it in the manner provided by the Code of Civil Procedure, 1908.

Explanation 1.—A trustee may sue under this section for the possession of movable property to the beneficial interest in which the person for whom he is trustee is entitled.

Explanation 2.—A special or temporary right to the present possession of movable property is sufficient to support a suit under this section.

SYNOPSIS

1. Weakness of Defendant's Case – Effect of
2. Specific Movable Property
3. Who can sue under this Section
4. Remedy Provided by Civil Procedure Code
5. *Explanation 1*: Trustee

COMMENTS

1. Weakness of Defendant's Case – Effect of – The plaintiff must succeed or fail on his own case and cannot take advantage of weakness in the defendant's case to get a decree; *Punjab Urban Planning and Development Authority* v. *Shiv Saraswati Iron and Steel Re-Rolling Mills*, AIR 1998 SC 2352: 1998 (2) SCALE 451: 1998 (4) SCC 539: 1998 (3) Supreme 269.

2. Specific Movable Property – Title deeds, share certificate, government securities etc., are movable property but money is not movable property; *Bhubaneswar Bhattcharjee* v. *Dwarkeswar Bhattacharjee*, AIR 1921 Cal 77: 66 IC 876.

Section 7 applies only when the property is specific. That is to say, property must be either ascertained or ascertainable; *Muguesa Mudali* v. *Jutharam Davay*, (1899) 22 Mad 478.

Besides this, the property must be such as can be seized and delivered; *Fadu Jhala* v. *Gour Jhala*, (1892) 19 Cal 544.

Trees, *Umed Ram* v. *Daulat Ram*, ILR 5 All 564 tiled huts; *Raj Chunder* v. *Dhurmo*, 10 Suth WR 416: 8 BLR 510 and standing corps; *Sadu* v. *Sambhu*, ILR 6 Bom 592; *Narasimham* v. *Venkiah*, 31 IC 796 are not movable property.

The suit was filed for issuing direction to defendant to hand over original sale-deed to plaintiff. No relief was claimed for declaration that *pro-forma* defendant was merely benamidar of plaintiff. There was nothing on record to show that *pro-forma* defendant had any knowledge of pendency of title suit. Therefore, the decree passed in suit on the basis of compromise that the defendants should hand over original sale-deed and in case of non-compliance, certified copy of sale-deed would be deemed to be original deed was held to be not binding on *pro-forma* defendant or his successor-in-interest; *Uma Shankar Mishra* v. *Pradeep Singh*, AIR 2008 (NOC) 1530 (Pat).

3. Who can sue under this Section – A person who has present or immediate possession may sue to recover specific movable property under section 7; *Patta Kumari Bibi* v. *Nirmal Kumar Sinha*, AIR 1948 Cal 97: 51 CWN 544: ILR (1948) 1 Cal 55.

A bailee, pawnee holder of lien or a finder of goods may also sue to recover movable property; *White* v. *Morsis*, (1852) 21 LJC 185.

4. Remedy Provided by Civil Procedure Code – A person entitled to recover property or to its delivery may also sue for its value; *Bhonajee* v. *Saraswati*, AIR 1924 Nag 176: 75 IC 833.

Where the defendant is not in possession of the property, the court may awarded a decree for its value; *Jaldu Venkatasubbarao* v. *Asiatic Steam Navigation Co. Ltd.*, AIR 1916 Mad 314: ILR 39 Mad 1.

This is the case when the goods cannot be delivered. If the good are capable of being delivered, they must be delivered; *Kashinath* v. *Debkristo,* 16 WR 240.

Where the plaintiff claims value of the goods, he can also claim special damages for the detention but for making such a claim the plaintiff will have to resort to the procedure laid down in Order XXI, rule 31 of the code of Civil Procedure; *Parathasathi Ray* v. *Ahindranath Ray,* AIR 1935 Cal 89: 61 Cal 711.

5. *Explanation 1*: Trustee – According to *Explanation* 1 a trustee may sue under this section for the possession of movable property and it is not at all necessary that the beneficiary must be the plaintiff. The Trustee may sue because he represents the beneficiary and may sue for the beneficial interest in which the person, for whom he is trustee is entitled; *Sathianama* v. *Sarav,* ILR 18 Mad 266 (272).

8. Liability of person in possession, not as owner, to deliver to persons entitled to immediate possession.—Any person having the possession or control of a particular article of movable property, of which he is not the owner, may be compelled specifically to deliver it to the person entitled to its immediate possession, in any of the following cases:—

(a) when the thing claimed is held by the defendant as the agent or trustee of the plaintiff;

(b) when compensation in money would not afford the plaintiff adequate relief for the loss of the thing claimed;

(c) when it would be extremely difficult to ascertain the actual damage caused by its loss;

(d) when the possession of the thing claimed has been wrongfully transferred from the plaintiff.

Explanation.—Unless and until the contrary is proved, the court shall, in respect of any article of movable property claimed under clause (b) or clause (c) of this section, presume—

(a) that compensation in money would not afford the plaintiff adequate relief for the loss of the thing claimed, or, as the case may be;

(b) that it would be extremely difficult to ascertain the actual damage caused by its loss.

SYNOPSIS

1. Sections 7 and 8—Distinction
2. Specific Delivery and Specific Performance
3. Clause (a): Defendant as Trustee or Agent
4. Clause (c): Damage Difficult to Ascertain
5. Clause (d): Possession Wrongfully Transferred from Plaintiff
6. *Explanation*—Presumption and Burden of Proof

COMMENTS

1. Sections 7 and 8—Distinction – Under section 8, a suit can not be instituted against the owner of the movable property. On the other hand, under section 7 a suit by a person having temporary or special right to possession of specific movable property is competent to file suit to recover possession even against owner of the movable property. Under section 8, the suit is for the return of movable property specifically under clause (b) or (c). But under section 7, the suit is for the return of movable property or for the money value of the article in the alternative. Under section 7 the suit instituted under Order 20, rule 10 and its execution is secured under Order 2, rules 30(31) of the Code of Civil Procedure, 1908.

2. Specific Delivery and Specific Performance – The specific delivery contemplated under section 8 is right to possess. On the other hand, specific performance is based on contract.

3. Clause (a): Defendant as Trustee or Agent – Where a beneficiary filed the suit for accounts against the trustee, he will be entitled to recover movable property from the trustee; *Maharaja Srish Chandra Nandy* v. *Supravat Chandra*, AIR 1946 Cal 337: 50 CWN 417.

Where a person delivered to the defendant a cinematograph project or under a contract to the effect that price of the projector would be payable in instalment and the ownership of the projector would remain with him until all the instalments have been paid. He also, resumed the right to cancel the contract on default of any instalment. The defendant having defaulted, he cancelled the contract and demanded the return of the projector. It was held that the contract having been cancelled, the defendant held the projector in a fiduciary position and was liable to return the projector; *G.J. Subbarayulu* v. *Arman Annamalai Chettiar*, AIR 1945 Mad 281: (1946) Mad 174.

4. Clause (c): Damage Difficult to Ascertain – Any person having the possession or control of a particular article of movable property, of which he is not the owner, may be compelled to deliver it to the person entitled to its immediate possession when it would be extremely difficult to ascertain the actual damage caused by its loss. This clause is applicable to things or articles which because of artistic quality, rareness or antiquity, because of association are such that it is very difficult to assess their value in terms of money. Moreover, beauty or preciousness of an artistic production such as a painting or sculptur is in the eye of beholder. Since it is difficult to assess damage for loss of such things, such things must be returned specifically. An article may be of special interest or special character that actual damage by its loss is extremely difficult to ascertain and the person in whose possession such an article is liable to return specifically to person who is entitled to its immediate possession; *Shankar Murlidhar* v. *Mohan Lal Jaduram*, (1887) 11 Bom 704.

5. Clause (d): Possession Wrongfully Transferred from Plaintiff – Clause (d) of section 8 deals with cases of specific movable property the possession of which has been wrongfully transferred from the plaintiff. For example, where the property has been wrongfully obtained by the defendant by fraud; *Kartic Charan Shetty* v. *Gopal Kisto Pandit*, ILR (1877) 3 Cal 264: ILR 3 Cal 264.

Where a purchaser of goods makes the payment by cheque and gives the cheque knowing that it would be dishonoured the seller would be entitled to get the value of goods form even receiver where the purchaser becomes insolvent; *Sankaralinga Nadar* v. *Ouseph Chacko*, (1963) 1 Ker LR 443: 1963 Ker LJ 387.

Where a lady pledged ornaments belonging exclusively to her husband without being authorized to the defendant the husband would be entitled to recover the ornaments; *Sagar* v. *Hukmakessa*, ILR 24 Bom 458.

So is the case where a servant pledged goods of his master without permission or authorization; *Biddomoye Dabee* v. *Sitaram*, (1878) 4 Cal 497.

6. *Explanation*—Presumption and Burden of Proof – Under section 8(b) and (c) a presumption arises that money would not afford the plaintiff adequate relief for loss of the thing claimed or that it would be extremely difficult to ascertain the actual damage caused by its loss. That is to say, burden of proving that compensation in money would afford the plaintiff adequate relief for the loss of the thing claimed or as the case may be, that it would not be extremely difficult to ascertain the actual damage caused by its loss, would be on the defendant. If the defendant fails to prove this, the plaintiff will be entitled to the return of the goods specifically. In cases where such a presumption arises, the plaintiff is in advantageous position. It is for the plaintiff to prove his case. But in cases where such a presumption arises the onus of proving shifts from the plaintiff to the defendant. If the defendant fails to rebut the presumption, the plaintiff will succeed and the court will compel the defendant to specifically deliver the thing. Where, however the defendant rebuts the presumption, court may not provide relief *in specie* and may award compensation for the loss of the thing. For getting the relief however, it is necessary for the plaintiff to allege and prove that the defendant is in possession of the thing and that he is entitled to its immediate possession; *Jaldu Venkatasubba Rao* v. *Asiatic Steam Navigation Co. Ltd.*, AIR 1916 Mad 314: 30 Mad 1: 30 IC 840 (FB).

CHAPTER II

SPECIFIC PERFORMANCE OF CONTRACTS

9. Defences respecting suits for relief based on contract.—Except as otherwise provided herein, where any relief is claimed under this Chapter in respect of a contract, the person against whom the relief is claimed may plead by way of defence any ground which is available to him under any law relating to contracts.

SYNOPSIS

1. Jurisdiction – Law on
2. Jurisdiction of Civil Court – Law on
3. Literal Construction – Law on
4. Words "Relating To" – Meaning of
5. Wrongdoer – Law on
6. Land Comprised in Tenancy – Law on
7. Vendor – Powers of

COMMENTS

1. Jurisdiction – Law on – Section 9 of the Civil Procedure Code, 1908 provides that whenever a question arises before the civil court whether its jurisdiction is excluded expressly or by necessary implication, the court naturally feels inclined to consider whether remedy afforded by an alternative provision prescribed by special statute is sufficient or adequate. In cases where exclusion of the civil court's jurisdiction is expressly provided for, the consideration as to the scheme of the statute in question and the adequacy or sufficiency of the remedy provided for by it may be relevant, but cannot be decisive. Where exclusion is pleaded as a matter of necessary implication such consideration would be very important and in conceivable circumstances might become even decisive; *Vatticherukuru Village Panchayat; Nori Madhusudan* v. *Nori Venkatarama Deekshithulu, Vatticherukuru Village Panchayat*, AIR 1991 SCW 1303: JT 1991 (5) SC 140: 1991 (Supp 2) SCC 228: 1991 (2) UJ 309.

2. Jurisdiction of Civil Court – Law on – It is settled law that the exclusion of the jurisdiction of the Civil Court is not to be readily inferred but such exclusion must either be explicitly expressed or clearly implied. It is also well-settled that where a statute creates a liability not existing at common law, and gives also a particular remedy for enforcing it with respect to that class it has always been held, that the party must adopt the form of remedy given by the statute; *State of Madhya Pradesh* v. *Balveer Singh*, AIR 2001 MP 268: 2001 (3) MPHT 255: 2001 (1) MPJR 546: 2001 (2) MPLJ 644.

3. Literal Construction – Law on – The main criticism against the literal construction of the language of the proviso is that it would put a premium on dishonest and cantankerous parties who can always see to it that the enquiry is delayed and that the party dispossessed is ultimately deprived of the benefit of the legal fiction created by the proviso; *Athiappa Gounder* v. *S.A. Athiappa Pandaram*, AIR 1967 Mad 445: 1967 Cr LJ 1650.

4. Words "Relating To" – Meaning of – The words used are "relating to recovery of rent or possession" and not "for recovery of rent or possession". The words "relating to" are very wide and would include any suit or proceeding in connection with or having a direct bearing on the question of possession of the premises. Even if, therefore, the suit is not for possession, if the relief claimed in the suit is in regard to or in respect of recovery of possession, it will come within the ambit of this section. Thus a suit, in which the plaintiff seeks to get rid of an order of his eviction by an injunction restraining the defendant from interfering with his possession, will also be covered by this section; *Dattatraya Krishna Jangam* v. *Jairam Ganesh Gore,* AIR 1965 Bom 177: 1964 (66) BLR 645: ILR 1965 Bom 730: 1964 Mah LJ 750.

5. Wrongdoer – Law on – Section 9 of the Specific Relief Act is in no way inconsistent with the position that as against a wrongdoer, prior possession of the plaintiff, in an action of ejectment, is sufficient title, even if the suit be brought more than six months after the act of dispossession complained of and that the wrongdoer cannot successfully resist the suit by showing that the title and right to possession are in a third person; *Somnath Berman* v. *S.P. Raju,* AIR 1970 SC 846: 1969 (3) SCC 129: 1970 (2) SCR 869.

6. Land Comprised in Tenancy – Law on – From the bare reading of section 65 of the Himachal Pradesh Abolition of Big Landed Estates and Land Reforms Act, 1954, it is clear that the provisions contained therein preserve the right of the possession of tenancy or of any land comprised in tenancy not recoverable under section 9 of the Specific Relief Act by a tenant dispossessed therefrom instead of destroying such rights. The vested right of a holder of property or property rights to file a suit to establish his claim in respect of any land or part thereof is a common law remedy and right and the same is found preserved and protected under section 92 which gives right to such person to establish his claim in the Civil Court having jurisdiction by a due process of law. The provision of a summary remedy under section 62 is no substitute to the right of suit and there is nothing in the Act which disclose any intention to destroy such right of suit otherwise available to a person as an adjunct to his rights to or in immovable property; *Joti Ram* v. *Bhagat Singh,* AIR 2000 HP 123: 2000 (2) Shim LC 195.

7. Vendor – Powers of – On a combined reading of section 9 of the Specific Relief Act and section 55 of The Indian Contracts Act it is clear that the vendor as a promisee, was within its right to terminate the contract by sending the letter in terms of Clause of the Contract while returning the advance money. It is clear that the plaintiff has not discharged its burden within the time specified and is not entitled to a specific performance of the contract. It is axiomatic that when discretionary remedy is prayed for by a party, such party must come to court on proper disclosure of facts. The plaint which it filed before the Court in such cases must state all facts with sufficient candour and clarity; *Citadel Fine Pharmaceuticals* v. *Ramaniyam Real Estates P. Ltd.,* AIR 2011 SC 3351: AIR 2011 SCW 5209: 2011 (8) SCALE 301: 2011 (9) SCC 147.

10. Cases in which specific performance of contract enforceable.—Except as otherwise provided in this Chapter, the specific performance of any contract may, in the discretion of the court, be enforced—

(a) when there exists no standard for ascertaining actual damage caused by the non-performance of the act agreed to be done; or

(b) when the act agreed to be done is such that compensation in money for its non-performance would not afford adequate relief.

Explanation.—Unless and until the contrary is proved, the court shall presume—

(i) that the breach of a contract to transfer immovable property cannot be adequately relieved by compensation in money; and

(ii) that the breach of a contract to transfer movable property can be so relieved except in the following cases:—

(a) where the property is not an ordinary article of commerce, or is of special value or interest to the plaintiff, or consists of goods which are not easily obtainable in the market;

(b) where the property is held by the defendant as the agent or trustee of the plaintiff.

SYNOPSIS

1. "Unless and Until the Contrary is Proved" – Inference from
2. Rights of Creditors – Law on
3. Rule of Perpetuity – Law on
4. Similar Interlocutory Relief – Law on
5. Terms of Document – Interpretation of
6. Untenable Ground – Rejection of
7. Breach of Contract – Law on
8. Provision – Comments on
9. Section 77 of the Registration Act, 1908 – Law on
10. Share Holder in Private Company – Law on
11. Contract – Essentials of
12. Promise to Transfer a Property – Law on
13. Compensation for Breach of Contract – Law on

COMMENTS

1. "Unless and Until the Contrary is Proved" – Inference from – Fact that the parties themselves have provided a sum to be paid by the party breaking the contract does not, by itself, remove the strong presumption contemplated by the use of the words "unless and until the contrary is proved" in section 10 of the Specific Relief Act of 1963. The sufficiency or insufficiency of any evidence to remove such a presumption is a matter of evidence; *Manzoor Ahmed Magray* v. *Gulam Hassan Aram*, AIR 2000 SC 191: JT 1999 (8) SC 34: 1999 (6) SCALE 350: 1999 (7) SCC 703.

2. Rights of Creditors – Law on – Sub-clause (7) of section 14 of Uttar Pradesh Encumbered Estates Act, 1934 uses the phrase "pass a simple money decree' and this terminology "simple money decree" has been used with some significance and if any doubt is left it has further been cleared by providing section 18. This provision clearly indicates that once a decree has been passed by the Special Judge under sub-section (7) of section 14 the effect of it will be to extinguish the previously existing rights in any of the claims or mortgage and the decree passed by the Special Judge will substitute all those rights. It is therefore clear that once the claim of a creditor even if he is secured is determined by the Special Judge under section 14 sub-clause (7) and a money decree is passed the rights of the creditors even if it was under mortgage come to an end although the scheme of the Act indicates that such debts which are secured may get priority over the debts which were not secured and on the basis of these provisions and the provisions contained in section 44; *Gaya Prasad* v. *Surendra Bahadur Singh*, AIR 1987 SC 925: JT 1987 (1) SC 652: 1987 (1) SCALE 514: 1987 (2) SCC 383: 1987 (2) SCR 542.

3. Rule of Perpetuity – Law on – When a contract has been executed in which no interest *in praesenti* has been created; the rule of perpetuity has no application. As a result, the agreement is in the nature of a pre-emptive right created in favour of the co-owner. Therefore, it is enforceable as and when an attempt is made by the co-owner to alienate the land to third parties. Therefore, rule against perpetuity has no application; *Shivji* v. *Raghunath*, AIR 1997 SC 1917: JT 1997 (3) SC 203: 1997 (2) SCALE 346: 1997 (10) SCC 309.

4. Similar Interlocutory Relief – Law on – There is now no justification to entertain a prayer for a similar interlocutory relief afresh; *Sunil D. Chedda* v. *Suresh Bansilal Sethi*, AIR 1992 SC 1200: AIR 1992 SCW 1165: 1993 (Supp 1) SCC 231.

5. Terms of Document – Interpretation of – It is well-settled that the terms of a document have to be read as a whole. Taking out a term in isolation and giving it a meaning torn from the context may tend to lead to a wrong interpretation causing injustice; *Deokabai* v. *Uttam*, JT 1993 (4) SC 374: 1993 (3) SCALE 255: 1993 (4) SCC 181.

6. Untenable Ground – Rejection of – Once it is held that the plaintiff did pay the amount and obtain the sale deed within the period prescribed by the trial Court; the main ground upon which the Court had dismissed his suit becomes untenable; *Kaulashwari Devi* v. *Nawal Kishore*, AIR 1994 SC 1200: AIR 1994 SCW 522: 1995 (Supp 1) SCC 141.

7. Breach of Contract – Law on – Damages and specific performance are both remedies available upon breach of obligations by a party to the contract. The former is considered to be a substantial remedy, whereas the latter is of course a specific remedy. It is true that *Explanation (i)* to section 10 of the Act provides that unless and until the contrary is proved, the Court shall presume that breach of contract to transfer immovable property cannot be adequately relieved by compensation in money. However, this presumption is not an irrefutable one. For a specific performance of a contract of sale of immovable property, there must be certainty with respect to the property to be sold; *Shanker Singh* v. *Narinder Singh*, 2012 (90) All LR 698: 2011 (13) SCALE 574: AIR 2012 SCW 3613: 2011 (8) Supreme 474.

8. Provision – Comments on – Section 10 of the Specific Relief Act, 1963 says that "Except as otherwise provided in this Chapter, the specific performance of any contract may, in the discretion of the Court, be enforced (a) when there exists no standard for ascertaining the actual damage caused by the non-performance of the act agreed to be done; or (b) when the act agreed to be done is such that compensation in money for its non-performance would not afford adequate relief." Clause (1) of the Explanation appended to the section says that "unless and until the contrary is proved, the Court shall presume (i) that the breach of a contract to transfer immovable property cannot be adequately relieved by compensation in money". Sub-section (1) of section 20 says that "the jurisdiction to decree specific performance is discretionary, and the Court is not bound to grant such relief merely because it is lawful to do so; but the discretion of the Court is not arbitrary but sound and reasonable, guided by judicial principles and capable of correction by a court of appeal". Sub-section (2) sets 'out ' the situations in which the Court may refuse specific performance. Sub-section (3) of section 20 says that "the Court may properly exercise discretion to decree specific performance in any case where the plaintiff has done substantial acts or suffered losses in consequence of a contract capable of specific performance". Section 21 sets out the circumstances in which the Court may award compensation in lieu of or in addition to specific performance. Section 23 says that merely because an agreement mentions a particular sum payable by the defaulting party to the other, that shall not be a ground for refusing the specific performance; *K.S. Vidyanadam* v. *Vairavan*, AIR 1997 SC 1751: JT 1997 (2) SC 375: 1997 (1) SCALE 739: 1997 (3) SCC 1: 1997 (1) SCR 993.

9. Section 77 of the Registration Act, 1908 – Law on – Section 77 of the Registration Act, 1908 is a complete Code in itself providing for the enforcement of a right to get a document registered by filing a civil suit which but for the special provision of that section could not be maintainable. Several difficulties have been considered in these decisions, such as, when the time has expired since the date of the execution of the document whether there could be a decree to direct the Sub-Registrar to register the document. On the other hand, it has also been noticed that an agreement for transfer of property implies a contract not only to execute the deed of transfer but also to appear before the registering officer and to admit execution thereby facilitating the registration of the document wherever it is compulsory. The provisions of the Specific Relief Act and the Registration Act may to a certain extent cover the same field but so that one will not supersede the other. Where the stage indicated in section 77 of the Registration Act, 1908 has reached and no other relief except a direction for registration of the document is really asked for, section 77 of the Act may be an exclusive remedy. However, in other cases it has no application, inasmuch as a suit for specific performance is of wider amplitude and is primarily one for enforcement of a contract and other consequential or further relief. If a party is seeking not merely the registration of a sale deed, but also recovery of possession and *mesne profits* or damages, a suit under section 77 of the Act is not adequate remedy. The analysis of the provisions of section 77 of the Act would indicate that it would apply only if a matter is pertaining to registration of a document and not for a comprehensive suit; *Kalavakurti Venkata Subbaiah* v. *Bala Gurappagari Guruvi Reddy*, AIR 1999 SC 2958: JT 1999 (5) SC 389: 1999 (4) SCALE 466: 1999 (7) SCC 114.

10. Share Holder in Private Company – Law on – A holder of shares in a private company may agree to sell his shares to a person of his choice. Such agreements are specifically enforceable under section 10 of the Specific Relief Act, 1963, which corresponds to section 12 of the Specific Relief Act, 1877. The section provides that specific performance of such contracts may be enforced when there exists no standard for ascertaining the actual damage caused by the non-performance of the act agreed to be done, or when the act agreed to be done is such that compensation in money for its non-performance would not afford adequate relief. In the case of a contract to transfer movable property, normally specific performance is not granted except in circumstances specified in the Explanation to section 10. One of the exceptions is where the property is "of special value or interest to the plaintiff, or consists of goods which are not easily obtainable in the market". It has been held by a long line of authority that shares in a private limited company would come within the phrase "not easily obtainable in the market"; *M.S. Madhusoodhanan* v. *Kerala Kaumudi Pvt. Ltd.*, AIR 2004 SC 909: JT 2003 (6) SC 560: 2003 (6) SCALE 191: 2004 (9) SCC 204; *See* Also: *Jainarain Ram Lundia* v. *Surajmull Sagarmull*, AIR (36) 1949 FC 211 (218); The Privy Council in the *Bank of India Ltd.* v. *J.A.H. Chinoy*, AIR 1950 PC 90 said: "It is also the opinion of the Board that, having regard to the nature of the company and the limited market for its shares, damages would not be an adequate remedy" specific performance of a contract for transfers of shares in a private limited company could be granted.

11. Contract – Essentials of – The essentials of contract set out in section 10 above are:—

(1) Free consent of the parties

(2) Competence of parties to contract

(3) Lawful consideration

(4) Lawful object.

Competence to contract is set out in section 11 which provides that every person is competent to contract who is of the age of majority and who is of sound mind and is not disqualified from contracting by any law to which he is subject. Section 12 provides that a person will be treated to be of sound mind if, at the time when he makes the contract, he is capable of understanding it and forming a rational judgment as to its effect upon its interests; *Tarsem Singh* v. *Sukhminder Singh*, AIR 1998 SC 1400: JT 1998 (2) SC 149: 1998 (1) SCALE 58: 1998 (3) SCC 471.

12. Promise to Transfer a Property – Law on – An agreement for sale of property and a promise to transfer a property convey the same meaning and effect in law. A promise to transfer a property is an agreement for sale of a property; *Bommaka Nagabhushana Reddy* v. W. *Srinivasa Rao*, 2001 (5) ALT (SC) 31: 2001 (3) CCC 116: JT 2001 (5) SC 487: 2002 (9) SCC 664: 2001 (5) Supreme 480.

13. Compensation for Breach of Contract – Law on – Section 10 deals with cases in which specific performance of contract is enforceable. It provides that except as otherwise provided in that Chapter (dealing with Specific Performance of Contracts) of the Act, specific performance of any contract may, in the discretion of the court, be enforced when the act agreed to be done is such that compensation in money for its non-performance would not afford adequate relief. *Explanation (i)* to section 10 provides that unless and until the contrary is proved, the court shall presume that the breach of a contract to transfer immovable property cannot be adequately relieved by compensation in money. Sub-sections (2) and (5) of section 21 of the Act provide that in a suit for specific performance, if the court decides that specific performance ought not to be granted, but that there is a contract between the parties which has been broken by the defendant, and that the plaintiff is entitled to compensation for that breach, it shall award him such compensation accordingly; and that no compensation shall be awarded under this section unless the plaintiff has claimed such compensation in his plaint. Section 23 of the Act provides that a contract otherwise proper to be specifically enforced, may be so enforced, though a sum be named in it as the amount to be paid in case of its breach and the party in default is willing to pay the same, if the court, having regard to the terms of the contract and other attending circumstances, is satisfied that the sum was named only for the purpose of securing performance of the contract and not for the purpose of giving to the party in default an option of paying money in lieu of specific performance; *Man Kaur (Dead) by LRs.* v. *Hartar Singh Sangha*, JT 2010 (10) SC 565: 2010 (10) SCC 512: 2010 (12) SCR 515.

11. Cases in which specific performance of contracts connected with trusts enforceable.—(1) Except as otherwise provided in this Act, specific performance of a contract may, in the discretion of the court, be enforced when the act agreed to be done is in the performance wholly or partly of a trust.

(2) A contract made by a trustee in excess of his powers or in breach of trust cannot be specifically enforced.

SYNOPSIS

1. Specific Performance of Contracts Connected with Trusts Enforceable
2. Contract by Trustee in Excess of Powers
3. Contract by Trustee in Breach of Trust

COMMENTS

1. Specific Performance of Contracts Connected with Trusts Enforceable – Sub-section (1) of section 11 provides that except as otherwise provided in this Act, specific performance of a contract may, in the discretion of the court, be enforced when the act agreed to be done is in performance wholly or partly of a trust. Thus, an agreement to lease their undivided property by all, except one brother who are members of an undivided Hindu Mitakshara family cannot be specifically enforced; *Jadu* v. *Abdul*, 11 IC 892.

But a compromise agreement entered into by an administrator, in excess of powers, cannot be specifically enforced; *Sarbesh* v. *Haridoyal*, 11 CLJ 346.

It has been held that an obligation annexed to the ownership of property, which does not amount to interest in the property will be regarded in the nature of a trust and can be specifically enforced; *Bai Dosabai* v. *Mathuradas*, AIR 1980 SC 1334: (1980) 3 SCC 545.

Where the agreement stipulated as to what will happen in the event of sale not going through such as refund of earnest money plus some more money, specific performance cannot be enforced; *Dadarao* v. *Ramrao*, 1999 (9) SLT 240: AIR 1999 SCW 4818: (1999) 8 SCC 416.

Similarly, where agreement of sale provides for claiming double amount of earnest money in case of default of execution of sale within time, specific performance of the agreement cannot be enforced and the plaintiff buyer can claim only that relief, which is provided for in the agreement; *Ashok Aggarwal* v. *Bhagwan Das Arora*, AIR 2001 Del 107 (109): 2002 (1) Civ LJ 780: 2000 (88) DLT 606: 2001 (57) DRJ 241.

2. Contract by Trustee in Excess of Powers – Similarly, a contract of sale by a father or *Karta* in a Hindu Mitakshara family without justifying necessity is not specifically enforceable; *Guruswami* v. *Ganapathia*, ILR 5 Mad 337.

3. Contract by Trustee in Breach of Trust – In this illustration, the contract is so disadvantageous so as to be in breach of trust. In such a case, the test is whether granting of specific enforcement would involve a breach of trust by the trustee; *Gajendra Nath* v. *Ashraf Hussain*, AIR 1923 Cal 130: 27 CWN 159.

Similarly, where the *Mahant* of a temple grants a permanent lease of temple property, which is in the hands of the successor, without justifying the necessity for the same, it cannot be specifically enforced; *Manohar* v. *Tarini*, AIR 1929 Cal 612: 34 CWN 135.

12. Specific performance of part of contract.—(1) Except as otherwise hereinafter provided in this section the court shall not direct the specific performance of a part of a contract.

(2) Where a party to a contract is unable to perform the whole of his part of it, but the part which must be left unperformed by only a small proportion to the whole in value and admits of compensation in money, the court may, at the suit of either party, direct the specific performance of so much of the contract as can be performed, and award compensation in money for the deficiency.

(3) Where a party to a contract is unable to perform the whole of his part of it, and the part which must be left unperformed either—

(a) forms a considerable part of the whole, though admitting of compensation in money; or

(b) does not admit of compensation in money,

he is not entitled to obtain a decree for specific performance; but the court may, at the suit of other party, direct the party in default to perform specifically so much of his part of the contract as he can perform, if the other party—

(i) in a case falling under clause (a), pays or has paid the agreed consideration for the whole of the contract reduced by the consideration for the part which must be left unperformed and a case falling under clause (b), [1][pays or had paid] the consideration for the whole of the contract without any abatement; and

(ii) in either case, relinquishes all claims to the performance of the remaining part of the contract and all right to compensation, either for the deficiency or for the loss or damage sustained by him through the default of the defendant.

(4) When a part of a contract which, taken by itself, can and ought to be specifically performed, stands on a separate and independent footing from another part of the same contract which cannot or ought not to be specifically performed, the court may direct specific performance of the former part.

Explanation.—For the purposes of this section, a party to a contract shall be deemed to be unable to perform the whole of his part of it if a portion of its subject matter existing at the date of the contract has ceased to exist at the time of its performance.

SYNOPSIS

1. Another Part of Same Contract – Law on
2. Contract is not Capable of Being Performed – Law on
3. Defendants – Duties of
4. Enforcement of Part of Whole Contract – Law on

---

1. Ins. by Act 52 of 1964, Sch. II (w.e.f. 29-12-1964).

5. Legislative Intent – Law on
6. Party to a Contract is Unable to Perform whole of his Part – Law on
7. Provision – Comments on
8. Relief – Entitlement for
9. Unregistered Award – Law on
10. Consolidation Proceedings – Law on
11. Execution of Sale Agreement – Law on
12. Provision – Comments on
13. Provision – Comments on
14. Provision – Nature of
15. Time Being Essence of Contract – Condition for

COMMENTS

1. Another Part of Same Contract – Law on – Section 12 provides for specific performance of part of contract. Sub-section (1) thereof postulates that except as otherwise hereinafter provided in the section, the Court shall not direct the specific performance of a part of a contract. Sub-section (4) thereto envisages that when a part of the contract which, taken by itself, can and ought to be specifically performed, stands on a separate and independent footing from another part of the same contract which cannot or ought not to be specifically performed, the Court may direct specific performance of the former part. Section 10(b) provides that "except as otherwise provided in this Chapter, the specific performance of any contract may, in the discretion of the Court, be enforced (b) when the act agreed to be done is such that compensation in money for its non-performance would not afford adequate relief; *Sardar Singh* v. *Krishna Devi*, AIR 1995 SC 491: 1994 (1) DNJ 204: JT 1994 (3) SC 465: 1994 (4) SCC 18.

2. Contract is not Capable of Being Performed – Law on – It must be clarified that Apex Court is not saying that merely because in correspondence or orally a party has insisted on performance of the whole contract he cannot thereafter elect to accept performance in part. A mere assertion that contract must be performed in full or even a filing of a suit for specific performance of the whole contract without averring that the plaintiff is willing to accept performance in part may not amount to electing not to accept performance in part. It is only in cases where a party has categorically refused to accept performance in part, *i.e.*, he has unambiguously elected not to accept part performance that he will be precluded from subsequently turning around and electing to accept performance in part. Whether a party has categorically elected or not will depend on facts of each case. It is also settled law that specific performance cannot be granted to a party who has not been ready and willing at all stages to perform the contract. But in cases where a contract is not capable of being performed in whole then the readiness and willingness, at all stages, is the readiness and willingness to accept part performance. If a contract is not capable of being performed in whole and a party clearly indicates that he is not willing to accept part performance, then there is no readiness and willingness, at all stages, to accept part performance. In that case there can be no specific performance of a part of the contract at a later stage; *Surjit Kaur* v. *Naurata Singh*, AIR 2000 SC 2927: JT 2000 (10) SC 520: 2000 (6) SCALE 364: 2000 (7) SCC 379.

3. Defendants – Duties of – According to mandate of section 53A of the Transfer of Property Act, 1882 the defendants had to prove that they were already in possession, continued in possession in part performance of the contract of sale and has done sonic act in furtherance of the contract and they were willing to perform their part of the contract. Section 53A of the T.P. Act does not provide for any limitation on expiry whereof the defence contemplated in the section will be lost or will extinguish. Limitation bars the remedy but not the right in possession. Thus the law of Limitation does not apply to section 53A of the T.P. Act; *Nand Lal* v. *Ramesh Chand*, 2000 (1) Raj LW 223 **[Hon'ble Judges:** Shiv Kumar Sharma, Jagdish Sharan Rastogi, B.P. Agrawal, R.P. Agraual].

4. Enforcement of Part of Whole Contract – Law on – If Courts hold that there were two contracts in an agreement of sale of undivided land, Courts would be setting up a new contract which cannot be enforced by the Court unless the plaintiff takes resort to sub-section (3) of section 12 of the Act. If there was only one contract for the entire land and what was pleaded in the plaint and enforcement of the agreement, was for the entire land covered by the agreement. If the plaintiff seeks enforcement of part of the whole contract, he must plead his readiness and willingness to perform his part of the whole contract; *A. Maria Angelena* v. *A.G. Balkis Bee*, AIR 2002 SC 2385: JT 2001 (10) SC 262: 2002 (9) SCC 597.

5. Legislative Intent – Law on – If the Legislative intent was that the mere proof that a sum is specified as liquidated damages or penalty for a breach should be enough to prove that a contract for the transfer of immovable property could be adequately compensated by the specified damages or penalty, section 20 of the old Act will certainly become meaningless. It is true that section 20 of the old Act does not mention the case of an express contract giving an option to a promiser to either carry out the contract to convey, or in the alternative, to pay the sum specified, in which case the enforcement of the undertaking to make the payment would be an enforcement of the contract itself and no occasion for rebutting the presumption in the explanation to section 21 would arise. In such cases the contract itself is specifically enforced when payment is directed in lieu of the conveyance to be made. Section 21 of the old Act, to which section 14 of the Act of 1963 corresponds, enacts, *inter alia*, that "a contract for the non-performance of which a compensation of money is adequate relief" cannot be specifically enforced. Hence, it is contended that, once the presumption contained in Explanation to section 12 is rebutted, by proof that the parties themselves contemplated a certain amount as liquidated damages for a breach of contract, the bar under section 21 of the old Act must be given effect to because it must be deemed to be proved that the non-performance complained of can be adequately compensated by money; *M.L. Devender Singh* v. *Syed Khaja*, AIR 1973 SC 2457: 1973 (2) SCC 515: 1974 (1) SCR 312.

6. Party to a Contract is Unable to Perform whole of his Part – Law on – Sub-section (3) of section 12 of the Specific Relief Act, 1963, provides that where a party to a contract is unable to perform the whole of his part of it, he is not entitled to obtain a decree for specific performance if the part which must be left unperformed forms a considerable part of the whole, though admitting of compensation in money, or if the part which must be left unperformed does not admit of compensation in money. However, at the suit of the other party, the Court may direct such a party in default to perform specifically so much of his part of the contract as he can perform if the party bringing the suit *i.e.*, the plaintiff fulfils the conditions laid down in clause (i) and (ii) of that sub-section. These conditions are: firstly, that in the case in which the part which must be left unperformed forms a considerable part of the whole and admits of compensation in money the plaintiff must pay the agreed consideration for the whole of the contract reduced by the consideration for the part which must be left unperformed, while in the case in which the unperformed part does not admit of compensation in money, the plaintiff must pay consideration for the whole of the contract without any abatement. The second condition is that in either of the above two cases the plaintiff must relinquish all claims to the performance of the remaining part of the contract and all right to compensation, either for the deficiency or for the loss or damage sustained by him through the default of the defendant; *Rakesh Kumar* v. *Sat Pal*, AIR 1986 P&H 335: 1986 (90) Punj LR 214.

7. Provision – Comments on – Section 12(3) of the Act is a beneficial provision so far as the purchasers are concerned. The relinquishment of claim as contemplated under section 12(3)(ii) of the Act as regard performance of the remaining part of the contract and all rights to compensation need not specifically be pleaded and can be made at any stage of the litigation. Such a plea can also be raised at the appellate stage. Delay by itself, it is trite, may not stand in the way of the plaintiff from claiming the relief unless the defendant establishes prejudice. The said provision postulates that where a defendant is unable to perform a part of the contract, and the part left unperformed forms a considerable portion of the whole but admits of compensation in money, the party not in default is entitled to specific performance on payment on the whole consideration, reduced by the consideration for the part left unperformed; *Surinder Singh* v. *Kapoor Singh*, JT 2005 (11) SC 8: 2005 (4) SCALE 596: 2005 (5) SCC 142: 2005 (3) SCR 1084.

8. Relief – Entitlement for – Section 12 of the Specific Relief act cannot be invoked by the vendee to obtain sale of undivided share of the two brothers with a right to force partition on the sisters who were not parties to the agreement of sale. Such a relief under section 12 cannot be obtained by a vendee, on purchase of an undivided share of the property of some of the co-owners, against other co-owners who were not parties to the sale agreement; *Shanmughasundaram* v. *Diravia Nadar (D) by LRs.*, 2005 (2) SCR 649: AIR 2005 SC 1836: 2005 (3) SCALE 62: 2005 (10) SCC 728.

9. Unregistered Award – Law on – Unregistered award *per se* is not inadmissible in evidence. It is a valid award and not a mere waste paper. It creates rights and obligations between the parties thereto and in conclusive between the parties. It can be set up as a defence as evidence of resolving the disputes and acceptance of it by the parties. If it is a foundation, creating right, title and interest *in praesenti* or future or extinguishes the right, title or interest in immovable property of the value of Rs. 100 or above it is compulsorily registrable and non-registration render it inadmissible in evidence. If it contains a mere declaration of a pre-existing right, it is not creating a right, title and interest *in praesenti*, in which event it is not a compulsorily registrable instrument. It can be looked into as evidence of the conduct of the parties of accepting the award, acting upon it that they have pre-existing right, title or interest in the immovable property; *Sardar Singh* v. *Krishna Devi*, AIR 1995 SC 491: 1994 (1) DNJ 204: JT 1994 (3) SC 465: 1994 (4) SCC 18.

10. Consolidation Proceedings – Law on – In Uttar Pradesh agricultural lands are subjected to consolidation proceedings under the relevant statute. During the pendency of the consolidation proceedings in a district, there is a provision in the statute that there should not be transfers, gifts and sales so that complications and confusions in the course of consolidation proceedings may be obviated. There is nothing at all in the Act which inhibits contracts for sale being entered into by owners of property; *Baikunthi Devi* v. *Mahendra Nath*, AIR 1977 SC 1514: 1977 (2) SCC 496: 1977 UJ 296.

11. Execution of Sale Agreement – Law on – It is difficult to believe that the sons had no knowledge of the execution of the sale agreement by their father. Even after institution of suit, no attempt was made by the sons to approach the authorities under the Act of 1953 for getting their names recorded on the lands as joint owners. In such circumstances, they cannot be heard to say that the father was not competent to execute the agreement of sale and it is not binding on them; *Narender Singh* v. *Jai Bhagwan*, AIR 2005 SC 582: JT 2004 (10) SC 345: 2004 (10) SCALE 335: 2005 (9) SCC 157.

12. Provision – Comments on – A perusal of sub-section (3) of section 12 shows that the first part of the said provisions mandates refusal of specific performance of a contract on certain conditions. However, latter part of the provisions permits a Court to direct the party in default to perform specifically so much of his part of the contract as he can perform if the other party pays or has paid the agreed consideration for the whole of the contract and relinquishes all claims to the performance of the remaining part of the contract and all the rights to compensation for the loss sustained by him. If a suit is laid by the other party, the Court may direct the defaulting party to perform that part of the contract which is performable on satisfying two pre-conditions, *i.e.*, (i) the plaintiff pays or has already paid the whole of the consideration amount under the agreement, and that (ii) plaintiff relinquishes all claims to the performance of other part of the contract which defaulting party is incapable to perform and all rights to compensation for loss sustained by him. Thus, the ingredients which would attract specific performance of the part of the contract, are: (i) if a party to an agreement is unable to perform a part of the contract, he is to be treated as defaulting party to that extent, and (ii) the other party to an agreement must, in a suit for such specific performance, either pays or has paid the whole of the agreed amount, for that part of the contract which is capable of being performed by the defaulting party to that extent, and (ii) the other party to an agreement must, in a suit for such specific performance, either pays or has paid the whole of the agreed amount, for that part of the contract which is capable of being performed by the defaulting party and also relinquish his claim in respect of other part of contract which defaulting party is not capable to perform and relinquishes the claim of compensation in respect of loss sustained by him. If such ingredients are satisfied, the discretionary relief of specific performance is ordinarily granted unless there is delay or laches or any other disability on the part of other party; *Rachakonda Narayana* v. *Ponthala Parvathamma*, AIR 2001 SC 3353: JT 2001 (7) SC 63: 2001 (5) SCALE 413: 2001 (8) SCC 173.

13. Provision – Comments on – The provision has been enacted for the benefit of the purchaser and, thus, cannot operate to his detriment. Under the old Specific Relief Act, the Plaintiff was not only required to relinquish his claim of specific contract as regard that part of the contract which cannot be performed but also was required to pay the entire amount of consideration; whereas in terms of section 12(3) of the new Specific Relief Act, 1963 he is now required to pay the amount of consideration proportionately; *P.C. Varghese* v. *Devaki Amma Balambika Devi*, AIR 2006 SC 145: JT 2005 (10) SC 278: 2005 (8) SCALE 320: 2005 (8) SCC 486.

14. Provision – Nature of – Section 12(3) of the Specific Relief Act can be invoked only where terms of contract permit segregation of rights and interest of parties in the property. The provision cannot be availed of when the terms of the contract specifically evince an intention contrary to segregating interest of the vendor having life interest. Neither law nor equity is in favour of the vendee to grant Specific Performance of the Contract. The power to grant partial relief, from the very language of the section 12(3) is discretionary with the Court to be exercised keeping in view the facts and circumstances of each case and the rights and interests of the parties involved; *H.P.A. International* v. *Bhagwandas Fateh Chand Daswani*, AIR 2004 SC 3858: JT 2004 (5) SC 408: 2004 (6) SCALE 188: 2004 (6) SCC 537.

Section 12 prohibits specific performance of a part of a contract except in the circumstances under sub-sections (2), (3) and (4). The circumstances mentioned in these sub-sections are exhaustive; *Kammana Sambamurthy (D) by LRs* v. *Kalipatnapu Atchutamma (D)*, AIR 2011 SC 103: JT 2010 (12) SC 92: 2011 (11) SCC 153.

15. Time Being Essence of Contract – Condition for – It is clear that in the case of sale of immovable property, there is no presumption as to time being the essence of the contract. Even where the parties have expressly provided that time is the essence of the contract, such a stipulation will have to be read along with other provisions of the contract. For instance, if the contract was to include clauses providing for extension of time in certain contingencies or for payment of fine or penalty for every day or week, the work undertaken remains unfinished on the expiry of the time provided in the contract, such clauses would be construed as rendering ineffective the express provision relating to the time being of the essence of contract. If the parties agreed that the sale deed is to be executed within six months and they made it clear that in the event of failure to execute the sale deed, the earnest money will be forfeited. In such circumstances, the clauses in the paragraphs of the agreement of sale would render ineffective the specific provision relating to the time being the essence of contract; *Balasaheb Dayandeo Naik* v. *Appasaheb Dattatraya Pawar*, AIR 2008 SC 1205: 2008 (1) SCALE 705: 2008 (1) Supreme 673: 2008 (2) Mad LJ 750.

13. Rights of purchaser or lessee against person with no title or imperfect title.—(1) Where a person contracts to sell or let certain immovable property having no title or only an imperfect title, the purchaser or lessee (subject to the other provisions of this Chapter), has the following rights, namely:—

(a) if the vendor or lessor has subsequently to the contract acquired any interest in the property, the purchaser or lessee may compel him to make good the contract out of such interest;

(b) where the concurrence of other persons is necessary for validating the title, and they are bound to concur at the request of the vendor or lessor, the purchaser or lessee may compel him to procure such concurrence, and when a conveyance by other persons is necessary to validate the title and they are bound to convey at the request of the vendor or lessor, the purchaser or lessee may compel him to procure such conveyance;

(c) where the vendor professes to sell unencumbered property, but the property is mortgaged for an amount not exceeding the purchase money and the vendor has in fact only a right to redeem it, the purchaser may compel him to redeem the mortgage and to obtain a valid discharge, and, where necessary, also a conveyance from the mortgagee;

(d) where the vendor or lessor sues for specific performance of the contract and the suit is dismissed on the ground of his want of title or imperfect title, the defendant has a right to a return of his deposit, if any, with interest thereon, to his costs of the suit, and to a lien for such deposit, interest and costs on the interest, if any, of the vendor or lessor in the property which is the subject-matter of the contract.

(2) The provisions of sub-section (1) shall also apply, as far as may be, to contracts for the sale or hire of movable property.

SYNOPSIS

COMMENTS

1. Rights of Purchaser – Law on – The section deals with rights of a purchaser in certain cases, where a person contracts to sell or let certain immovable property having no title or only an imperfect title. These rights enable the purchaser to take action when title of vendor is bettered in the circumstances given in this section. The vendor is under a duty to prove his title and to convey what he has contracted to convey. The section gives right to purchaser in the event there is a defect in title as enumerated in clauses (a) to (d) to compel the vendor to convey the title or to secure the concurrence or conveyance or to redeem the mortgaged etc., as the case may be; *Waheed Baig* v. *Bangi Lakshmamma*, AIR 2008 SCW 4176: 2008 (7) SCALE 302: 2008 (6) SCR 726: 2008 (7) SCJ 226.

2. Scope and Application – Section 13 deals with the rights of the purchaser or lessee against persons who have no title or imperfect title to sell the property. Sub-section (1) of section 13 deals with immovable property and sub-section (2) makes the provision of sub-section (1) applicable to sale or hire of movable property. Section 13 applies to executory contracts. It does not apply where the vendor or lessor has no title or imperfect title in a suit property; *Silla Chandrasekharan* v. *Ram Chander Sahu*, AIR 1964 SC 1789: (1964) 7 SCR 858.

Section 13 applies to the principle of estoppel. It applies in cases where parties enter into contract for sale of party, without having title or having imperfect title at the time of the contract but subsequently acquire the title, they are estopped from denying that they had no power of performance of the contract. Thus, where a lessee, having no right to sub-let without the consent of lessor, enters into a contract to sub-let, and subsequently, of the lessee obtains the consent of lessors, the contract may be specifically enforced; *Gokul Chandra* v. *Haji Mohammad,* AIR 1986 Cal 136: 1938 LR 1 Cal 563.

Where the purchaser is willing to take such title as the vendor has, the vendor cannot refuse specific performance on the ground that his title is defeasible; *C.V. Munisamappa* v. *Kolala Gurunanjappa,* AIR 1950 Mad 90: (1949) 2 Mad 342.

Where the vendor claims to be the sole owner of the property but the property in fact is that of joint Hindu family of which he is a *Karta,* he is estopped from showing that he was mistaken about the property; *Kalyanpur Lime Works Ltd.* v. *State of Bihar,* AIR 1954 SC 165: 1954 SCR 958.

3. Clause (a) of sub-section (1): Vendor or Lessor Acquiring Title Subsequently – The words "imperfect title" mean a defective title for example, where the property is in charge of the collector in execution of a money decree; *Magniram* v. *Bakubai,* 36 Bom 510: 16 IC 570.

The vendor or lessor who seeks to convey immovable property must have a present right or some interest in immovable property. An imperfect title is, therefore, not one which has not been perfected; *Rajendrakumar Bhandari* v. *Poosammal,* AIR 1975 Mad 379: (1975) 2 Mad LJ 59: 88 Mad LW 484.

A person having some contingent interest may be said to have an imperfect title in the property; *Pandlik Daryaji* v. *Jainarayan Maliram,* AIR 1949 Nag 83: ILR 1948 Nag 815: 1948 NLJ 424.

Where a vendor has agreed to transfer agricultural land subject to the condition that he would obtain permission from collector to convert the land for agricultural purposes, such a contract can be specifically enforced only when on account of passing of some Act, conversion of the said land for non-agricultural purposes becomes possible. This has been held by the Supreme Court in *Rojasara Ramjibhai Dayabhai* v. *Jain Narotamdas Lallubhai,* AIR 1986 SC 1912 (1916-1918): (1986) 3 SCC 300.

Where the defendant entered into agreement to sell property in dispute but during pendency of suit, the patta of property was granted to the defendant so that he became title-holder, the plaintiff was entitled to specific performance of contract. Section 13 of the S.R. Act is based on the doctrine "feeding the grant by estoppel." If a person represents a valid title and enters into contract to sell the property and subsequently acquires a valid title, he cannot evade the performance thereof; *P.C. Hawaldar* v. *Jogen Das,* AIR 2009 MP 129 (130): 2009 AIHC 654 (NOC): (2009) 4 ALJ (NOC) 770 (DB).

4. Lessee – Where the defendant had been allotted the land by the Government on lease-cum-sale basis and there was a clear stipulation that lessee was not the owner of the property and could not sell the same till the sale price as determined by the Commissioner of Labour was paid in full and there was no condition that after payment of price, the lessee would become owner of the same, the property having not been registered in favour of lessee, he had no right to alienate the property in favour of another person. In the agreement which was made between the plaintiff and the defendant for the sale of that property to the plaintiff, the Government was not a party to it and therefore the agreement could not be enforced. The plaintiff had no right to invoke section 13; *Waheed Bag* v. *Bangi Lakshmamma,* (2008) 14 SCC 435 (442).

5. Imperfect Title – The buyer cannot avoid contract of sale on the ground of alleged imperfect title of seller in the property as it is neither void nor voidable *per se.* It is the prerogative of the buyer to raise a reasonable doubt and seek reasonable information which is within the knowledge of the seller and also recognized principle of law that the buyer can also compel the vendor to rectify the defects and pass on unencumbered title to the buyer in which event the contract does not become voidable; *A.K. Lakshmipathy* v. *Rai Sahab Pannalal Hirlal Lahoti Charilable Trust, Hyderabad,* AIR 2006 (NOC) 497 (AP): (2005) 6 Andh LJ 238.

6. Clause (b) of Sub-section (1): Sale Subject to Concurrence of other Persons – Clause (b) of sub-section (1) deals with a situation where a person contracts to sell or let certain immovable property and for validating the title in concurrence of other persons is necessary for validating the title and they are bound to concur at the request of the vendor or lessor, the purchaser or the lessor may compel him to procure such concurrence, and when a conveyance by other persons is necessary to validate the title and they are bound to convey at the request of the vendor or lessor, the purchase may compel him to procure such conveyance. Thus, where a lessee agrees to assign the lease to a person but the assignment of the lease is not possible without the consent of the lessor who cannot unreasonably withhold such assignment, the lessee cannot oppose specific performance of the suit and the lessee may be compelled to obtain the consent of the lessor; *Kamla Ranjan Roy* v. *Baijnath Bajoria,* AIR 1951 SC 1: 1950 SCR 840.

Similarly, a contract for sale of Sirdari land can be specifically enforced because sirdari land can be transferred after converting it into Bhumidari land under the U.P. Zamindari Abolition and Land Reforms Act by depositing ten times of the land revenue; *Pahunchi Lal* v. *Man Singh,* AIR 1971 All 444: 1971 AWR (HC) 338.

Where the concurrence of a third party is necessary for validity of the title and conveyance but cannot be obtained or is refused in the specific performance, it cannot be enforced but the court in its exercise of equitable jurisdiction may award damages; *Chandnee Widyavati Madden* v. *Dr. C.L. Katial,* AIR 1964 SC 978: (1954) 2 SCR 495.

7. Clause (c) of Sub-section (1): Property Being Subject to Encumbrances – The words "property is mortgaged for an amount not exceeding the purchase money" are important. Thus, where the vendor has not undertaken to clear the mortgage debt before executing the sale deed, the decree can be enforced only when the price is sufficient; *Venkataranga Aiyar* v. *C.S. Ramasamy Aiyar,* AIR 1926 Mad 173: 93 IC 670.

But where, the vendor has undertaken to discharge the mortgage debt or any other encumbrance, the court may direct discharge of the encumbrance on the property, before he is paid consideration money; *Kathamuthu Pillai* v. *Subramaniam Chettiar,* AIR 1926 Mad 569: 1926 MWN 271: 50 MLJ 228.

8. Clause (d) of sub-section (1): Dismissal of Suit for Specific Performance and Return of Deposit – Thus, where the purchaser successfully resists the suit of specific performance, he would be entitled to the refund of his deposit; *Meenakshi Ammal* v. *A. Munnuswamy Pillai,* 1966 (1) Mad 114.

Where the defendant entered into an agreement to sell property to the plaintiff for a sum of Rs. 6 lakh, the property was owned jointly by him and his sister. By misrepresenting the property to be his own, the defendant received a sum of Rs. 2,43,000 from the plaintiff as part payment. Since the defendant misrepresented that he was the sole owner of the property, no valid agreement to sell had come into existence. The court, therefore, refused to decree the specific performance. The court held that the plaintiff is, however, entitled to a refund of Rs. 2,43,000 and Rs. 3,50,000 as damages from the defendant on account of his failure to perform his part of the agreement, on account of which the plaintiff suffered a lot of inconvenience and harassment and failed to own a property of his choice; *Ramesh Kumar* v. *Chaman Lal,* AIR 2003 Del 202 (204): (2002) 100 DLT 512.

In case, however, where the purchaser's suit is dismissed without setling his relief, it is not a bar to filing a separate suit for getting back his deposit; *Parangodan Nair* v. *Perumtoduka Illot Chata,* (1903) 27 Mad 380.

But where the plaintiff himself abandons his claim for specific performance, he cannot file a separate suit for return of deposit; *Ardeshir H. Mama* v. *Flora Sassoon*, AIR 1928 PC 208: 1928 IA 360.

Contracts which cannot be specifically enforced

14. Contracts not specifically enforceable.—(1) The following contracts cannot be specifically enforced, namely:—

(a) a contract for the non-performance of which compensation in money is an adequate relief;

(b) a contract which runs into such minute or numerous details or which is so dependent on the personal qualifications or volition of the parties, or otherwise from its nature is such, that the court cannot enforce specific performance of its material terms;

(c) a contract which is in its nature determinable;

(d) a contract the performance of which involves the performance of a continuous duty which the court cannot supervise.

(2) Save as provided by the Arbitration Act, 1940 (10 of 1940), no contract to refer present or future differences to arbitration shall be specifically enforced; but if any person who has made such a contract (other than an arbitration agreement to which the provisions of the said Act apply) and has refused to perform it, sues in respect of any subject which he has contracted to refer, the existence of such contract shall bar the suit.

(3) Notwithstanding anything contained in clause (a) or clause (c) or clause (d) of sub-section (1), the court may enforce specific performance in the following cases:—

(a) where the suit is for the enforcement of a contract,—

(i) to execute a mortgage or furnish any other security for securing the repayment of any loan which the borrower is not willing to repay at once:

Provided that where only a part of the loan has been advanced the lendor is willing to advance the remaining part of the loan in terms of the contract; or

(ii) to take up and pay for any debentures of a company;

(b) where the suit is for,—

(i) the execution of a formal deed of partnership, the parties having commenced to carry on the business of the partnership; or

(ii) the purchase of a share of a partner in a firm;

(c) where the suit is for the enforcement of a contract for the construction of any building or the execution of any other work on land:

Provided that the following conditions are fulfilled, namely:—

(i) the building or other work is described in the contract in terms sufficiently precise to enable the court to determine the exact nature of the building or work;

(ii) the plaintiff has a substantial interest in the performance of the contract and the interest is of such a nature that compensation in money for non-performance of the contract is not an adequate relief; and

(iii) the defendant has, in persuance of the contract, obtained possession of the whole or any part of the land on which the building is to be constructed or other work is to be executed.

SYNOPSIS

1. Continuous Duty – Law on
2. Damages or Back Wages for Payment – Law on
3. Necessary Parties – Law on
4. Pre-Existing Right of Hindu Female – Law on
5. Semi Agreement – Law on
6. Social Justice – Comments on
7. Civil Court – Powers of
8. Contract of Personal Service – Enforcement of
9. Expressed Terms of Contract – Law on
10. Service Matters – Law on
11. Writ Petition – Maintainability of
12. Contract of Personal Service – Law on
13. Industrial Dispute – Law on
14. Contracts Involving Performance of Continuous Duty cannot be Specifically Enforced

COMMENTS

1. Continuous Duty – Law on – The provision provides that a contract the performance of which involves the performance of a continuous duty which the Court cannot supervise is not specifically enforceable; *Her Highness Maharani Shantadevi P. Gaekwad* v. *Savjibhai Haribhai Patel,* AIR 2001 SC 1462: JT 2001 (4) SC 43: 2001 (2) SCALE 647: 2001 (5) SCC 101.

2. Damages or Back Wages for Payment – Law on – Legal profession may not be considered as an employment but the income from profession of avocation if not negligible, cannot be ignored while determining damages or back wages for payment. It must also be taken into consideration; *Kayastha Pathshala, Allahabad* v. *Rajendra Prasad,* AIR 1990 SC 415: 1989 (2) SCALE 1394: 1989 (Supp 2) SCC 732: 1990 (1) SLR 820; In *S.M. Saiyad* v. *Baroda Municipal Corporation, Baroda,* 1984 (Supp) SCC 378: AIR 1984 SC 1829 the Court gave deduction of even a small income of Rs. 150 per month earned by the worker turned advocate while awarding backwages upon reinstatement.

3. Necessary Parties – Law on – Necessary parties are those persons in whose absence no decree can be passed by the Court or that there must be a right to some relief against some party in respect of the controversy involved in the proceedings and proper parties are those whose presence before the Court would be necessary in order to enable the Court effectually and completely to adjudicate upon and settle all the questions involved in the suit although no relief in the suit was claimed against such person. Second part of Order I, rule 10 sub-rule (2) of the C.P.C. would clearly show that the necessary parties in a suit for specific performance of a contract for sale are the parties to the contract or if they are dead their legal representatives as also a person who had purchased the contracted property from the vendor. In equity as well as in law, the contract constitutes rights and also regulates the liabilities of the parties. A purchaser is a necessary party as he would be affected if he had purchased with or without notice of the contract, but a person who claims adversely to the claim of a vendor is, however, not a necessary party. From the above, it is now clear that two tests are to be satisfied for determining the question who is a necessary party. Tests are - (1) there must be a right to some relief against such party in respect of the controversies involved in the proceedings (2) no effective decree can be passed in the absence of such party; *Kasturi* v. *Iyyamperumal,* 2005 (2) BLJR 1114: 2005 (2) Civ CC 379: 2005 (2) RCR (Civ) 691: 2005 (3) SCR 864.

4. Pre-Existing Right of Hindu Female – Law on – Sub-section (2) of section 14 of the Act is in the nature of proviso or exception to sub-section (1) and being in the nature of an exception it must be construed strictly so as to impinge as little as possible on the broader sweep of the ameliorative provision contained in sub-section (1). Further sub-section (2) cannot, therefore, be interpreted in a manner, which would rob sub-section

(1) of its efficacy and deprive a Hindu female of the protection sought to be given to her by sub-section (1). According to the Court sub-section (2) must be confined to cases where a property is acquired by a Hindu female for the first time as a grant, without any pre-existing right under a gift, will, instrument, the terms of which prescribe a restricted estate in the property and that is the legislative intendment; *V. Muthusami* v. *Angammal*, AIR 2002 SC 1279: JT 2002 (2) SC 410: 2002 (2) SCALE 308: 2002 (3) SCC 316.

5. Semi Agreement – Law on – Sale-deed was executed in respect of the land and there was specific provision in a preceding agreement that four persons were to be given employment. Allegation was that only three had been provided employment and in spite of assurance the defendants did not give the job to the plaintiff which is contrary to policy so illegal; *General Manager, Pench Area, Parasia, M.P.* v. *Barkan @ Kanhaiya*, AIR 2008 SC 1228: JT 2008 (1) SC 163: 2007 (14) SCALE 411: 2007 (14) SCC 47.

6. Social Justice – Comments on – The legal aid movement and public interest litigation seeks to bring justice to these forgotten specimens of humanity who constitute the bulk of the citizens of India and who are really and truly the "People of India", who gave to themselves this magnificent Constitution. It is true that there are large arrears pending in the courts but that cannot be any reason for denying access to justice to the poor and weaker sections of the community. No State has a right to tell its citizens that because a large number of cases of the rich and the well-to-do are pending in our courts, we will not help the poor to come to the courts for seeking justice until the staggering load of cases of people who can afford is disposed of. The time has now come, when the courts must become the courts for the poor and struggling masses of this country. They must shed their character as upholders of the established order and the *status quo*. They must be sensitised to the need of doing justice to the large masses of people to whom justice has been denied by a cruel heartless society for generations. The realisation must come to them that social justice is the signature tune of our Constitution, and it is their solemn duty under the Constitution to enforce the basic human rights of the poor and vulnerable sections of the community and actively help in the realisation of the constitutional goals; *Peoples Union for Democratic Rights* v. *Union of India*, AIR 1982 SC 1473: 1982 (1) SCALE 818: 1982 (3) SCC 235: 1983 (1) SCR 456.

7. Civil Court – Powers of – State is bound to comply with the requirements of article 14 of the Constitution of India as also other provisions of Part III of the Constitution. It is also bound to comply with the mandatory provisions of the statute or the regulations framed by it. It is also bound to follow the principles of natural justice. In the event, it is found that the action on the part of a State is violative of the Constitutional Provisions or the mandatory requirements of a statute or statutory rules, the Civil Court would have the jurisdiction to direct reinstatement with full back wages; *Rajasthan SRTC* v. *Mohar Singh*, AIR 2008 SC 2553: 2008 (7) SCALE 339: 2008 (5) SCC 542: 2008 (3) SLJ 357.

8. Contract of Personal Service – Enforcement of – Section 14(b) states that a contract of personal service cannot be enforced in a civil suit. If the plaintiff had any grievance and if he is a workman as defined in the Industrial Disputes Act, 1947, he should have raised an industrial dispute and sought relief under the Industrial Disputes Act, 1947 before the Labour Court or Industrial Tribunal. There are many powers which the Labour Court or Industrial Tribunal enjoy which the Civil Court does not enjoy *e.g.*, the power to enforce contracts of personal service, to create contracts, to change contracts etc. These things can only be done by the labour Court or Industrial Tribunal but cannot be done by a Civil Court. A contract for personal service includes all matters relating to the service of the employee *e.g.* confirmation, suspension, transfer, termination etc., *Apollo Tyres Ltd.* v. *C.P. Sebastian*, JT 2009 (8) SC 182: 2009 (8) SCALE 748: 2009 (14) SCC 360.

9. Expressed Terms of Contract – Law on – Just as the principles of natural justice ensure fair decision where function is quasi-judicial the doctrine of fairness is evolved to ensure fair action when the function is administrative. But the said principle cannot be invoked to amend, alter or vary the expressed terms of the contract between the parties. The duty to act fairly and reasonably is a doctrine developed in administrative law field to ensure the rule of law and to prevent failure of justice when the action is administrative in nature; *Puravankara Projects Limited* v. *Hotel Venus International*, 2007 (2) Ker LT 943: 2007 (2) SCALE 471: 2007 (10) SCC 33: 2007 (2) Supreme 532.

10. Service Matters – Law on – Civil Court may have a limited jurisdiction in service matters but it cannot be said to have no jurisdiction at all to entertain a suit. It may not be entitled to sit in appeal over the order passed in the disciplinary proceedings or on the quantum of punishment imposed. It may not in a given case direct reinstatement in service having regard to section 14(1)(b) of the Specific Relief Act, 1963 but, it is a trite law that where the right is claimed by the plaintiff in terms of common law or under a statute other than the one which created a new right for the first time and when a forum has also been created for enforcing the said right, the Civil Court shall also have jurisdiction to entertain a suit where the plaintiff claim benefit of a fundamental right as adumbrated under article 14 of the Constitution of India or mandatory provisions of statute or statutory rules governing the terms and conditions of service; *Rajasthan SRTC* v. *Mohar Singh*, AIR 2008 SC 2553: 2008 (7) SCALE 339: 2008 (5) SCC 542.

11. Writ Petition – Maintainability of – When an action of the party is *de hors* the terms and conditions contained in an agreement as also beyond the scope and ambit of the domestic forum created therefore, the writ petition may be held to be maintainable; but indisputably therefore such a case has to be made out. The arbitrator may not have the requisite jurisdiction to direct restoration of distributorship having regard to the provisions contained in section 14 of the Specific Relief Act, 1963; but while entertaining a writ petition even in such a case, the court may not lose sight of the fact that if a serious disputed question of fact is involved arising out of a contract *qua* contract, ordinarily a writ petition would not be entertained. A writ petition, however, will be entertained when it involves a public law character or involves a question arising out of public law functions on the part of the respondent; *Empire Jute Co. Ltd.* v. *Jute Corporation of India Limited*, 2007 (11) SCR 388: AIR 2007 SCW 6930: JT 2007 (12) SC 391: 2007 (12) SCALE 514.

12. Contract of Personal Service – Law on – Section 14(b) of the Specific Relief Act provides that a contract of personal service shall not be enforced. The Court does not thrust an employee upon an unwilling master. However there exists four exceptions to the aforementioned rules.

(1) Where an employee enjoys the status which is being protected under article 311 of the Constitution of India.

(2) An employee who has been dismissed from service by a statutory corporation in violation of the mandatory provisions of a statute.

(3) A workman under the Industrial Disputes Act.

(4) Employees whose services are protected by a statute.

A distinction as to co-operative societies which are merely registered under Co-operative Societies Act on the one hand and those cooperative societies although registered under the Co-operative Societies Act are fully funded and controlled by the State and conditions of service of its employee are governed by the statutory rules; *Sum Prasad* v. *Andhra Pradesh State Federation of Co-operative Spinning Mills Limited, Hyderabad*, 2001 (6) ALD 741: 2001 (6) ALT 233.

13. Industrial Dispute – Law on – A dispute arising in between an employer and employee may or may not be an industrial dispute. The dispute may be in relation to or arising out of a fundamental right of the employee, or his right under a Parliamentary Act and the Regulations framed thereunder, and/or a right arising under the provisions of the Industrial Disputes Act or the sister laws and may relate to same or similar rights or different rights, or even may be based on common law right or contractual right. The question in regard to the jurisdiction of the civil court must, therefore, be addressed having regard to the fact as to which rights or obligations are sought to be enforced for the purpose of invoking or excluding the jurisdiction of a civil court. If an employee intends to enforce his constitutional rights or a right under a statutory Regulation, the civil court will have the necessary jurisdiction to try a suit. If, however, he claims his right and corresponding obligations only in terms of the provisions of the Industrial Disputes Act or the sister laws so called, the civil court will have none. In this view of the matter, in our considered opinion, it would not be correct to contend that only because the employee concerned is also a workman within the meaning of the provisions of the 1947 Act or the conditions of his service are otherwise governed by the Standing Order certified under the 1946 Act *ipso facto* the Civil Court will have no jurisdiction; *Rajasthan State Road Transport Corporation* v. *Bal Mukund Bairwa*, AIR 2009 SCW 2566: JT 2009 (2) SC 423: 2009 (2) SCALE 428: 2009 (4) SCC 299.

14. Contracts Involving Performance of Continuous Duty cannot be Specifically Enforced – Where in a contract the performance of material terms involves performance of continuous duty which court cannot supervise, such contract cannot be specifically enforced; *Amar Nagar (SRA) Sah. Gruhanirman Sanstha, Mumbai* v. *Vikas Narayan Raikar*, AIR 2015 Bom 31.

Persons for or against whom contracts may be specifically enforced

15. Who may obtain specific performance.—Except as otherwise provided by this Chapter, the specific performance of a contract may be obtained by—

(a) any party thereto;

(b) the representative in interest or the principal, of any party thereto:

Provided that where the learning, skill, solvency or any personal quality of such party is a material ingredient in the contract, or where the contract provides that his interest shall not be assigned, his representative in interest or his principal shall not be entitled to specific performance of the contract, unless such party has already performed his part of the contract, or the performance thereof by his representative in interest, or his principal, has been accepted by the other party;

(c) where the contract is a settlement on marriage, or a compromise of doubtful rights between members of the same family, any person beneficially entitled thereunder;

(d) where the contract has been entered into by a tenant for life in due exercise of a power, the reminderman;

(e) a reversioner in possession, where the agreement is a covenant entered into with his predecessor in title and the reversioner is entitled to the benefit of such covenant;

(f) a reversioner in remainder, where the agreement is such a covenant, and the reversioner is entitled to the benefit thereof and will sustain material injury by reason of its breach;

(g) when a company has entered into a contract and subsequently becomes amalgamated with another company, the new company which arises out of the amalgamation;

(h) when the promoters of a company have, before its incorporation, entered into a contract for the purposes of the company, and such contract is warranted by the terms of the incorporation, the company:

Provided that the company has accepted the contract and has communicated such acceptance to the other party to the contract.

SYNOPSIS

1. Legal Right of Assignment – Law on
2. Parties to Contract – Law on
3. Personal Performance – Law on
4. Promoters of a Company – Law on
5. Representative-in-Interest – Right of
6. Right of Repurchase – Law on

COMMENTS

1. Legal Right of Assignment – Law on – As is to be seen from the provisions of section 15(b) of the Specific Relief Act, 1963, specific performance of the contract may be obtained by 'any party thereto' or 'their representative in interest.' This expression clearly includes the transferees and assignees from the contracting party in whose favour the right exists. Such right of seeking specific performance would, however, be not available in terms of proviso below clause (b) where the contract provides that the 'interest shall not be assigned.' In the absence of any words or expressions in the documents indicating prohibition on assignment or transfer of right of repurchase and in the face of clear provisions of section 15(b) of the Specific Relief Act, 1963, an implied prohibition cannot be read into the terms of the documents. Merely because in the documents, there is mention of 'heirs' of the contracting parties but not their 'assignees' or 'transferees,' the legal right of assignment available to the benefit of original contracting party under section 15(b) of the Act cannot be denied to it; *Shyam Singh* v. *Daryao Singh*, AIR 2004 SC 348: 2003 (9) SCALE 802: 2003 (12) SCC 160.

2. Parties to Contract – Law on – Specific performance of a contract can be enforced by any party to the contract. If there are more parties than one, specific performance of a contract cannot be decreed in the absence of some of the parties to the contract. If some of the parties entitled to the benefit of the contract are not willing to be arrayed as plaintiffs they should be impleaded as defendants. Section 23(a) of the Specific Relief Act (now section 22) covers such a case; *Mukesh Kumar* v. *Col. Harbans Waraiah*, AIR 2000 SC 172: JT 1999 (8) SC 563: 1999 (6) SCALE 644: 1999 (9) SCC 380.

3. Personal Performance – Law on – Section 15 of the new Act provides for the specific performance of a contract. Under this section, unless the contract itself provides that the agreement to sell shall not be assigned, or the terms of the contract laid down conditions which may indicate that the contract has to be personally performed by the parties to it, an agreement to sell a property is assignable; *Munawwar Husen* v. *Zakir Husen*, 1984 AWC 1 [**Hon'ble Judges:** K.C. Agrawal, S.D. Agarwala, O.P. Saxena]

4. Promoters of a Company – Law on – In terms of section 15(h) of the Specific Relief Act, the Promoters of a company before its incorporation could enter into a contract for the benefit of the company and such contract may be warranted by the terms of incorporation of the company. The said provision is subject to the proviso that the company should accept the said transaction. Under the 1877 Act, not only ratification and adoption of the contract was mandatory, such contract was to be warranted by the terms of the incorporation. The words 'ratified and adopted" have been dropped from the main section and in section 19 of the 1963 Act, a proviso has been added that the company has accepted the contract and communicated such acceptance to the other party of the contract. An express ratification of the contract, therefore, is no longer warranted; *Jai Narain Parasurampuria* v. *Pushpa Devi Saraf*, 2006 (133) Comp Cas 794: 2006 (8) SCALE 477: 2006 (7) SCC 756: 2006 (8) SCJ 524.

5. Representative-in-Interest – Right of – Section 23(b) of the Specific Relief Act, 1877 is analogous to section 15(b) of the Specific Relief Act, 1963. It lays down that except as otherwise provided the specific performance of a contract may be obtained by the representative-in-interest or the principal, of any party thereto. Thus normally any interest in a contract could be assigned to any representative-in-interest who also can enforce the specific performance of the contract against the contracting party. However, if the terms of the contract, expressly or by necessary implication, prohibited the beneficiary from transferring his contractual interest to third parties, then only such an assignee cannot sue for specific performance; *Habiba Khatoon* v. *Ubaidul Huq*, AIR 1997 SC 3236: 1997 (5) SCALE 380: 1997 (7) SCC 452: 1997 (7) Supreme 286.

6. Right of Repurchase – Law on – It must at once be stated that right to repurchase flowing from the document was independent of the obligation of the said beneficiary enforcing the contract of repurchase to defray the cost of repair of the house, if at all any, carried out by the purchaser-executant of the document. That is an independent obligation which would get attached to the property and consequently whoever is the purchaser of the property on the basis of the enforcement of the right of repurchase will have to bear that burden; *Habiba Khatoon* v. *Ubaidul Huq*, AIR 1997 SC 3236: JT 1997 (7) SC 298: 1997 (5) SCALE 380: 1997 (7) SCC 452.

16. Personal bars to relief.—Specific performance of a contract cannot be enforced in favour of a person—

(a) who would not be entitled to recover compensation for its breach; or

(b) who has become incapable of performing, or violates any essential term of, the contract that on his part remains to be performed, or acts in fraud of the contract, or wilfully acts at variance with, or in subversion of, the relation intended to be established by the contract; or

(c) who fails to aver and prove that he has performed or has always been ready and willing to perform the essential terms of the contract which are to be performed by him, other than terms the performance of which has been prevented or waived by the defendant.

Explanation.—For the purposes of clause (c),—

(i) where a contract involves the payment of money, it is not essential for the plaintiff to actually tender to the defendant or to deposit in court any money except when so directed by the court;

(ii) the plaintiff must aver performance of, or readiness and willingness to perform, the contract according to its true construction.

SYNOPSIS

COMMENTS

1. 'Contract' – Law on – 'Contract' is a bilateral transaction between two or more than two parties. Every contract has to pass through several stages beginning with the stage of negotiation during which the parties discuss and negotiate proposals and counter-proposals as also the consideration resulting finally in the acceptance of the proposals. The proposal when accepted gives rise to an agreement. It is at this stage that the agreement is reduced into writing and a formal document is executed on which parties affixed their signatures or thumb impression so as to be bound by the terms of the agreement set out in that document. Such an agreement has to be lawful as the definition of contract, as set out in section 2(h) provides that "an agreement enforceable by law is a contract". Section 2(g) sets out that "an agreement not enforceable by law is said to be void"; *Tarsem Singh* v. *Sukhminder Singh,* AIR 1998 SC 1400: JT 1998 (2) SC 149: 1998 (1) SCALE 58.

2. Alternative Plea – Law on – The plaintiff in a suit for specific performance of contract may raise an alternative plea that the transaction is a mortgage by way of conditional sale but he must be ready and willing either to repay the debt or pay the amount of consideration as agreed upon; *Umabai* v. *Nilkanth Dhondiba Chavan,* 2005 (3) SCR 521: JT 2005 (4) SC 292: 2005 (4) SCALE 142: 2005 (6) SCC 243.

3. Amendment – Law on – Thus, the oldest golden case law and the latest modern case law by interpreting the law clearly says and clarifies that the settled position is that amendment of pleadings can be allowed at any stage of the proceedings, provided it is necessary for the purpose of deciding the controversies between the parties. They further clarified that even if such an amendment is barred by time, that factor is to be taken into consideration in exercise of the discretion as to whether amendment should be allowed or not and when it does not affect the cause of action and when it does not introduce a new case and when there is no serious prejudice caused to the opposite party and when such amendment is required to do justice, the Court has wide discretionary power to allow such amendment; *Hi Sheet Industries* a *Partnership Firm* v. *Litelon Limited, Rep by its Managing Partner, S. Gokul,* 2007 AIHC 1281: AIR 2007 Mad 78: 2007 (1) Mad LJ 320: 2007 (1) Rent LR 177.

4. Argument for First Time at Stage of Second Appeal – Maintainability of – In the absence of any plea or an issue to effect, it was not open to the High Court to entertain the argument, for the first time, at the stage of the second appeal; *Sheikh Farjan Mian* v. *Teju Sahu,* JT 2001 (8) SC 645: 2002 (1) AWC 441 (SC).

5. Contract Involves Payment of Money – Law on – *Explanation* to clause (c) of section 16 makes it clear that where a contract involves the payment of money, it is not essential for the Plaintiff to actually render to the Defendant or to deposit in court any money, except when so directed by the court. The Court must see as to how consistent the testimony of the witness is and as to how that answer fits in with the rest of the evidence and probabilities of the case; *Boramma* v. *Krishna Gowda*, 2000 ACJ 504: JT 2000 (8) SC 13: 2000 (9) SCC 214: 2000 (7) Supreme 80.

6. Contract with Union of India – Law on – No contract is enforceable against the Union of India, unless the mandatory requirements of article 299 of the Constitution have been complied within the absence of any enforceable contract, It was clearly wrong in passing a law for specific performance against the Union of India. No decree for specific performance can be made without proof of a valid and enforceable contract between the plaintiff and the Union of India; *Sohan Lal* v. *Union of India*, AIR 1991 SC 955: JT 1991 (5) SC 102: 1990 (2) SCALE 1267: 1991 (1) SCC 438; *See* also: *State of Haryana* v. *Lal Chand*, AIR 1984 SC 1326: (1984) 3 SCR 715; *State of Punjab* v. *M/s. Om Parkash Baldev Krishan*, (1988) Supp SCC 722: AIR 1988 SC 21419 and *Mulamchand* v. *State of Madhya Pradesh*, (1968) 3 SCR 214: AIR 1968 SC 1218.

7. Copy of Agreement – Law on – It is not in dispute that in the absence of the original document, the copy of the agreement which was typed as a duplicate of the document could be received as secondary evidence in the case. The son of the vendor (deceased) has admitted the signatures on the document to be those of his father. In such circumstances, no exception could be taken to acceptance of the document as genuine and its contents as true. On the evidence on record, sufficient foundation for accepting the document by way of secondary evidence in terms of section 65 of the Evidence Act can be laid; *T. Mohan* v. *Kannammal*, JT 2002 (2) SC 163: 2002 (10) SCC 82: 2002 (3) Supreme 176: 2002 (3) ICC 708.

8. Cross Appeal – Law on – It is necessary that both the appeals arising from the judgment and decree of the trial Court are heard and disposed of together. Cross appeal against the decree of the trial Court should have been considered by the High Court; *Thakamma Mathew* v. *M. Azamathulla Khan*, AIR 1993 SC 1120: JT 1993 (1) SC 35: 1992 (3) SCALE 454: 1993 (2) SCJ 47 **[Hon'ble Judges:** M.N. Venkatachaliah, S.C. Agrawal, A.S. Anand]

9. Deficiency in Payment of Court Fee – Law on – Any deficiency in payment of court fee at one stage will not disentitle plaintiff to pursue the suit for specific performance; *Satya Narain Misra* v. *Har Pratap Singh (Dead) by LRs.*, 2007 (15) SCC 585.

10. Died Witness – Law on – It has come on evidence on record that Mr. X, one of the attesting witnesses, after his examination-in- chief died and, therefore, he could not put up for cross-examination. Under such circumstances, the evidence of Mr. X could not have been excluded; *Satnam Singh* v. *Sadhu Singh*, 2001 (Supp 1) JT 545: 2001 (8) Supreme 574: 2002 (1) Apex CJ 79.

11. Enforcement of Agreement – Law on – Under section 16(c) of Specific Relief Act, 1963, the plaintiff must plead in the plaint, his readiness and willingness from the date of the contract till date of the decree. The plaintiff who seeks enforcement of the agreement is enjoined to establish the same. Equally, when transferee seeks to avail of section 53A to retain possession of the property which he had under the contract, it would also be incumbent upon the transferee to plead and prove his readiness and willingness to perform his part of the contract. He who comes to equity must do equity. The doctrine of readiness and willingness is an emphatic way of expression to establish that the transferee always abides by the terms of the agreement and is willing to perform his part of the contract. Part performance, as statutory right is conditioned upon the transferee's continuous willingness to perform his part of the contract in terms covenanted thereunder. Even otherwise, a transferee can avail of section 53A only as a shield but not as a sword. It contemplates that where any person contracts to transfer for consideration any immovable property by writing signed by him or on his behalf from which the terms necessary to constitute the transfer can be ascertained with reasonable certainty and the transferee has performed or is willing to perform his part of the contract, he would be entitled to retain possession and to continue in possession which he has already received from the transferor so long as he is willing to perform his part of contract. Agreement does not create title on interest in the property. Since the agreement had met with dismissal of the suit his willingness to perform his part of the contract does not arise; *Mohan Lal* v. *Mira Abdul Gaffar*, AIR 1996 SC 910: JT 1995 (9) SC 436: 1996 (1) SCALE 5: 1996 (1) SCC 639.

12. Essence of Contract – Law on – It is a well-settled principle that in the case of sale of immovable property, time is never regarded as the essence of the contract. In fact, there is a presumption against time being the essence of the contract. This principle is not in any way different from that obtainable in England. Under the law of equity which governs the rights of the parties in the case of specific performance of the contract to sell real estate, law looks not at the letter but at the substance of the agreement. It has to be ascertained whether under the terms of the contract the parties named a specific time within which completion was to take place, really and in substance it was intended that it should be completed within a reasonable time. An intention to make time the essence of the contract must be expressed in unequivocal language; *P. Purushottam Reddy* v. *Pratap Steels Ltd.*, AIR 2002 SC 771: JT 2002 (5) SC 5: 2002 (1) SCALE 447: 2002 (2) SCC 686.

13. Essential Part of Contract – Law on – Section 16 of the Specific Relief Act, 1963 corresponds with section 24 of the old Act of 1877 which lays down that the person seeking specific performance of the contract, must file a suit wherein he must allege and prove that he has performed or has been ready and willing to perform the essential terms of the contract, which are to be performed by him. The specific performance of the contract cannot be enforced in favour of the person who fails to aver and prove his readiness and willingness to perform essential terms of the contract. *Explanation (ii)* to clause (c) of section 16 further makes it clear that plaintiff must aver performance of, or readiness and willingness to perform, the contract according to its true construction. The compliance of the requirement of section 16(c) is mandatory and in the absence of proof of the same that the plaintiff has been ready and willing to perform his part of the contract suit cannot succeed. The first requirement is that he must aver in plaint and thereafter prove those averments made in the plaint. The plaintiff's readiness and willingness must be in accordance with the terms of the agreement. The readiness and willingness of the plaintiff to perform the essential part of the contract would be required to be demonstrated by him from the institution of the suit till it is culminated into decree of the court; *Bal Krishna* v. *Bhagwan Das (Dead)*, AIR 2008 SC 1786: 2008 (4) SCALE 805: 2008 (12) SCC 145: 2008 (2) Supreme 752.

14. Fresh Cause of Action – Law on – It was only one averment required under section 16(c) of the Specific Relief Act to be made in a plaint in a suit for specific performance which was not made, probably on account of some oversight or mistake of the lawyer who drafted the plaint and that error was sought to be rectified by the amendment applied for. There was no fresh cause of action sought to be introduced by the amendment and hence, no question of causing any injustice to the respondent on that account arose; *Lakhi Ram* v. *Trikha Ram*, AIR 1998 SC 1230: JT 1998 (1) SC 665: 1998 (1) SCALE 551: 1998 (2) SCC 720: 1998 (1) SCR 705; *Gajanan Jaikishan Joshi* v. *Prabhakar Mohanlal Kalwar*, (1990) 1 SCC 166.

15. High Courts – Guidelines for – The purpose of the establishment of courts of justice is to render justice between the parties. Is it necessary to unduly curtail the jurisdiction of the High Courts, either under section 100 of the Code of Civil procedure or under section 115 of the Code of Civil Procedure in that context? Of course, the High Courts have to act with circumspection while exercising these jurisdictions. Certainly, it is for the Parliament to take into account all the relevant aspects; *Rajeshwari* v. *Puran Indoria*, JT 2005 (7) SC 630: 2005 (6) SCALE 762: 2005 (7) SCC 60: 2005 (6) Supreme 1.

16. Hindu Law – Comments on – The minors were, admittedly, not party to the agreement. Under law, the Person could not have sold the property without any legal necessity. It was not proved that there was any legal necessity for sale of the property. Under such circumstances, the court is justified in refusing the relief for specific performance; *Mohamed Asgar Mohamed Mazhar* v. *Arvind Raghunath Sawant*, 2001 (5) ALD (SC) 30: 2001 (44) All LR 576: JT 2001 (5) SC 563: 2001 (5) Supreme 396.

17. Mandatory Obligations of Plaintiff – Law on – Section 16 of the Specific Relief Act, 1963 mandates the plaintiff to aver in the plaint and establish as a fact by evidence *aliunde* that he has always been ready and willing to perform his part of the contract. The failure thereof is fatal to maintain the suit and entails with its dismissal. Though the decree for specific performance is a discretionary power, yet the court is not bound to grant such a relief merely because it is lawful to do so; but the discretion of the court is not arbitrary, but sound and reasonable, guided by judicial principles of law and capable of correction by a court of appeal. Therefore, the discretion should be properly exercised keeping in view the settled principles of law as envisaged in section 20 of the Act; AIR 1994 SC 105: 1995 (Supp 4) SCC 542.

18. Mortgage – Law on – There exists a distinction between mortgage by conditional sale and a sale with a condition of repurchase. In a mortgage, the debt subsists and a right to redeem remains with the debtor; but a sale with a condition of repurchase is not a lending and borrowing arrangement. There does not exist any debt and no right to redeem is reserved thereby. An agreement to sell confers merely a personal right which can be enforced strictly according to the terms of the deed and at the time agreed upon. Proviso appended to section 58(c) of the Transfer of Property Act, 1882, however, states that if the condition for re-transfer is not embodied in the document which effects or purports to effect a sale, the transaction will not be regarded as a mortgage; *Umabai* v. *Nilkanth Dhondiba Chavan*, 2005 (3) SCR 521: JT 2005 (4) SC 292: 2005 (4) SCALE 142: 2005 (6) SCC 243.

19. Newly Framed Issue – Law on – It is considered view that the High Court should frame an issue whether there has been unexplained delay on the part of the plaintiff in taking recourse to law in filing suit (though it is filed within the prescribed period of limitation) and whether on facts and in the circumstances of the case such delay defeats the relief of specific performance of the contract for sale of the suit property and call for the finding of the trial court on the issue and on receipt of the same decide, the first appeal afresh after giving opportunity of hearing to the parties. It goes without saying that the trial court will give opportunity to the parties to adduce further evidence in the case on the newly framed issue and record its finding on the question; *Ram Niwas Gupta* v. *Mumtaz Hasan*, JT 2002 (2) SC 384: 2008 (17) SCC 362: 2002 (7) Supreme 591.

20. No Written Statement Filed – Law on – It is clear that the Court, at no stage, can act blindly or mechanically. While enabling the Court to pronounce judgment in a situation where no written statement is filed by the defendant, the Court has also been given the discretion to pass such order as it may think fit as an alternative. This is also the position under Order VIII, rule 10, C.P.C. where the Court can either pronounce judgment against the defendant or pass such order as it may think fit; *Balraj Taneja* v. *Sunil Madan*, AIR 1999 SC 3381: JT 1999 (6) SC 473: 1999 (5) SCALE 400: 1999 (8) SCC 396.

21. Normal Presumption – Law on – Apart from the normal presumption that in the case of an agreement of sale of immovable property time is not the essence of the contract; *Govind Prasad Chaturvedi* v. *Hari Dutt Shastri*, AIR 1977 SC 1005: 1977 (2) SCC 539: 1977 (2) SCR 877.

22. Purchaser – Restriction for – There was no need for the purchaser to have backed out from the agreement to purchase because the property prices were going up and the vendor would have known that on the date of settlement the property would have fetched much larger money; *Manicklal Mukherjee* v. *Commr. of Sanchaita Investments, Calcutta*, AIR 1993 SC 1571: 1992 (2) SCALE 812: 1993 (1) SCC 505: 1992 (3) SCJ 595 **[Hon'ble Judges:** S. Ranganathan, V. Ramaswami, Yogeshwar Dayal].

23. Readiness to Perform Contract and Willingness to Perform Contract – Law on – There is a distinction between readiness to perform the contract and willingness to perform the contract. By readiness may be meant the capacity of the plaintiff to perform the contract which includes his financial position to pay the purchase price. For determining his willingness to perform his part of the contract, the conduct has to be properly scrutinised. The factum of readiness and willingness to perform plaintiff's part of the contract is to be adjudged with reference to the conduct of the party and the attending circumstances. The Court may infer from the facts and circumstances whether the plaintiff was ready and was always ready and willing to perform his part of the contract; *His Holiness Acharya Swami Ganesh Dassji* v. *Sita Ram Thapar*, AIR 1996 SC 2095: JT 1996 (5) SC 460: 1996 (4) SCALE 476: 1996 (4) SCC 526.

24. *Res Judicata* – Law on – That the basis on which the rule rests is founded on consideration of public policy and it is in the interest of public at large that a finality should attach to the binding decision pronounced by a Court of competent jurisdiction and it is also in the public interest that individuals should not be vexed twice over in the same kind of litigation; *Daryao* v. *State of Uttar Pradesh,* (1962) 1 SCR 574: AIR 1961 SC 1457 [Constitution Bench].

25. Status of Tenant after an Agreement of Sale with Landlord – Law on – Whether status of a tenant would continue to be so even after an agreement of sale is executed by such tenant with the landlord in respect of the same tenanted premises. The status of such tenant, after execution of the said agreement of sale ceases to be such which is changed to that of a purchaser and when a sale deed is executed, as in this case of the half share of the said property such tenant becomes co-owner with the landlord; *Imambi* v. *Azeeza Bee,* 2001 ACJ 125: JT 2000 (9) SC 562: 2001 (3) Supreme 517: 2000 (4) ICC 549.

26. Time – Importance of – As a matter of law time becomes essence of the contract; *Bismillah Begum* v. *Rahmatullah Khan*, AIR 1998 SC 970: JT 1998 (1) SC 262: 1998 (1) SCALE 178: 1998 (2) SCC 226.

27. Time Being Essence of Contract – Presumption Against – It is a well-accepted principle that in the case of sale of immovable property, time is never regarded as the essence of the contract. In fact, there is a presumption against time being the essence of the contract. This principle is not in any way different from that obtainable in England. Under the law of equity which governs the rights of the parties in the case of specific performance of contract to sell real estate, law looks not at the letter but at the substance of the agreement. It has to be ascertained whether under the terms of the contract the parties named a specific time within which completion was to take place, really and in substance it was intended that it should be completed within a reasonable time. An intention to make time the essence of the contract must be expressed in unequivocal language; *Chand Rani* v. *Kamal Rani*, AIR 1993 SC 1742: JT 1993 (1) SC 74: 1992 (1) LJR 368: 1992 (3) SCALE 544: 1993 (1) SCC 519 **[Hon'ble Judges:** L.M. Sharma, S. Ratnavel Pandian, S. Mohan, B.P. Jeevan Reddy, S.P. Bharucha].

28. Valuation of Superstructure – Law on – Before sale deed is to be executed; valuation of the superstructure is to be ascertained. For this vendor and purchaser was to nominate an engineer or architect and in the case of their difference each has to appoint as such and if, there be any difference between them, then the matter was to be referred to an Umpire. Section 16(c) of the Specific Relief Act, requires that not only there be a plea of readiness and willingness but has to be proved so. It is not in dispute except for a plea there is no other evidence on record to prove the same except the two circumstances. It is true that mere absence of plaintiff coming in the witness box that by itself may not be a factor to conclude that he was not ready and willing; *Pushparani S. Sundaram* v. *Pauline Manomani James (Deceased),* AIR 2001 SCW 2347: 2000 (4) CCC 83: JT 2000 (8) SC 95: 2002 (9) SCC 582.

29. Void Agreement – Law on – Section 73 stipulates a valid and binding contract between the parties. It deals with one of the remedies available for the breach of contract. It is provided that where a party sustains a loss on account of breach of contract; he is entitled to receive, from the party who has broken the contract, compensation for such loss or damage. Under section 74 of the Act, however, the parties to the agreement stipulate either a particular amount which is to be paid in case of breach or an amount may be mentioned to be paid by way of penalty. The party complaining of the breach is entitled, whether or not actual damage or loss is proved to have been caused, to receive from the party who has committed the breach of contract, compensation not exceeding the amount mentioned in the agreement or the penalty stipulated therein. But this section also contemplates a valid and binding agreement between the parties. Since the stipulation for forfeiture of the earnest money is part of the contract, it is necessary for the enforcement of that stipulation, that the contract between the parties is valid. If the forfeiture clause is contained in an agreement which is void on account of the fact that the parties were suffering from mistake of fact in respect of a matter which was essential to the contract, it cannot be enforced as the agreement itself is void under section 20 of the Contract Act. A void agreement cannot be split up. None of the parties to the agreement can be permitted to seek enforcement of a part only of the contract through a Court of law. If the agreement is void, all its terms are void and none of the terms, except in certain known exceptions, especially where the clause is treated to constitute a separate and independent agreement, severable from the main agreement, can be enforced separately and independently. This section 65 of the Contract Act is based on equitable doctrine, provides for the restitution of any benefit received under a void agreement or contract and, therefore, mandates that any "person" which obviously would include a party to the agreement, who has received any advantage under an agreement which is discovered to be void or under a contract which becomes void, has to restore such advantage or to pay compensation for it, to the person from whom he received that advantage or benefit; *Tarsem Singh* v. *Sukhminder Singh*, AIR 1998 SC 1400: JT 1998 (2) SC 149: 1998 (1) SCALE 58: 1998 (3) SCC 471.

30. Cancellation – Condition for – After the decree was passed by the trial Court, the litigant through their power of attorney sold large extent of properties including the subject-matter of the suit in favour of certain other persons .Once there is a conveyance the concept would be different and the primary relief could be only cancellation; *M.M.S. Investments* v. *V. Veerappan*, AIR 2007 SC 2663: 2007 (5) SCALE 582: 2007 (9) SCC 660: 2007 (3) SCJ 662.

31. Capacity to Perform Contract – Law on – There can be no quarrel with the proposition that in a suit for specific performance of the contract, the plaintiff must prove that he was ready and willing to perform his part of the contract continuously between the date of the contract and the date of hearing of the suit. But the finding that the plaintiff has not proved his capacity to perform his part of the contract as he was not even ready to deposit the money in terms of the trial court's order is factually wrong. The High Court should not have acted on an oral submission made by the defendant without granting of an opportunity to the plaintiff to have their say in the matter; *Mst. Etwari Devi* v. *Mst. Parvati Devi*, AIR 2006 SC 970: JT 2006 (2) SC 419: 2006 (1) SCALE 366: 2006 (2) SCC 327.

32. Conduct of Plaintiff – Law on – The basic principle behind section 16(c) read with *Explanation (ii)* is that any person seeking benefit of the specific performance of contract must manifest that his conduct has been blemishless throughout entitling him to the specific relief. The provision imposes a personal bar. The Court is to grant relief on the basis of the conduct of the person seeking relief. If the pleadings manifest that the conduct of the plaintiff entitles him to get the relief on perusal of the plaint he should not be denied the relief. Section 16(c) of the Act mandates the plaintiff to aver in the plaint and establish as the fact by evidence that he has always been ready and willing to perform his part of the contract; *Aniglase Yohannan* v. *Ramlatha,* AIR 2005 SC 3503: JT 2005 (8) SC 499: 2005 (7) SCALE 471: 2005 (7) SCC 534.

The requirements to be fulfilled for bringing in compliance of the section 16(c) of the Act have been delineated by Apex Court in several judgments. The language in section 16(c) of the Specific Relief Act, 1963 does not require any specific phraseology but only that the plaintiff must aver that he has performed or has always been and is willing to perform his part of the contract. So the compliance of 'readiness and willingness' has to be in spirit and substance and not in letter and form. "It is thus clear that an averment of readiness and willingness in the plaint is not a mathematical formula which should only be in specific words. If the averments in the plaint as a whole do clearly indicate the readiness and willingness of the plaintiff to fulfill his part of the obligations under the contract which is the subject-matter of the suit, the fact that they are differently worded will not militate against the readiness and willingness of the plaintiff in a suit for specific performance of contract for sale. "The basic principle behind section 16(c) read with *Explanation (ii)* is that any person seeking benefit of the specific performance of contract must manifest that his conduct has been blemishless throughout entitling him to the specific relief. The provision imposes a personal bar. The Court is to grant relief on the basis of the conduct of the person seeking relief. If the pleadings manifest that the conduct of the plaintiff entitles him to get the relief on perusal of the plaint he should not be denied the relief. Section 16(c) of the Act mandates the plaintiff to aver in the plaint and establish as the fact by evidence that he has always been ready and willing to perform his part of the contract; *H.P. Pyarejan* v. *Dasappa,* AIR 2006 SC 1144: JT 2006 (2) SC 228: 2006 (2) SCALE 241: 2006 (2) SCC 496.

33. Decree for Specific Performance – Requirement for – If Plaintiff had fulfilled the conditions as stated in section 16(c) of the Specific Relief Act and in that event the plaintiff is entitled to decree for specific performance; *Aloka Bose* v. *Parmatma Devi,* AIR 2009 SC 1527: 2008 (16) SCALE 281: 2009 (2) SCC 582.

34. Deposit of Balance Amount – Law on – The language in section 16(c) does not require any specific phraseology but only that the plaintiff must aver that he has performed or has always been and is willing to perform his part of the contract. So the compliance of "readiness and willingness" has to be in spirit and substance and not in letter and form. So to insist for mechanical production of the exact words of an statute is to insist for the form rather than essence. So absence of form cannot dissolve an essence if already pleaded. It is significant that this explanation carves out contract which involves payment of money as a separate class from section 16(c). *Explanation (i)* uses the words "it is not essential for the plaintiff to actually tender to the defendant or to deposit in Court any money except when so directed by the Court. This speaks in negative term what is not essential for plaintiff to do. This is more in support of plaintiff that he need not tender to the defendant or deposit in Court any money but the plaintiff must (as per *Explanation (ii)* at least aver his performance or readiness and willingness to perform his part of the contract. This does not mean that unless the Court directs the plaintiff cannot tender the amount to the defendant or deposit in the Court. Plaintiff can always tender the amount to the defendant or deposit it in Court, towards performance of his obligation under the contract. Such tender rather exhibits willingness of the plaintiff to perform his part of the obligation. What is 'not essential' only means need not do but does not mean he cannot do so. Hence, when the plaintiff has tendered the balance amount in Court even without Court's order it cannot be construed adversely against the plaintiff under *Explanation (i); Syed Dastagir* v. *T.R. Gopalakrishnasetty,* AIR 1999 SC 3029: JT 1999 (5) SC 642: 1999 (4) SCALE 697: 1999 (6) SCC 337.

35. Essence of Contract – Law on – In terms of the article 54 of the Limitation Act, 1963, a suit for specific performance of a contract is required to be filed within three years; in the event no date is fixed for the performance, within a period of three years from the date when the plaintiff has notice that performance is refused. The notice is required to be construed in the context of the agreement entered into by and between the parties. There cannot be any doubt whatsoever that in respect of a contract for sale of immovable property, time is not of the essence of the contract, but the question as regard the conduct of the parties must be considered in the backdrop of the events noticed Limitation Act; *R.K. Parvatharaj Gupta* v. *K.C. Jayadeva Reddy*, JT 2006 (2) SC 156: 2006 (2) SCALE 156: 2006 (2) SCC 428: 2006 (2) SCJ 239.

36. High Court – Guidelines for – Full Bench should be constrained to disapprove the approach adopted by the single Judge in ignoring the decision of the Division Bench and preferring to agree to the view expressed by the single Judges. The proper course is that if he disagrees to the Division Bench judgment and merely wants to follow the single Judge's view, he ought to have referred the matter to a Larger Bench; *P. Maragathamani; V. Ramasamy; K. Thangavelu* v. *General Manager (In-Charge), Bharat Heavy Electricals Limited*, 2006 (1) CTC 497: 2007 (1) JCR 283: 2006 (1) Mad LJ 480.

37. High Court – Powers of – It is not within the domain of the High Court to investigate the grounds on which the findings were arrived at, by the last court of fact. It is true that the lower appellate court should not ordinarily reject witness accepted by the trial court in respect of credibility but even where it has rejected the witnesses accepted by the trial court, the same is no ground for interference in second appeal, when it is found that the appellate court has given satisfactory reasons for doing so. In a case where from a given set of circumstances two inferences are possible. One drawn by the lower appellate court is binding on the High Court in second appeal. Adopting any other approach is not permissible. The High Court cannot substitute its opinion for the opinion of the first appellate court unless it is found that the conclusions drawn by the lower appellate court were erroneous being contrary to the mandatory provisions of law applicable or its settled position on the basis of pronouncements made by the Apex Court, or was based upon inadmissible evidence or arrived at without evidence; *Sugani* v. *Rameshwar Das*, AIR 2006 SC 2172: 2006 (4) SCALE 491: 2006 (11) SCC 587: 2006 (5) SCJ 59.

38. Judicial Discipline – Rule of – The High Court should have given respect to the view of the Supreme Court, in the light of the settled principles of law that the judicial discipline requires that clear pronouncements by the Supreme Court, about what the law on a matter is, must be treated as binding by all the Courts in India. Where the Supreme Court has stated that the law laid down in a particular case is the applicable law, it is not open to the High Court to consider or rely on any supposedly conflicting decision. Judicial discipline to abide by declaration of law by the Supreme Court cannot be forsaken under any pretext by any authority or Court, be it even the highest Court in a State, oblivious to article 141 of the Constitution; *P. Maragathamani; V. Ramasamy; K. Thangavelu* v. *General Manager (In-Charge), Bharat Heavy Electricals Limited*, 2006 (1) CTC 497: 2007 (1) JCR 283: 2006 (1) Mad LJ 480.

39. Maxim "*Equity Acts* in Personam and Jurisdiction – Law on – Sections 15 to 20 of the Code contain detailed provisions relating to jurisdiction of courts. They regulate forum for institution of suits. They deal with the matters of domestic concern and provide for the multitude of suits which can be brought in different courts. Section 15 requires the suitor to institute a suit in the court of the lowest grade competent to try it. Section 16 enacts that the suits for recovery of immovable property, or for partition of immovable property, or for foreclosure, sale or redemption of mortgage property, or for determination of any other right or interest in immovable property, or for compensation for wrong to immovable property shall be instituted in the court within the local limits of whose jurisdiction the property is situate. Proviso to section 16 declares that where the relief sought can be obtained through the personal obedience of the defendant, the suit can be instituted either in the court within whose jurisdiction the property is situate or in the court where the defendant actually or voluntarily resides or carries on business, or personally works for gain. Section 17 supplements section 16 and is virtually another proviso to that section. It deals with those cases where immovable property is situated within the jurisdiction of different courts. Section 18 applies where local limit of jurisdiction of different courts is uncertain. Section 19 is a special provision and applies to suits for compensation for wrongs to a person or to movable property. Section 20 is a residuary section and covers all those cases not dealt with or covered by sections 15 to 19. Section 16 thus recognizes a well established principle that actions against *res* or property should be brought in the forum where such *res* is situate. A court within whose territorial jurisdiction the property is not situate has no power to deal with and decide the rights or interests in such property. In other words, a court has no jurisdiction over a dispute in which it cannot give an effective judgment. Proviso to section 16, no doubt, states that though the court cannot, in case of immovable property situate beyond jurisdiction, grant a relief *in rem* still it can entertain a suit where relief sought can be obtained through the personal obedience of the defendant. The proviso is based on well known maxim "*equity acts in personam*, recognized by Chancery Courts in England. Equity Courts had jurisdiction to entertain certain suits respecting immovable properties situated abroad through personal obedience of the defendant. The principle on which the maxim was based was that courts could grant relief in suits respecting immovable property situate abroad by enforcing their judgments by process *in personam, i.e.*, by arrest of defendant or by attachment of his property; *Harshad Chiman Lal Modi* v. *DLF Universal Ltd.*, AIR 2005 SC 4446: JT 2005 (8) SC 561: 2005 (7) SCALE 533: 2005 (7) SCC 791.

40. Obligations – Duty of Court for – The obligation imposed by section 16 is upon the Court not to grant specific performance to a plaintiff who has not met the requirements of clauses (a), (b) and (c) thereof. A Court may not, therefore, grant to a plaintiff who has failed to aver and to prove that he has performed or has always been ready and willing to perform his part of the agreement the specific performance whereof he seeks. There is, therefore, no question of the plea being available to one defendant and not to another. It is open to any defendant to contend and establish that the mandatory requirement of section 16(c) has not been complied with and it is for the Court to determine whether it has or has not been complied with and, depending upon its conclusion, decree or decline to decree the suit; *Ram Awadh* v. *Achhaibar Dubey*, AIR 2000 SC 860: JT 2000 (1) SC 535: 2000 (1) SCALE 41502: 2000 (2) SCC 428; *Jugraj Singh* v. *Labh Singh*, 1995 (2) SCC 31: 1995 AIR SCW 901: AIR 1995 SC 945 – Overruled.

41. Plaintiff – Duties of – In terms of section 16(c) of the Specific Relief Act, 1963, it is incumbent on the party, who wants to enforce the specific performance of a contract, to aver and prove that he has performed or has always been ready and willing to perform the essential terms of the contract. *Explanation* appended to this sub-section (c) makes it clear that if a contract involves the payment of money, it is not essential for the plaintiff to actually tender to the defendant or to deposit in Court any money except when so directed by the Court. However, the plaintiff must aver performance of, or readiness and willingness to perform, the contract according to its true construction; *Coromandel Indag Products (P) Ltd.* v. *Garuda Chit & Trading Co. P. Ltd.*, JT 2011 (10) SC 34: 2011 (4) RCR (Civ) 677: 2011 (9) SCALE 139: 2011 (8) SCC 601.

42. Plaintiff – Obligations of – To succeed in a suit for specific performance, the plaintiff has to prove: (a) that a valid agreement of sale was entered by the defendant in his favour and the terms thereof; (b) that the defendant committed breach of the contract; and (c) that he was always ready and willing to perform his part of the obligations in terms of the contract. If a plaintiff has to prove that he was always ready and willing to perform his part of the contract, that is, to perform his obligations in terms of the contract, necessarily he should step into the witness box and give evidence that he has all along been ready and willing to perform his part of the contract and subject himself to cross examination on that issue. A plaintiff cannot obviously examine in his place, his attorney holder who did not have personal knowledge either of the transaction or of his readiness and willingness. Readiness and willingness refer to the state of mind and conduct of the purchaser, as also his capacity and preparedness on the other. One without the other is not sufficient. Therefore a third party who has no personal knowledge cannot give evidence about such readiness and willingness, even if he is an attorney holder of the person concerned; *Man Kaur (Dead) by LRs.* v. *Hartar Singh Sangha*, AIR 2010 SCW 6198: JT 2010 (10) SC 565: 2010 (10) SCC 512: 2010 (12) SCR 515.

43. Time Being Essence of Contract – Condition for – In the case of sale of immovable property there is no presumption as to time being the essence of the contract. Even if it is not of the essence of the contract the Court may infer that it is to be performed in a reasonable time if the conditions are:

1. from the express terms of the contract;
2. from the nature of the property; and
3. from the surrounding circumstances, for example: the object of making the contract; *Chand Rani* v. *Kamal Rani*, AIR 1993 SC 1742: JT 1993 (1) SC 74: 1992 (3) SCALE 544: 1993 (1) SCC 519 **[Hon'ble Judges:** L.M. Sharma, S. Ratnavel Pandian, S. Mohan, B.P. Jeevan Reddy, S.P. Bharucha].

44. Provision – Basic Principle of – The basic principle behind section 16(c) read with *Explanation (ii)* is that any person seeking benefit of the specific performance of contract must manifest that his conduct has been blemishless throughout entitling him to the specific relief. The provision imposes a personal bar. The Court is to grant relief on the basis of the conduct of the person seeking relief. If the pleadings manifest that the conduct of the plaintiff entitles him to get the relief on perusal of the plaint he should not be denied the relief; *Sita Ram* v. *Radhey Shyam*, AIR 2008 SC 143: 2008 (1) Mad LJ 146: 2007 (11) SCALE 626: 2007 (14) SCC 415: 2007 (10) SCR 552.

45. Right of Vendor to Rescind Contract – Law on – That time is presumed not to be of essence of the contract relating to immovable property, but it is of essence in contracts of reconveyance or renewal of lease. The onus to plead and prove that time was the essence of the contract was on the person alleging it, thus giving an opportunity to the other side to adduce rebuttal evidence that time was not of essence. When the plaintiff pleads that time was not of essence and the defendant does not deny it by evidence, the court is bound to accept the plea of the plaintiff. In cases where notice is given making time of the essence, it is duty of the court to examine the real intention of the party giving such notice by looking at the facts and circumstances of each case. That a vendor has no right to make time of the essence, unless he is ready and willing to proceed to completion and secondly, when the vendor purports to make time of the essence, the purchaser must be guilty of such gross default as to entitle the vendor to rescind the contract; *Swarnam Ramachandran* v. *Aravacode Chakungal Jayapalan*, 2005 (2) BCR 887: 2004 (7) SCALE 211: 2004 (8) SCC 689: 2004 (6) Supreme 385.

46. Specific Performance of Contract – Law on – Section 16(c) mandates that the discretionary relief of specific performance of the contract can be granted only in the event, the plaintiff not only makes necessary pleadings but also establishes that he had all along been ready and willing to perform his part of contract. Such readiness and willingness on the part of the plaintiff is not confined only to the stage of filing of the plaint but also at the subsequent stage means at the hearing; *Inderchand Jain (D) through LRs.* v. *Motilal (D) through LRs.*, AIR 2009 SCW 5364: 2009 (5) CTC 365: 2009 (9) SCALE 777: 2009 (14) SCC 663: 2009 (11) SCR 252.

47. Specific Performance of Contract – Limitation for – Section 16(c) of the Specific Relief Act, 1963 postulates continuous readiness and willingness on the part of the plaintiff. It is a condition precedent for obtaining a relief of grant of specific performance of contract. The court, keeping in view the fact that it exercises a discretionary jurisdiction, would be entitled to take into consideration as to whether the suit had been filed within a reasonable time. What would be a reasonable time would, however, depend upon the facts and circumstances of each case. No hard and fast law can be laid down therefore; *Azhar Sultana* v. *B. Rajamani*, AIR 2009 SC 2157: JT 2009 (2) SC 622: 2009 (3) SCALE 159: 2009 (17) SCC 27: 2009 (2) SCR 537.

48. Suit for Specific Performance – Duty of plaintiff for – Section 16(c) bars the specific performance of a contract in favour of a plaintiff who fails to aver and prove that he has performed or has always been ready and willing to perform the essential terms of the contract which are to be performed by him (other than terms of the performance of which has been prevented or waived by the defendant). *Explanation (ii)* to section 16 provides that for purposes of clause (c) of section 16, the plaintiff must aver performance of, or readiness and willingness to perform, the contract according to its true construction. Thus in a suit for specific performance, the plaintiff should not only plead and prove the terms of the agreement, but should also plead and prove his readiness and willingness to perform his obligations under the contract in terms of the contract; *Man Kaur (Dead) by LRs.* v. *Hartar Singh Sangha*, JT 2010 (10) SC 565: 2010 (10) SCC 512: 2010 (12) SCR 515: 2010 (9) UJ 4569.

49. Surrounding Circumstances – Law on – Section 16(c) of the Specific Relief Act lays down that specific performance of a contract cannot be enforced in favour of a person who fails to aver and prove that he has performed or has always been ready and willing to perform the essential terms of the contract which are to be performed by him, other than terms the performance of which has been prevented or waived by the defendant. *Explanation II* to this sub-section provides that the plaintiff must aver performance of, or readiness and willingness to perform, the contract according to its true construction. The requirement of this provision is that plaintiff must aver that he has always been ready and willing to perform the additional terms of the contract. Therefore not only there should be such an averment in the plaint but the surrounding circumstances must also indicate that the readiness and willingness continue from the date of the contract till the hearing of the suit. It is well-settled that equitable remedy of specific performance cannot be had on the basis of pleadings which do not contain averments of readiness and willingness of the plaintiff to perform his contract in terms of Forms 47 and 48 of C.P.C.; *Pukhraj D. Jain* v. *G. Gopalakrishna*, AIR 2004 SC 3504: JT 2004 (5) SC 329: 2004 (4) SCALE 688: 2004 (7) SCC 251.

50. Conduct of Parties – Law on – It is now well-settled that the conduct of the parties, with a view to arrive at a finding as to whether the plaintiff-respondents were all along and still are ready and willing to perform their part of contract as is mandatorily required under section 16(c) of the Specific Relief Act must be determined having regard to the entire attending circumstances. A bare averment in the plaint or a statement made in the examination-in-chief would not suffice. The conduct of the plaintiff-respondents must be judged having regard to the entirety of the pleadings as also the evidences brought on record; *Umabai* v. *Nilkanth Dhondiba Chavan*, 2005 (3) SCR 521: JT 2005 (4) SC 292: 2005 (4) SCALE 142: 2005 (6) SCC 243.

51. Performance of Contract – Law on – If upon reading the plaint in its entirety, the Court comes to the conclusion that for all intent and purport, the requirements of section 16(c) of the Specific Relief Act stood complied with, no exception thereto can be taken. As a vendee what he could do was to offer the balance amount of consideration to the vendor and make arrangements for getting the sale deed executed and registered. If he has done all that, Courts are of the opinion he was ready and willing to perform his part of the contract; *Gurdial Kaur* v. *Piara Singh*, AIR 2008 SC 2019: 2008 (4) SCALE 695: 2008 (14) SCC 735: 2008 (4) SLT 346.

52. Plaintiff – Requirement for – The language under section 16(c) of the Act does not require any specific phraseology but only that the plaintiff must aver that he has performed or has always been ready and willing to perform his part of the contract. Therefore, the compliance with the readiness and willingness has to be in spirit and substance and not in letter and form; *Faquir Chand* v. *Sudesh Kumari*, 2006 (9) SCALE 554: 2006 (12) SCC 146: 2006 (7) SCJ 712: 2006 (Supp 6) SCR 466: 2006 (7) Supreme 388.

53. Provision – Comments on – It is an undisputed fact that section 16 of the Act confers power upon the Board to dispose of its property as per rule 3 of the U.P. Avas Avam Vikas Parishad (Delegation of Powers by the Board and the Housing Commissioner) Rules, 1968. The Board has power under section 12(1) of the Act to delegate its power either to a Committee or the Housing Commissioner or any other officer in exercise of its power to discharge its functions; *U.P. Avas Evam Vikas Parishad* v. *Om Prakash Sharma*, JT 2013 (5) SC 548: 2013 (6) SCALE 202: 2013 (3) All LJ 762: 2013 (5) SCC 182.

54. Specific Performance – Duties of Plaintiff for – In a suit for specific performance it is absolutely necessary for the plaintiff to assert that he/she was always ready and willing to perform the essential terms of the contract sought to be enforced against the defendant. Section 16(c) of the Specific Relief Act, 1963 makes that requirement mandatory; *Raj Kishore (Dead) by LRs.* v. *Prem Singh*, AIR 2011 SC 382: JT 2010 (13) SC 535: 2011 (1) SCC 657.

55. Terms "Readiness" and "Willingness" – Meaning of – Section 16(c) of the Specific Relief Act, 1963 mandates "readiness and willingness" on the part of the plaintiff and it is a condition precedent for obtaining relief of grant of specific performance. It is also clear that in a suit for specific performance, the plaintiff must allege and prove a continuous "readiness and willingness" to perform the contract on his part from the date of the contract. The onus is on the plaintiff. The words "ready" and "willing" imply that the person was prepared to carry out the terms of the contact. The distinction between "readiness" and "willingness" is that the former refers to financial capacity and the latter to the conduct of the plaintiff wanting performance. Generally, readiness is backed by willingness; *J.P. Builders* v. *A. Ramadas Rao*, JT 2010 (12) SC 588: 2010 (12) SCALE 400: 2011 (1) SCC 429: 2010 (8) SLT 546.

17. Contract to sell or let property by one who has no title, not specifically enforceable.—(1) A contract to sell or let any immovable property cannot be specifically enforced in favour of a vendor or lessor—

(a) who, knowing not to have any title to the property, has contracted to sell or let the property;

(b) who, though he entered into the contract believing that he had a good title to the property, cannot at the time fixed by the parties or by the court for the completion of the sale or letting, give the purchaser or lessee a title free from reasonable doubt.

(2) The provisions of sub-section (1) shall also apply, as far as may be, to contracts for the sale or hire of movable property.

SYNOPSIS

1. Mujavars – Powers of
2. Clause (a) of Sub-section (1): Contract by a Person Having no Title
3. Clause (b) of Sub-section (1): Doubtful Title
4. Sub-section (2): Applicability to Movable Property

COMMENTS

1. Mujavars – Powers of – If Mujavars have no authority to sell the property, the agreement of sale could not have been directed to be specifically performed. In any event, as no permission had been granted by the Wakf Board, the Courts below had committed a serious error in passing the impugned judgment. A mutwalli is a manager or trustee of the property. Mujavars were not even that. Mujavars, prior to the amendment of the Act, were not even authorized to enter into the agreement for sale. That was not the purpose for which they were appointed. They were appointed as the Dargah in question was not being properly looked after and the then surviving Mutawallis failed and/or neglected to perform their statutory duties. The functions of the Mutwalli and/or Mujavars in the light of the provisions of the Wakf Act and the Rules framed thereunder must be viewed in the context of the statute and on the basis of the common concept. Mutwallis have no ownership right or estate in the Wakf property unless the deed of wakf says so; *Mohammedia Co-op. Building Society Ltd.* v. *Lakshmi S. Co-op. Building Society Ltd.*, AIR 2009 SC 590: JT 2008 (6) SC 250: 2008 (7) SCALE 172: 2008 (7) SCC 310.

2. Clause (a) of Sub-section (1): Contract by a Person Having no Title – Under clause (a) of section 17 of the Specific Relief Act, 1963, if a person having no title to immovable property contracts to sell or let it, he cannot claim successfully, the specific performance of his contract. This seems to be based on the famous maxim, *nemo dat quod nan habet* of the law of sale of goods. This maxim means that a person cannot confer a better title than he himself has. If a person has no title, how can he pass a good title to the transferee since he cannot pass a good title to the transferee, it was quite just and equitable that his contract must not specifically be enforced. If such a vendor sues for specific performance, the purchaser can resist the suit on the ground that the vendor has no title or a defective title; *Mir Abdul Hakeem Khan* v. *Abdul Mannan Khadri,* AIR 1972 AP 178.

If the purchaser sues for specific performance, the vendor cannot resist the suit on the ground of defect in his title; *Netyam Venkataramanna* v. *Mahankali Narasimhan,* AIR 1994 AP 244: (1993) 2 APLJ 381.

Where the defendant who was coparcener but not *karta* of the family had agreed to sell the property of the family to the plaintiff without permission of other coparceners, the plaintiff was entitled to specific performance of the agreement relating to share of the defendant; *Uma Kant & Co. Ltd.* v. *Niranjan Prasad Mahesh,* AIR 2006 Raj 46 (48): 2006 AIHC 1038: (2006) 1 Raj LR 95: (2005) 4 WLC 716.

3. Clause (b) of Sub-section (1): Doubtful Title – Clause (b) of sub-section (1) mandates that for obtaining the decree of specific performance, the vendor must be able to 'give the purchaser or lessee a title free from reasonable doubt'. Thus a person having a doubtful or defective title is not competent to claim successfully; the specific performance of his contract. But there is nothing in section 17 to invalidate such a contract. The contract may be repudiated by the other party which may also claim damages for the breach of contract; *Kisanlal Rudmal Agarwal* v. *Namdeo Krushanji Dhangar,* AIR 1943 Nag 299: ILR 1944 Nag 90: 211 IC 525.

Where the title of the vendor is doubtful or not free from reasonable doubt, the purchaser cannot be compelled to complete his part of the contract. Illustration (ii) noted above which is an illustration to section 25 of the repealed Act of 1877 makes it clear that specific performance cannot be claimed unless the title of the vendor is 'free from reasonable doubt'. It has been held that where there are certain restrictive conditions in the nature of easements on the property and the vendor does not disclose them, the court would deny the specific performance of such a contract; *Lallubhai Rupchand* v. *Mohanlal Sakarchand,* AIR 1935 Bom 16: 36 Bom LR 1041.

4. Sub-section (2): Applicability to Movable Property – Sub-section (2) makes applicable as far as may be, provisions of sub-section (1) for the sale or hire of movable property. Section 25 of the repealed Act of 1877 applied to all kinds of property-immovable as well as movable. Under the present section, *i.e.,* section 17 sub-section (1) applies to immovable property and sub-section (2) makes provisions of sub-section (1) applicable as far as may be for the sale or hire of movable property; *Kidambi Vatapatra Sayi* v. *V. Venkata Punnayya,* AIR 1965 AP 353: (1965) 1 Comp LJ 257: (1965) 1 Andh WR 441.

18. Non-enforcement except with variation.—Where a plaintiff seeks specific performance of a contract in writing, to which the defendant sets up a variation, the plaintiff cannot obtain the performance sought, except with the variation so set up, in the following cases, namely:—

(a) where by fraud, mistake of fact or misrepresentation, the written contract of which performance is sought is in its terms or effect different from what the parties agreed to, or does not contain all the terms agreed to between the parties on the basis of which the defendant entered into the contract;

(b) where the object of the parties was to produce a certain legal result which the contract as framed is not calculated to produce;

(c) where the parties have, subsequently to the execution of the contract, varied its terms.

SYNOPSIS

1. Expression "Any Interest" – Law on
2. High Courts – Right of

COMMENTS

1. Expression "Any Interest" – Law on – Section 18 of the Specific Relief Act has been applied also to cases where a person, at the time of agreement of sale, had no title in the property agreed to be sold. Clause (a) of section 18 gives right to the purchaser to compel the vendor to make good the contract out of any interest the vendor has acquired in the property after the contract of sale. The expression "any interest" is very wide in its amplitude and also denotes a case in which a vendor who has no title to the property acquires title after the contract of sale. There is nothing in clause (a) to limit the expression "any interest" only to cases where a person has title to the property and later he acquires an interest which enables him to give a valid title to the purchaser; *Muthabathula Arjayya* v. *Rambala Venkata Surya Gopala Krishanamurthy,* AIR 1974 AP 240.

2. High Courts – Right of – As a bare perusal of the provision shows that nothing in sub-section (5) takes away or abridges power of the High Court to hear for reasons to be recorded, the appeal on any other substantial question, not formulated earlier, if it is satisfied that the case involves such question; *Phool Pata* v. *Vishwanath Singh,* AIR 2005 SC 3079: JT 2005 (6) SC 483: 2005 (6) SCALE 3: 2005 (6) SCC 40.

19. Relief against parties and persons claiming under them by subsequent title.—Except as otherwise provided by this Chapter, specific performance of a contract may be enforced against—

(a) either party thereto;

(b) any other person claiming under him by a title arising subsequently to the contract, except a transferee for value who has paid his money in good faith and without notice of the original contract;

(c) any person claiming under a title which, though prior to the contract and known to the plaintiff, might have been displaced by the defendant;

(d) when a company has entered into a contract and subsequently becomes amalgamated with another company, the new company which arises out of the amalgamation;

(e) when the promoters of a company have, before its incorporation, entered into a contract for the purpose of the company and such contract is warranted by the terms of the incorporation, the company:

Provided that the company has accepted the contract and communicated such acceptance to the other party to the contract.

SYNOPSIS

COMMENTS

1. Contract for Specific Performance – Parties for – Persons seeking addition in the suit for specific performance of the contract for sale who were not claiming under the vendor but they were claiming adverse to the title of the vendor do not fall in any of the categories enumerated in sub-sections (a) to (e) of section 19 of the Specific Relief Act. From a plain reading of section 19 of the Act, it appears that this section is exhaustive on the question as to who are the parties against whom a contract for specific performance may be enforced; *Kasturi* v. *Iyyamperumal*, 2005 (5) All MR 721: 2005 (2) BLJR 1114: 2005 (2) Civ CC 379: 2005 (3) KCCR 1545: 2005 (2) RCR (Civ) 691: 2005 (3) SCR 864 .

2. Necessary Parties in a Suit for Specific Performance of a Contract – Law on – From a plain reading of the expression used in sub-rule (2), Order I, rule 10 of the C.P.C. "all the questions involved in the suit" it is abundantly clear that the legislature clearly meant that the controversies raised as between the parties to the litigation must be gone into only, that is to say, controversies with regard to the right which is set up and the relief claimed on one side and denied on the other and not the controversies which may arise between the plaintiff and the defendants inter se or questions between the parties to the suit and a third party. Second part of Order I, rule 10, sub-rule (2) of the C.P.C. would clearly show that the necessary parties in a suit for specific performance of a contract for sale are the parties to the contract or if they are dead their legal representatives as also a person who had purchased the contracted property from the vendor. In equity as well as in law, the contract constitutes rights and also regulates the liabilities of the parties. A purchaser is a necessary party as he would be affected if he had purchased with notice of the contract, but a person who claims adversely to the claim of a vendor is, however, not a necessary party. From the above, it is now clear that two tests are to be satisfied for determining the question who is a necessary party. Tests are - (1) there must be a right to some relief against such party in respect of the controversies involved in the proceedings (2) no effective decree can be passed in the absence of such party; *Kasturi* v. *Iyyamperumal*, AIR 2005 SC 2813: 2005 (3) Mad LJ 124: 2005 (3) MPLJ 261.

3. Onus of Proof of Good Faith – Law on – As can be seen from section 19(a) and (b) , specific performance of a contract can be enforced against (a) either party thereto and (b) any person claiming under him by a title arising subsequent to the contract, except a transferee for value who has paid his money in good faith and without notice of the original contract. Section 19(b) protects the *bona fide* purchaser in good faith for value without notice of the original contract. This protection is in the nature of exception to the general rule. Hence the onus of proof of good faith is on the purchaser who takes the plea that he is an innocent purchaser. Good faith is a question of fact to be considered and decided on the facts of each case. Section 52 of the Penal Code emphasizes due care and attention in relation to the good faith. In the General Clauses Act emphasis is laid on honesty; *R.K. Mohammed Ubaidullah* v. *Hajee C. Abdul Wahab*, AIR 2001 SC 1658: JT 2000 (8) SC 1: 2000 (5) SCALE 186: 2000 (6) SCC 402.

4. Parties to Suit – Law on – As per sub-sections (a) to (e) of section 19 of the Specific Relief Act the persons seeking addition in the suit for specific performance of the contract for sale who were not claiming under the vendor but they were claiming adverse to the title of the vendor do not fall, in any of the categories enumerated in sub-sections (a) to (e) of section 19 of the Specific Relief Act. This section is exhaustive on the question as to who are the parties against whom a contract for specific performance may be enforced; *Kasturi* v. *Iyyamperumal*, AIR 2005 SC 2813: AIR 2005 SCW 2368: 2005 (4) SCALE 363: 2005 (6) SCC 733: 2005 (4) SCJ 196.

5. Revenue Record – Presumption for – A revenue record is not a document of title. It merely raises a presumption in regard to possession. Presumption of possession and/ or continuity thereof both forward and backward can also be raised under section 110 of the Indian Evidence Act. The courts below, were, therefore, required to appreciate the evidence keeping in view the correct legal principles in mind; *Gurunath Manohar Pavaskar* v. *Nagesh Siddappa Navalgund*, AIR 2008 SC 901: 2007 (14) SCALE 283: 2007 (13) SCC 565: 2007 (8) Supreme 561.

6. Specific Performance of Contract – Law on – Section 19(b) of the Specific Relief Act, which occurs in Chapter II, applies to movables by virtue of the provisions of section 58 of the Sale of Goods Act. Under section 19(b) a specific performance of a contract can be enforced not only against either party thereto against any other person claiming under him by a title arising subsequently to the contract, except a transferee for value who has paid his money in good faith and without notice of original contract. Further, section 91 of the Indian Trust Act, 1882 lays down that where a person acquires property with notice that another person as entered into an existing contract affecting that property, of which a specific performance could be enforced, the former must hold the property for the benefit of the latter to the extent necessary to give effect to the contract. Apex Court is of the view that the High Court was quite justified in passing a decree against them as well; *Gramophone Company of India Ltd.* v. *Mars Recording Pvt. Limited*, AIR 2001 SC 2885: JT 2001 (7) SC 352: 2002 (2) SCC 103: 2001 (9) SRJ 220.

7. Subsequent Transferee – Law on – It is well-settled that the initial burden to show that the subsequent purchaser of suit property covered by earlier suit agreement was a *bona fide* purchaser for value without notice of the suit agreement squarely rests on the shoulders of such subsequent transferee; *Jagan Nath* v. *Jagdish Rai*, AIR 1998 SC 2028: JT 1998 (3) SC 551: 1998 (3) SCALE 275: 1998 (5) SCC 537.

8. Execution Proceedings – Law on – In interpreting the provisions of Order XXI, rule 97 of the Code and the other provisions in the Order, the aims and objects for introducing amendment to the Code cannot be lost sight of. Under the unamended Code, third parties adversely affected or dispossessed from the property involved, were required to file independent suits for claiming title and possession. The Legislature purposely amended provisions in Order XXI to enable the third parties to seek adjudication of their rights in execution proceedings themselves with a view to curtail the prolongation of litigation and arrest delay caused in execution of decrees; *Ashan Devi* v. *Phulwasi Devi*, AIR 2004 SC 511: 2003 (9) SCALE 783: 2003 (12) SCC 219: 2003 (7) SLT 385. See *Bhag Mal* v. *Ch. Parbhu Ram*, 1985 (1) SCC 61.

9. Principle of *Lis Pendens* – Attraction of – Subsequent purchaser has to be aware before he purchases the suit property. Principle of *lis pendens* will be applicable as the second sale has taken place after the filing of the suit; *Guruswamy Nadar* v. *P. Lakshmi Ammal (D) through LRs.*, AIR 2008 SC 2560: JT 2008 (6) SC 555: 2008 (7) SCALE 611: 2008 (5) SCC 796.

10. Registration – Law on – Section 54 of the Transfer of Property Act, 1882 mandatorily requires that the sale of any immovable property of the value of hundred rupees and upward can be made only by a registered instrument. Section 47 of the Registration Act, 1908 Act, 1908, provides that registration of the document shall relate back to the date of the execution of the document. Thus, the two provisions make it crystal clear that sale deed in question requires registration. Even if registration had been done subsequent to the filing of Suit, it related back to the date of execution of the sale deed, which was prior to institution of the Suit; *Har Narain (Dead) by LRs.* v. *Mam Chand (Dead) by LRs.*, JT 2010 (11) SC 641: 2010 (4) Ker LT 359: 2010 (13) SCC 128: 2010 (7) Supreme 1.

11. Right of Purchaser – Law on – The purchasers have acquired a legal right under sale deed. The right of the tenant under, if it is true and valid, though earlier in time, is only an equitable right and it does not affect the purchasers if they are *bona fide* purchasers for valuable consideration without notice of that equitable right; *Ram Niwas* v. *Bano*, AIR 2000 SC 2921: JT 2000 (8) SC 340: 2000 (5) SCALE 363: 2000 (6) SCC 685.

12. Sale Deed Executed During Pendency of Suit – Law on – The requirement of section 41 of the Transfer of Property Act, 1882 and the proviso thereto was not a requirement for the applicability of section 43 of the Transfer of Property Act, 1882 and hence even if a subsequent purchaser was aware of the pending litigation at the time of purchase of the suit property, it would disentitle him to the benefit of section 43. Section 52 did not operate to render a sale deed executed during the pendency of the suit void, as the said transaction was not hit either by section 52 of the Transfer of Property Act or section 23 of the Contract Act, 1872; *S. Abdul Khader* v. *Abdul Wajid (D)*, JT 2008 (10) SC 413: 2008 (12) SCALE 473: 2008 (9) SCC 522.

Discretion and powers of Court

20. Discretion as to decreeing specific performance.—(1) The jurisdiction to decree specific performance is discretionary, and the court is not bound to grant such relief merely because it is lawful to do so; but the discretion of the court is not arbitrary but sound and reasonable, guided by judicial principles and capable of correction by a court of appeal.

(2) The following are cases in which the court may properly exercise discretion not to decree specific performance:—

(a) where the terms of the contract or the conduct of the parties at the time of entering into the contract or the other circumstances under which the contract was entered into are such that the contract, though not voidable, gives the plaintiff an unfair advantage over the defendant; or

(b) where the performance of the contract would involve some hardship on the defendant which he did not foresee, whereas its non-performance would involve no such hardship on the plaintiff; or

(c) where the defendant entered into the contract under circumstances which though not rendering the contract voidable, makes it inequitable to enforce specific performance.

Explanation 1.—Mere inadequacy of consideration, or the mere fact that the contract is onerous to the defendant or improvident in its nature, shall not be deemed to constitute an unfair advantage within the meaning of clause (a) or hardship within the meaning of clause (b).

Explanation 2.— The question whether the performance of a contract would involve hardship on the defendant within the meaning of clause (b) shall, except in cases where the hardship has resulted from any act of the plaintiff subsequent to the contract, be determined with reference to the circumstances existing at the time of the contract.

(3) The court may properly exercise discretion to decree specific performance in any case where the plaintiff has done substantial acts or suffered losses in consequence of a contract capable of specific performance.

(4) The court shall not refuse to any party specific performance of a contract merely on the ground that the contract is not enforceable at the instance of the party.

SYNOPSIS

COMMENTS

1. Term "Reasonable" – Meaning of – The word "reasonable" has in law *prima facie* meaning of reasonable in regard to those circumstances of which the person concerned is called upon to act reasonably knows or ought to know as to what was reasonable. It may be unreasonable to give an exact definition of the word "reasonable." The reason varies in its conclusion according to ideosyncrasy of the individual and the time and circumstances in which he thinks. The dictionary meaning of the "reasonable time" is to be so much time as is necessary, under the circumstances, to do conveniently what the contract or duty requires should be done in a particular case. In other words it means as soon as circumstances permit. In Law Lexicon it is defined to mean "A reasonable time, looking at all the circumstances of the case; a reasonable time under ordinary circumstances; as soon as circumstance will permit; so much time as is necessary under the circumstances, conveniently to do what the contract requires should be done; some more protracted space than 'directly'; such length of time as may fairly, and properly, and reasonably be allowed or required, having regard to the nature of the act or duty and to the attending circumstances; all these convey more or less the same idea"; *Veerayee Ammal* v. *Seeni Ammal*, AIR 2001 SC 2920: JT 2001 (9) SC 145: 2001 (7) SCALE 403: 2002 (1) SCC 134.

2. Adverse Possession – Law on – The Court has also given a finding regarding adverse possession in a suit for specific performance which is not proper; *B.K. Sri Harsha* v. *Bharath Heavy Electricals Ltd.*, AIR 2008 SC 1267: 2008 (2) SCALE 338: 2008 (4) SCC 48: 2008 (1) Supreme 615.

3. Agreement of Sale – Effect of – Every conduct of the landlady right from the date of entering into agreement of sale, accepting money towards the sale consideration, delivering possession in lieu of such agreement all clearly indicates and has to be construed in law that she repudiated her old relationship of landlord and tenant. Thus after this parties enter into new cloak of seller and purchaser and their relationship to be governed under the said terms of the agreement. Every right and obligation thereafter would flow from it. Even if parties under the agreement of sale do not perform their obligations remedy may be availed in law as permissible under the law. When Person is no more tenant how can non-payment be construed as wilful default; *R. Kanthimathi* v. *Beatrice Xavier*, AIR 2003 SC 4149: AIR 2001 SCW 2369: 2000 (2) Mad LW 805: 2000 (9) SCC 339.

4. Anticipatory Breach of Contract – Effect of – It is settled in law that where a party to a contract commits an anticipatory breach of the contract, the other party to the contract may treat the breach as putting an end to the contract and sue for damages, but in that event he cannot ask for specific performance. The other option open to the other party, namely, the aggrieved party, is that he may choose to keep the contract alive till the time for performance and claim specific performance but, in that event, he cannot claim specific performance of the contract unless he shows his readiness and willingness to perform the contract; *Jawahar Lal Wadhwa* v. *Haripada Chakroberty*, AIR 1989 SC 606: JT 1988 (4) SC 138: 1988 (2) SCALE 1033: 1989 (1) SCC 76 **[Hon'ble Judges:** Sabyasachi Mukherjee, M.H. Kania, S. Ranganathan].

5. Benami Transaction – Law on – The benami transaction is one which evidences an operative and valid transfer resulting in the passing of title in the transferee, whereas in the sham transaction, there is no valid transfer of interest, though ostensibly the deed incorporating the transaction seeks to clothe the transferee with the title in the property. Sham transaction takes place, *inter alia,* when there is no consideration for the transfer. In such a case, if the transferor wants to assail the validity of the transaction, he shall have to seek cancellation of the document because so long as the document stands, the transferee would remain clothed with the title to the property. In case of benami transaction, however, what happens is that the document has legal effect being perfectly valid document in the sense that if it be a sale deed, the same having been executed on the passing of consideration, but the question involved is who is the person who is the true owner of the of the property — whether it is the transferee named in the deed of somebody else, the transferee being a benami. In such a case, the aggrieved person does not demand, indeed would not demand, cancellation of the sale deed because, if the deed would be cancelled, he as well would not be clothed with any right, title or interest over the property which had been the subject-matter of the sale deed; *Keshab Chandra Nayak* v. *Laxmidhar Nayak*, AIR 1993 Ori 1: 2003 (1) LJR 668: 2002 (4) RCR (Civ) 75 **[Hon'ble Judges:** B.L. Hansaria, P.C. Misra, L. Rath].

6. Bidders – Law on – Section 18A of the Kerala Abkari Act shows that the exclusive or other privilege of selling liquor by retail may be granted on payment of rental in consideration of the grant. Section 18A(2) lays down that "no grantee of any privilege under sub-section (1) shall exercise the same until he has received a licence in that behalf from the Commissioner." It will be seen that this provision contemplates the statutory status of a "grantee" even before he becomes entitled, as of right, to exercise of privileges of a grantee on the receipt of a licence. What is noticeable is that even before he receives his license he is described as a "grantee". The successful bidders, in the case before us, had been permitted by the excise authorities, in recognition of their rights to receive and in anticipation of receipt of licences, to exercise the privileges of grantees. They were thus treated as grantees in anticipation of execution, of contracts and grants of licenses. Grantees under section 28 of the Act are those who have received the privilege and not necessarily only those who have received the written contracts and licenses. The word "grantee" used there seems to us to carry this wider connotation with it; *A. Damodaran* v. *State of Kerala*, AIR 1976 SC 1533: 1976 (3) SCC 61: 1976 (3) SCR 780.

7. Conduct of Party and Attending Circumstances – Law on – It is settled law that remedy for specific performance is an equitable remedy and is in the discretion of the Court, which discretion requires to be exercised according to settled principles of law and not arbitrarily as adumbrated under section 20 of the Specific Relief Act, 1963 (for short, 'the Act'). Under section 20, the court is not bound to grant the relief just because there was valid agreement of sale. Section 16(c) of the Act envisages that plaintiff must plead and prove that he had performed or has always been ready and willing to perform the essential terms of the contract which are to be performed by him, other than those terms the performance of which has been prevented or waived by the defendant. The continuous readiness and willingness on the part of the plaintiff is a condition precedent to grant the relief of specific performance. This circumstance is material and relevant and is required to be considered by the court while granting or refusing to grant the relief. If the plaintiff fails to either aver or prove the same, he must fail. To adjudge whether the plaintiff is ready and willing to perform his part of the contract, the court must take into consideration the conduct of the plaintiff prior and subsequent to the filing of the suit along with other attending circumstances. The amount of consideration which he has to pay to the defendant must of necessity be proved to be available. Right from the date of the execution till date of the decree he must prove that he is ready and has always been willing to perform his part of the contract. As stated, the factum of his readiness and willingness to perform his part of the contract is to be adjudged with reference to the conduct of the party and the attending circumstances. The court may infer from the facts and circumstances whether the plaintiff was ready and was always ready and willing to perform his part of contract; *N.P. Thirugnanam* v. *R. Jagan Mohan Rao*, AIR 1996 SC 116: JT 1995 (5) SC 553: 1995 (4) SCALE 465: 1995 (5) SCC 115.

8. Contract – Essence of – There can be no dispute with the broad proposition of law. Normally time is not of the essence of the Contract unless parties make it so; *Surjit Kaur* v. *Naurata Singh*, AIR 2000 SC 2927: JT 2000 (10) SC 520: 2000 (6) SCALE 364: 2000 (7) SCC 379.

9. Contract of Employment – Law on – Principles of law are well-established. A contract of employment depending on the volition of parties cannot be specifically enforced; *Indian Institute of Technology* v. *Mangat Singh*, 1973 (9) DLT 475: 1973 (2) ILR (Del) 6: 1973 RLR 44: 1973 (2) SLR 46.

10. Damages in a Suit for Specific Performance – Law on – Merely, because the plaintiff claims damages in a suit for specific performance of contract as alternative relief, it cannot be said that he is not entitled to the main relief of specific performance of contract itself. If Plaintiff had already deposited the balance of consideration pursuant to the judgment and decree of the trial Court, the legal representatives of the defendant should be ordered to execute the sale deed in favour of the plaintiff; *Motilal Jain* v. *Ramdasi Devi*, AIR 2000 SC 2408: JT 2000 (8) SC 59: 2000 (5) SCALE 232: 2000 (6) SCC 420.

11. Declaration for Ownership of Vehicle – Law on – It is true that in case a declaration is sought for and granted that the plaintiff was the owner of the bus along with the permits and that he was entitled to run the same. But in spite of such a declaration no injunction was granted restraining the defendant not to interfere with the plaintiff's right to run the same under the permit. This was because till then the transport authorities had not granted the requisite permission under section 59 of the Motor Vehicles Act, 1939. This type of decision leads to the conclusion that a person who has become the owner of the vehicle as well as the permit can legally ply or run the vehicle under that permit only after the requisite permission has been granted by the transport authorities. In other words, the plaintiff has not only to be the owner of the permit but also its holder; *Khawaz Bux* v. *Mirza Mohammad Ismail*, AIR 1984 All 83: 1984 (1) ACC 171: 1984 AWC 35 - **[Hon'ble Judges:** Satish Chandra, B.N. Sapru, Amarendra Nath Verma].

12. Declaratory Judgment – Law on – Under Order I, rule 10(2) Apex court held that in a suit for declaration as regards status or legal character under section 42 of the Specific Relief Act, the rule that in order that a person may be added as a party must have a present or direct interest in the subject-matter of the suit, is not wholly applicable, and the rule may be relaxed in a suitable case where the court is of the opinion that by adding that party it would be in a better position to effectually and completely adjudicate upon the controversy. In such suits the court is not bound to grant the declaration prayed for, on a mere admission of the claim by the defendant, if the court has reasons to insist upon clear proof, apart from the admission. It was therefore, held that since a declaratory judgment binds not only the parties actually before the court but also the persons claiming through them respectively within the meaning of section 43 of the Specific Relief Act, they are proper parties; *Anil Kumar Singh* v. *Shivnath Mishra* alias *Gadasa Guru*, AIR 1995 SCW 1782: 1994 (4) SCALE 953: 1995 (3) SCC 147.

13. Decree for Specific Performance of Contract – Law on – Section 20 of the Specific Relief Act confers a discretionary jurisdiction upon the courts. Undoubtedly such a jurisdiction cannot be refused to be exercised on whims and caprice; but when with passage of time, contract becomes frustrated or in some cases increase in the price of land takes place, the same being relevant factors can be taken into consideration for the said purpose. While refusing to exercise its jurisdiction, the courts are not precluded from taking into consideration the subsequent events. Only because the Plaintiff are ready and willing to perform their part of contract and even assuming that the Defendant was not entirely vigilant in protecting their rights in the proceedings before the competent authority under the Urban Land (Ceiling and Regulation) Act, 1976 , the same by itself would not mean that a decree for specific performance of contract would automatically be granted. While considering the question as to whether the discretionary jurisdiction should be exercised or not, the orders of a competent authority must also be taken into consideration; *M. Meenakshi* v. *Metadin Agarwal*, AIR 2006 SCW 4323: 2006 (8) SCALE 566: 2006 (7) SCC 470: 2006 (6) Supreme 768.

14. Defendants – Duties of – It is the duty of the defendants to specifically plead and prove their case by leading proper evidence in the matter; *Sanjay Gera* v. *Haryana Urban Development Authority,* AIR 2005 SC 1303: JT 2005 (2) SC 532: 2005 (2) SCALE 290: 2005 (3) SCC 207.

15. Denial of Relief of Specific Performance – Compensation for – Denial of relief of specific performance can be right, but there should be some compensation to be given, in view of the particular facts and circumstances of the case; *B.R. Mulani* v. *A.B. Aswathanarayana,* AIR 1993 SC 1318: AIR 1993 SCW 533: 1993 (Supp 4) SCC 743 **[Hon'ble Judges:** M.N. Venkatachaliah, P.B. Sawant, N.P. Singh].

16. Discretionary Powers – Law on – Section 20 of the Act specifically provides that the court's jurisdiction to grant decree of specific performance is discretionary but not arbitrary. The discretion must be exercised in accordance with the sound and reasonable judicial principles; *K. Prakash* v. *B.R. Sampath Kumar,* AIR 2015 SC 9.

Section 20 of the Specific Relief Act provides that the jurisdiction of the court to decree specific performance of agreement is discretionary and the court is not bound to grant such relief merely because it is lawful to do so; *Sahadeva Gramani* v. *Perumal Gramani,* 2005 (11) SCC 454.

17. Earnest Money – Law on – The right to demand back the earnest money necessarily implies the right to rescind the contract. The refund could not be claimed as long as the contract remained in force; *Jiwan Lal* v. *Brij Mohan Mehra,* AIR 1973 SC 559: 1972 (2) SCC 757: 1973 (2) SCR 230: 1973 (2) SCJ 594.

18. Educational Institution – Status of – If the object of the educational institution or the school is such as recognised as charitable or religious under the Hindu Law such an educational institution or school will be regarded as possessing a juristic personality and will be capable of holding property; *D.A.V. College, Hoshiarpur Society, Hoshiarpur* v. *Sarvada Nand Anglo Sanskrit Higher Secondary School, Managing Committee,* AIR 1972 P&H 245: 1972 (74) PunLR 673.

19. Equitable Jurisdiction – Law on – If the agreement to sell was executed way back in the year 1982 and the value of the real estate has shoot up very high, therefore, while exercising jurisdiction under section 20 of the Specific Relief Act, 1963 Courts would like to be equitable and would not allow the sale of property to be executed for a petty sum of that time and if the litigation has prolonged for almost 25 years and now at last reached at the end of the journey. Therefore, Courts have to settle the equity between the parties; *Pratap Lakshman Muchandi* v. *Shamlal Uddavadas Wadhwa,* AIR 2008 SC 1378: JT 2008 (1) SC 531: 2008 (1) SCALE 520: 2008 (12) SCC 67.

It is settled law that the party who seeks to avail of the equitable jurisdiction of a Court and specific performance being equitable relief, must come to the Court with clean hands. In other words the party who makes false allegations does not came with clean hands and is not entitled to the equitable relief; *Lourdu Mari David* v. *Louis Chinnaya Arogiaswamy,* AIR 1996 SC 2814: JT 1996 (7) SC 499: 1996 (6) SCALE 184: 1996 (5) SCC 589.

20. Equitable Principles – Law on – The equitable discretion of courts to grant or not to grant a relief of specific performance also depends upon the conduct of the parties. The necessary ingredient has to be proved and established by the plaintiff so that discretion would be exercised judiciously in favour of the plaintiff. At the same time, if the dependent does not come with clean hands and suppresses material facts and evidence and mislead the court then such discretion should not be exercised by refusing to grant specific performance; *Zarina Siddiqui* v. *Ramalingam @ R. Amarnathan,* AIR 2015 SC 580.

The jurisdiction to decree specific relief is discretionary and the court can consider various circumstances to decide whether such relief is to be granted. Merely because it is lawful to grant specific relief, the Court need not grant the order for specific relief; but this discretion shall not be exercised in an arbitrary or unreasonable manner. Certain circumstances have been mentioned in section 20(2) of the Specific Relief Act, 1963 as to under what circumstances the Court shall exercise such discretion. If under the terms of the contract the plaintiff gets an unfair advantage over the defendant, the Court may not exercise its discretion in favour of the plaintiff. So also, specific relief may not be granted if the defendant would be put to undue hardship which he did not foresee at the time of agreement. If it is inequitable to grant specific relief, then also the Court would desist from granting a decree to the plaintiff. Granting of specific performance is an equitable relief, though the same is now governed by the statutory provisions of the Specific Relief Act, 1963. These equitable principles are nicely incorporated in section 20 of the Act. While granting a decree for specific performance, these salutary guidelines shall be in the forefront of the mind of the Court. The trial Court, which had the added advantage of recording the evidence and seeing the demeanour of the witnesses considered the relevant facts and reached a conclusion. The appellate Court should not have reversed that decision disregarding these facts; *A.C. Arulappan* v. *Ahalya Naik*, AIR 2001 SC 2783: JT 2001 (6) SC 394: 2001 (5) SCALE 154: 2001 (6) SCC 600.

21. Equitable Remedy – Comments on – It is a case where the plaintiff seeks specific performance of a contract stated to be evidenced by an allegedly sham document which did not come into effect. Plaint does not contain the requisite pleadings necessary to obtain a decree for specific performance. This equitable remedy recognised by the Specific Relief Act cannot be had on the basis of such pleadings and evidence; *Abdul Khader Rowther* v. *P.K. Sara Bai*, AIR 1990 SC 682: 1990 (67) Comp Cas 316: JT 1989 (3) SC 527: 1989 (2) SCALE 1464: 1989 (4) SCC 313.

22. Equity – Law on – Section 20 deals with discretion and jurisdiction to the court. It says that the court is not bound to grant such relief merely because it is lawful to do so, but at the same time it enjoins that the discretion of the court should not be arbitrary but sound and reasonable, guided by judicial principles and capable of correction by a court of appeal. It would thus be seen that the discretion given to the court of equity is required to be exercised not arbitrarily but on sound and reasonable basis guided by judicial principles; *Kallathil Sreedharan* v. *Komath Pandyala Prasanna*, JT 1996 (8) SC 40: 1997 (1) Mad LJ 61: 1996 (6) SCALE 311: 1996 (6) SCC 218.

23. Facts and Circumstances – Consideration of – It is true that since the High Court and the Courts below have exercised discretion, it may not normally be interfered with under article 136 of the Constitution, but the fact remains that the Mr. R are money-lenders and that they sought to recover the amounts due to them. Since the Mr. A was not in a position to pay the amount due on the promissory note, he entered into the agreement to sell the property and the agreement was sought to be enforced. Though the Mr. A had agreed to sell the property to Mr., the predominant object thereby would be for recovery of the dues with interest. He who demands equity must do equity. Court has discretion. Court is not bound to grant specific performance. It depends on facts and circumstances in each case; *S. Rangaraju Naidu* v. *S. Thiruvarakkarasu*, AIR 1995 SC 1769: 1995 (2) SCALE 504: 1995 (2) SCR 617.

24. Identification of Property – Law on – It is well-settled that unless the property in question for which the relief has been sought for is identifiable, no decree can be granted in respect of the same; *Nahar Singh* v. *Harnak Singh*, JT 1996 (9) SC 701: 1996 (8) SCALE 119: 1996 (6) SCC 699.

25. Intention of Parties – Law on – A document, as is well known, must be read in its entirety. The intention of the parties, it is equally well-settled, must be gathered from the document itself. All parts of the deed must be read in their entirety so as to ascertain the nature thereof; *P.S. Ranakrishna Reddy* v. *M.K. Bhagyalakshmi*, AIR 2007 SC 1256: JT 2007 (4) SC 223: 2007 (3) SCALE 409: 2007 (10) SCC 231.

26. Joint Property – Law on – Even where any property is held jointly, and once any party to the contract has agreed to sell such joint property agreement, then, even if other co-sharer has not joined at least to the extent of his share, he is bound to execute, the sale deed. However, in the absence of other co-sharer there could not be any decree of any specified part of the property to be partitioned and possession given; *A. Abdul Rashid Khan* v. *P.A.K.A. Shahul Hamid*, AIR 2001 SCW 2361: JT 2000 (7) SC 483: 2000 (10) SCC 636: 2000 (6) Supreme 575.

27. *Lis Pendens* – Law on – In the light of these principles we have got to consider whether in the event of a conflict arising between the doctrine of *lis pendens* enshrined in section 52 of the Transfer of Property Act and the rule availing a subsequent transferee without notice, contained in section 19(b) of the Specific Relief Act either the one or the other should prevail. Ordinarily, it is true that the title acquired by the subsequent purchaser is good, the sale to him being not void. But he who purchases during the pendency of the suit is bound by the decree that may be made against the person from whom he derives title. The litigating parties are exempted from the necessity of taking any notice of a title so acquired, As to the vendor and the prior contractor it is as if no such title existed. Section 52 places a complete embargo on the transfer of any right to immovable property pending suit, which is directly and specifically in question in such a litigation; it enacts that during the pendency of the suit in which any right to immovable property is "directly and specifically in question, the property cannot be transferred or otherwise alienated by any party to the suit so as to affect the rights of any other party thereto under any decree; *Ram Peary* v. *Gauri*, AIR 1978 All 318; see *Samarendra Nath Sinha* v. *Krishna Kumar Nag*, AIR 1967 SC 1440.

28. Material Alteration – Comments on – In *Halsbury's Laws of England*, 4th Edn., p. 552, para 1378 it is observed: "A material alteration is one which varies the rights, liabilities, or legal position of the parties as ascertained by the deed in its original state, or otherwise varies the legal effect of the instrument as originally expressed, or reduces to certainty some provision which was originally unascertained and as such void, or which may otherwise prejudice the party bound by the deed as originally executed. The effect of making such an alteration without the consent of the party bound is exactly the same as that of cancelling the deed;" *Ram Khilona* v. *Sardar*, AIR 2002 SC 2548: JT 2002 (5) SC 503: 2002 (5) SCALE 210: 2002 (6) SCC 375.

29. More Courts Possess Jurisdiction to Entertain a Suit – Law on – Plain reading of section 20 of the code leaves no room of doubt that it is a residuary provision and covers those cases not falling within the limitations of sections 15 to 20. The opening words of the section "subject to the limitations aforesaid" are significant and make it abundantly clear that the section takes within its sweep all personal actions. A suit falling under section 20 thus may be instituted in a court within whose jurisdiction the defendant resides, or carries on business, or personally works for gain or cause of action wholly or partly arises. Where two or more courts have jurisdiction to entertain a suit, parties may by agreement submit to the jurisdiction of one court to the exclusion of the other court or courts. Such agreement is not hit by section 28 of the Contract Act, 1872 nor can such a contract be said to be against public policy. It is legal, valid and enforceable; *Harshad Chiman Lal Modi* v. *DLF Universal Ltd.*, AIR 2005 SC 4446: JT 2005 (8) SC 561: 2005 (7) SCALE 533: 2005 (7) SCC 791.

30. Mortgagor's Right – Law on – In India, the word "transfer" is defined with reference to the word "convey." The word "transfer" in English law in its narrower and more usual sense refers to the transfer of an estate in land. Section 205 of the Law of Property Act in England defines: "Conveyance" includes a mortgage, charge, lease, assent, vesting declaration, vesting instrument. The word "conveys" in section 5 of the Transfer of Property Act is used in the wider sense of conveying ownership. The right of redemption which is embodied in section 60 of the Transfer of Property Act is available to the Mortgagor unless it has been extinguished by the act of parties. The combined effect of section 54 of the Transfer of Property Act and section 17 of the Indian Registration Act is that a contract for sale in respect of immovable property of the value of more than one hundred rupees without registration cannot extinguish the equity of redemption. In India it is only on execution of the conveyance and registration of transfer of the mortgagor's interest by registered instrument that the mortgagor's right of redemption will be extinguished. The conferment of power to sell without intervention of the Court in a Mortgage Deed by itself will not deprive the mortgagor of his right to redemption. The extinction of the right of redemption has to be subsequent to the deed conferring such power. The right of redemption is not extinguished at the expiry of the period. The equity of redemption is not extinguished by mere contract for sale. The mortgagor's right to redeem will survive until there has been completion of sale of by the mortgagee by a registered deed. In England a sale of property takes place by agreement but it is not so in our country. The power to sell shall not be exercised unless and until notice in writing requiring payment of the principal money has been served on the mortgagor. Further section 69(3) of the Transfer of Property Act shows that when a sale has been made in professed exercise of such a power, the title of the purchaser shall not be impeachable on the ground that no case had arisen to authorise the sale. Therefore, until the sale is complete by registration the mortgagor does not lose right of redemption. It is erroneous to suggest that the mortgagee is acting as the agent of the mortgagor in selling the property. The mortgagor exercises his right under a different claim. The mortgagee's right is different from the mortgagor's. The mortgagee exercises his right under a totally superior claim which is not under the mortgagor, but against him. In other words, the sale is against the mortgagor's wishes. Rights and interests of the mortgagor and the mortgagee in regard to sale are conflicting; *Narandas Karsondas* v. *S.A. Kamtam*, AIR 1977 SC 774: 1977 (3) SCC 247: 1977 (2) SCR 341.

31. Multiplicity of Proceedings – Law on – It is thus clear that the Legislature has given ample power to the Court to allow amendment of the plaint at any stage, including the execution proceedings. The limitation would start against the decree-holders only after they had obtained a sale in respect of the disputed property. It is, therefore, difficult to accept that a valuable right had accrued to the judgment-debtor by lapse of time. Section 22 has been enacted only for the purpose of avoiding multiplicity of proceedings which the law Courts always abhor; *Babu Lal* v. *Hazari Lal Kishori Lal*, AIR 1982 SC 818: 1982 (1) SCALE 79: 1982 (1) SCC 525: 1982 (3) SCR 94; *Rameshwar Nath* v. *Uttar Pradesh Union Bank Ltd.*, AIR 1956 All 586.

32. Necessary Parties – Law on – Therefore, the expression "all the questions involved in the suit" can very well be said to mean the questions as between the parties to the litigation. The scope of the suit cannot be widened. The judgment in this suit is not going to affect the title of the applicants, if any. The plaintiff is the *dominus litus* and cannot be forced to add parties against whom he does not want to fight unless it is a compulsion of the rule of law and, as already discussed herein-above, these applicants are not necessary parties and as such, the plaintiff cannot be forced upon to join them as parties. Merely on this ground, a party which does not fall within the scope of the aforesaid expression which governs the question of determining as to who is a proper party cannot be joined as proper party. If this is taken as the only test, in any litigation, no party can be termed as an 'improper party' even if its addition in effect is to compel the plaintiff to enlarge or change the nature of his suit; *Panne Khushali* v. *Jeewanlal Mathoo Khatik*, AIR 1976 MP 148: 1976 Jab LJ 84: 1976 MPLJ 170.

33. Necessary Party – Law on – Sub-rule (2) of rule 10 of Order I provides that the court may either upon or without an application of either party, add any party whose presence before the court may be necessary in order to enable the court effectually and completely to adjudicate upon and settle all questions involved in the suit. Since the Mr. R is not a party to the agreement of sale, it cannot be said that without his presence the dispute as to specific performance cannot be determined. Therefore, he is not a necessary party. A person may be added as a party-defendant to the suit though no relief may be claimed against him/her provided his/her presence is necessary for a complete and final decision on the question involved in the suit. Such a person is only a proper party as distinguished from a necessary party; *Anil Kumar Singh* v. *Shivnath Mishra* alias *Gadasa Guru*, AIR 1995 SCW 1782: JT 1995 (1) SC 273: 1994 (4) SCALE 953: 1995 (3) SCC 147.

34. Negotiations – Law on – The specific performance of a contract is the actual execution of the contract according to its stipulations and terms, and the courts direct the party in default to do the very thing which he contracted to do. The stipulations and terms of the contract have, therefore, to be certain and the parties must have been consensus *ad idem*. The burden of showing the stipulations and terms of the contract and that the minds were ad idem is, of course, on the plaintiff. If the stipulations and terms are uncertain, and the parties are not *ad idem*, there can be no specific performance, for there was no contract at all. Where there are negotiations, the court has to determine at what point, if at all, the parties have reached agreement. Negotiations thereafter would also be material if the agreement is rescinded; *Mayawanti* v. *Kaushalya Devi*, JT 1990 (3) SC 205: 1990 (1) SCALE 724: 1990 (3) SCC 1: 1990 (2) SCR 350.

35. No Specific Plea – Law on – Merely because the plaint says in the prayer such other relief be granted to the plaintiff it does not mean that without a specific plea for possession and disregarding bar under section 42 (proviso) of the Specific Relief Act, the suit could be decreed even with reference to the portions of which the plaintiff has been in possession; *Vinay Krishna* v. *Keshav Chandra*, AIR 1993 SC 957: AIR 1992 SCW 3652: 1993 (2) APLJ 4: 1993 (Supp 3) SCC 129.

36. Payment – Modes of – The payment by way of bank draft is as good a payment as cash-in-hand. Instead of bringing the cash, he had brought bank draft; *Sohan Singh* v. *Sarwan Singh*, JT 1996 (7) SC 508: 1996 (6) SCALE 253: 1996 (5) SCC 759: 1996 (6) Supreme 585.

37. Plaintiff – Duties of – Plaintiff in a suit for specific performance of contract not only must raise a plea that he had all along been and even on the date of filing of suit was ready and willing to perform his part of contract, but also prove the same. Only in certain exceptional situation where although in letter and spirit, the exact words had not been used but readiness and willingness can be culled out from reading all the averments made in the Plaintiff as a whole coupled with the materials brought on record at the trial of the suit, to the said effect, the statutory requirement of section 16(c) of the Specific Relief Act may be held to have been complied with; *Manjunath Anandappa Urf Shivappa Hansi* v. *Tammanasa*, AIR 2003 SC 1391: 2003 (3) SCALE 331: 2003 (10) SCC 390: 2003 (2) SCR 1068.

38. Plaintiff – Obligations of – In a suit for specific performance, the plaintiff should allege that he is ready and willing to perform his part of the contract and in the absence of such an allegation in the plaint, the suit is not maintainable; *Gajanan Jaikishan Joshi* v. *Prabhakar Mohanlal Kalwar*, JT 1989 (4) SC 524: 1989 (2) SCALE 1323: 1990 (1) SCC 166.

39. Plea of Hardship – Law on – When the plea of hardship had not been raised by the party concerned, examination of the provisions of section 20(2)(b) of the Specific Relief Act would not arise at all. When the party concerned did not raise this plea as to how the Court could imagine it might result in hardship to the party concerned, is beyond Court's comprehension; *Sarita Rani* v. *Deepak Raj*, JT 2000 (10) SC 270: 2001 (4) Supreme 510.

40. Premature Suit – Law on – A suit of a civil nature disclosing a cause of action even if filed before the date on which the plaintiff became actually entitled to sue and claim the relief founded on such cause of action is not to be necessarily dismissed for such reason. A plea as to non-maintainability of the suit on the ground of its being premature should be promptly raised by the defendant and pressed for decision. It will equally be the responsibility of the court to examine and promptly dispose of such a plea. The plea may not be permitted to be raised at a belated stage of the suit. However, the court shall not exercise its discretion in favour of decreeing a premature suit in the following cases: (i) When there is a mandatory bar created by a statute which disables the plaintiff from filing the suit on or before a particular date or the occurrence of a particular event; (ii) when the institution of the suit before the lapse of a particular time or occurrence of a particular event would have the effect of defeating a public policy or public purpose; (iii) if such premature institution renders the presentation itself patently void and the invalidity is incurable such as when it goes to the root of the court's jurisdiction, and

(iv) where the *lis* is not confined to parties alone and affects and involves persons other than those arrayed as parties, such as in an election petition which affects and involves the entire constituency; *Vithalbhai Pvt. Ltd.* v. *Union of India,* 2005 (2) SCR 680: AIR 2005 SC 1891: JT 2005 (3) SC 278: 2005 (3) SCALE 132: 2005 (4) SCC 315.

41. Properties Scattered at Different Places – Specific Performance of – It is clear from section 12 that it relates to the specific performance of a part of a contract. Courts also do not see any difficulty in granting specific performance merely because the properties are scattered at different places. There is no law that the properties to be sold must be situated at one place; *Kartar Singh* v. *Harjinder Singh,* AIR 1990 SC 854: JT 1990 (1) SC 253: 1990 (1) SCALE 276: 1990 (3) SCC 517.

42. Purchasing of Stamp Paper – Effect of – It will be unfair and inequitable not to grant a decree for specific relief in favour of the plaintiff because he is a *bona fide* purchaser and he has done everything which is possible that he has purchased the stamp paper and was ready and willing to perform his part of the contract; *Devalsab (D) by LRs.* v. *Ibrahimsab F. Karajagi,* AIR 2005 SC 1940: JT 2005 (3) SC 40: 2005 (2) SCALE 540: 2005 (3) SCC 342.

43. Readiness and Willingness – Burden of Proof for – It is indisputable that in a suit for specific performance of contract the plaintiff must establish his readiness and willingness to perform his part of contract. The question is whether the onus was discharged by the plaintiff or not will depend upon the fact and circumstance of each case. No strait-jacket formula can be laid down in this behalf. The readiness and willingness on the part of the plaintiff to perform his part of contract would also depend upon the question as to whether the defendant did everything which was required of him to be done in terms of the agreement for sale; *P. Dsouza* v. *Shondrilo Naidu,* AIR 2004 SC 4472: 2004 (6) SCALE 364: 2004 (6) SCC 649: 2004 (4) SLT 893.

44. Relief of Specific Performance – Circumstances for – Section 20 provides that relief of the specific performance lies in the discretion of the Court and the Court is not bound to grant such relief merely because it is lawful to do so. The discretion cannot be exercised arbitrarily. It has to be exercised in a sound and reasonable manner guided by judicial principles. Sub-section (2) enumerates the circumstances in which the Court may exercise its discretion in not granting the decree of specific performance; sub-section (3) gives guidelines for proper exercise of the discretion in decreeing the relief of specific performance; and sub-section (4) does away with the requirement of mutuality as a condition for grant of relief of specific performance. The circumstances enumerated in sub-sections (2) and (3) are not exhaustive; *Nirmala Anand* v. *Advent Corporation Pvt. Ltd.,* AIR 2002 SC 2290: 2003 (1) Mad LJ 72: 2002 (4) SCALE 601: 2002 (5) SCC 481.

45. Rise in Prices of Properties – Law on – Because of the normal trend of rise in prices of properties situate especially in metropolitan city . If merely because the prices have risen during the pendency of litigation, Courts were to deny the relief of specific performance if otherwise due, this relief could hardly be granted in any case, because by the time the litigation comes to an end sufficiently long period is likely to elapse in most of the cases. This factor, therefore, should not normally weigh against the suitor in exercise of discretion by a Court; *S.V.R. Mudaliar* v. *Rajabu F. Buhari,* AIR 1995 SC 1607: JT 1995 (3) SC 614: 1995 (2) SCALE 720: 1995 (4) SCC 15.

46. Scribe of Document – Testimony of – It is well-known that is the scribe of a document which has been found to be forged by the lower appellate court and therefore a person who can go to the extent of manufacturing a document to suit one of the parties to the litigation cannot be said to be an independent witness and the court is right in discarding his testimony; *Annapoorani Ammal* v. *G. Thangapalam,* 1989 (Supp 1) JT 164: 1989 (1) SCALE 1417: 1989 (3) SCC 287: 1989 (2) SCR 833.

47. Specific Performance – Denial of – The ordinary rule is that specific performance should be granted. It ought to be denied only when equitable considerations point to its refusal and the circumstances show that damages would constitute an adequate relief; *Prakash Chandra* v. *Angadlal*, AIR 1979 SC 1241: 1979 (4) SCC 393: 1979 UJ 277 **[Hon'ble Judges:** Jaswant Singh, R.S. Pathak, A.P. Sen].

48. Specific Performance of Enforceable Contract – Law on – In a case of specific performance it is settled law, and indeed it cannot be doubted, that the jurisdiction to order specific performance of a contract is based on the existence of a valid and enforceable contract. The Law of Contract is based on the ideal of freedom of contract and it provides the limiting principles within which the parties are free to make their own contracts. Where a valid and enforceable contract has not been made, the court will not make a contract for them. Specific performance will not be ordered if the contract itself suffers from some defect which makes the contract invalid or unenforceable. The discretion of the court will be there even though the contract is otherwise valid and enforceable and it can pass a decree of specific performance even before there has been any breach of the contract. It is, therefore, necessary first to see whether there has been a valid and enforceable contract and then to see the nature and obligation arising out of it. The contract being the foundation of the obligation the order of specific performance is to enforce that obligation; *Mayawanti* v. *Kaushalya Devi*, JT 1990 (3) SC 205: 1990 (1) SCALE 724: 1990 (3) SCC 1: 1990 (2) SCR 350.

49. Suit for Specific Performance – Limitation for – Under article 113 of the Limitation Act, 1963, the limitation prescribed for a suit for specific performance is a period of three years which runs from the date when the cause of action accrues; *Rojasara Ramjibhai Dahyabhai* v. *Jani Narottamdas Lallubhai*, AIR 1986 SC 1912: 1986 (1) SCALE 566: 1986 (3) SCC 300: 1986 (2) SCR 447.

50. Tenure-Holder – Rights of – A bare perusal of the section reveals that the rights, title, interests and liabilities of the tenure-holder in his original holding cease. The tenure-holder acquires the same rights, title, interests and liabilities in the chaks allotted to him, it is the rights, title, interests and liabilities of the tenure-holder which stand transferred to the chak allotted to him under Uttar Pradesh Consolidation of Holdings Act, 1954; *Mahendra Nath* v. *Baikunthi Devi*, AIR 1976 All 150: 1975 AWC 596.

51. Time not Essence of Contract – Law on – It is settled law that unless the deed of agreement of sale stipulated a date for performance, time is not always essence of the contract. The cause of action arose on expiry of eight years from the date of execution of later sale deed; *D.S. Thimmappa* v. *Siddaramakka*, AIR 1996 SC 1960: JT 1996 (4) SC 324: 1996 (3) SCALE 704: 1996 (8) SCC 365: 1996 (3) SCR 1045.

52. Violation of Term of Agreement – Effect of – The person had failed to comply with the term of the agreement relating to payment of amount. In these circumstances, in any case, a decree for specific performance cannot be granted as it would be unfair and unreasonable to do so; *P.R. Deb* v. *Sunanda Roy*, AIR 1996 SC 1504: JT 1996 (2) SC 684: 1996 (2) SCALE 551: 1996 (4) SCC 423.

53. *Void Ab Initio* Agreement of Sale – Law on – It is well-settled that any agreement of sale in regard to property which cannot be transferred is void *ab initio*, and it is further well-settled that an agreement which is *void ab initio* cannot be specifically enforced; *Muthabathula Arjayya* v. *Rambala Venkata Surya Gopala Krishanamurthy*, AIR 1974 AP 240.

54. Void Order – Law on – It is a well-settled principle of law that even a void order is required to be set aside by a competent court of law inasmuch as an order may be void in respect of one person but may be valid in respect of another. A void order is necessarily not *non est*. An order cannot be declared to be void in a collateral proceeding and that too in absence of the authorities who were the authors thereof; *M. Meenakshi* v. *Metadin Agarwal*, AIR 2006 SCW 4323: 2006 (8) SCALE 566: 2006 (7) SCC 470: 2006 (3) SCC (Cri) 538.

55. Voluntary Performance of Conditions Specified by Owner – Law on – An agreement for sale and purchase simpliciter is a reciprocal arrangement imposing obligations and benefits on both parties and is enforceable at the instance of either. The interpretation of such a contract would be governed by the laws of contract relating to the performance of reciprocal promises. An agreement for sale is described as a reconveyance does not by itself mean that it is not an option to repurchase nor does it in any way alter the substance of the deed. It merely records a historical fact that the property which is to be sold was being purchased by the person who used to be the owner. No logical distinction can be drawn between an agreement to re-purchase and an ordinary agreement of purchase just because the vendor happens to be the original purchaser and the purchaser happens to be the original vendor. The agreement remains an agreement for sale of immovable property and must be governed by the same provisions of law. Whether an agreement is an option to purchase or an "ordinary" agreement would depend on the interpretation of its provisions. Sometimes the option is expressly and in terms granted. In others the right may be implicit. Thus when an agreement provides that the right to obtain a sale is subject to the fulfilment of certain conditions by the purchaser, the agreement would in effect be an option to purchase, as the right to purchase would only accrue upon the voluntary performance of the conditions specified by the owner. The vendor cannot compel the performance of the conditions by the purchaser and then ask for the contract to be specifically performed; *V. Pechimuthu* v. *Gowrammal*, AIR 2001 SC 2446: JT 2001 (6) SC 162: 2001 (4) SCALE 650: 2001 (7) SCC 617.

56. Agreement Entered into Subject to Ratification – Law on – When an agreement is entered into subject to ratification by others, a concluded contract is not arrived at. Whenever ratification by some other persons, who are not parties to the agreement is required, such a clause must be held to be a condition precedent for coming into force of a concluded contract. The word 'subject to' has been defined in *Black's Law Dictionary*, 5th Edn., p. 1278, *inter alia*, as "subservient, inferior, obedient to; governed or affected by; provided that; provided; answerable for". In Collins' English the words 'subject to' has been stated to mean as: "under the condition that.

57. Agreement to Sell – Credibility of – The plaintiff who has examined himself as PW-1 has raised mutually inconsistent pleas, as is evident from the pleadings in the plaint wherein he had stated that it has been agreed that the sale deed would be executed within a period of 4 months, however, in his deposition, he has stated that the sale deeds were agreed to be executed only after the expiry of the term of the lease. The agreement to sell has been transcribed on the non-judicial stamp paper, though not registered. Admittedly, the said stamp paper had been purchased 11 months prior to the date mentioned in the agreement for sale. More so, it had been purchased from a different place. Further, there is nothing on record to show as in whose name, the non-judicial stamp paper had been purchased and who had purchased it. The Court should not rely upon untrustworthy, shaky and vague evidence to grant the discretionary relief of specific performance in contravention of the mandate of section 20; *Garre Mallikharjuna Rao (D) by LRs.* v. *Nalabothu Punniah*, 2013 (3) SCALE 344: JT 2013 (9) SC 341: 2013 (4) Supreme 717.

58. Agreement to Sell Holder – Compensation for – Agreement to sell holder filed the suit for specific performance on the last day of limitation. Since the Agreement to sell holder filed the suit within the period of limitation and his readiness and willingness to conclude the sale transaction was quite obvious from the fact that he had taken upon himself the burden of pursuing the matter with the authorities for obtaining sale permission and Income Tax Clearance Certificate. The role played by the Agreement to sell holder in this regard cannot, therefore, be applied to his disadvantage. Agreement to sell holder should be compensated for the time spent by him in pursuing his remedy in respect of the Agreement to Sell; *Rattan Lal* v. *S.N. Bhalla*, AIR 2012 SC 3094: JT 2012 (7) SC 380: 2012 (8) SCC 659: 2012 (7) SCALE 257.

59. Agreement under a Mistake as to a Matter of Fact – Effect of – Sections 15, 16, 17 and 18 define "Coercion", "Undue Influence", "Fraud" and "Misrepresentation". Section 19 provides that when consent to an agreement is caused by coercion, fraud or misrepresentation, such agreement is voidable at the option of the party whose consent was so caused. So also is the agreement to which consent of a party was obtained by undue influence. Section provides that an agreement would be void if both the parties to the agreement were under a mistake as to a matter of fact essential to the agreement. The mistake has to be mutual and in order that the agreement be treated as void, both the parties must be shown to be suffering from mistake of fact. Unilateral mistake is outside the scope of this section; *Tarsem Singh* v. *Sukhminder Singh*, AIR 1998 SC 1400: JT 1998 (2) SC 149: 1998 (1) SCALE 58: 1998 (3) SCC 471.

60. Compensatory Amount – Law on – Grant of relief of specific performance being discretionary, it cannot be claimed as a matter of right. It is governed by sound judicial principles and one of the foremost principle is that the Court should be satisfied that circumstances are such that it is equitable to grant the relief of specific performance of the contract. Under this principle one of the questions which has been considered at times by the Courts is: as to whether due to delay in the grant of decree and the escalation of prices of the real estate during the period is a ground to deny the relief of specific performance. It has repeatedly been held that *per se* the delay or the escalation of price is no ground to deny the relief of specific performance. In certain cases the Courts in equity and to mitigate the hardship to the vendor have directed the vendee to pay further compensatory amount. But this is not a principle of universal application. It would depend upon the facts and circumstances of each case; *Nirmala Anand* v. *Advent Corporation Pvt. Ltd.*, AIR 2002 SC 2290: 2002 (4) SCALE 601: 2002 (5) SCC 481: 2002 (4) Supreme 255.

61. Conduct of Plaintiff – Consideration of – I find that there is absolutely no scope for holding that the plaintiff had committed breach of contract. If the conduct of the plaintiff throughout shows that she/he was always ready and willing to perform her part of the contract within the stipulated time. I find that there are absolutely no grounds to deny the relief of specific performance to the plaintiff. Hence the plaintiff is entitled to get a decree for specific performance; *Annapoorani Ammal (Died)* v. *Ramaswamy Naicker*, AIR 1990 Mad 361 **[Hon'ble Judges:** Nainar Sundaram, K.M. Natarajan, Bellie].

62. Coparcenary Property – Law on – For the purpose of assigning one's interest in the property, it was not necessary that partition by metes and bounds amongst the coparceners must take place. When an intention is expressed to partition the coparcenary property, the share of each of the coparceners becomes clear and ascertainable. Once the share of a co-parcener is determined, it ceases to be a coparcenary property. The parties in such an event would not possess the property as "joint tenants" but as "tenants in common"; *Hardeo Rai* v. *Sakuntala Devi*, AIR 2008 SC 2489: 2008 (7) SCALE 662: 2008 (7) SCC 46; For contrary view *vide*; *State Bank of India* v. *Ghamandi Ram*, AIR 1969 SC 1330.

63. Discretionary Jurisdiction – Law on – It is now well-settled that fraud vitiated all solemn act. Any order or decree obtained by practicing fraud is a nullity. The doctrine of estoppel by acquiescence was not restricted to cases where the representor was aware both of what his strict rights were and that the representee was acting on the belief that those rights would not be enforced against him. The application of the said doctrine becomes relevant in view of the fact that in the Memorandum of Association of the company alone were shown to be the subscriber members of the company. If both the parties are guilty of serious misconduct and both of them have abused the process of court and they initiated unnecessary frivolous proceedings against each another. Both the parties took recourse to abuse of judicial process against the other upon suppression of material fact, which would amount to fraud on court. The question in regard to exercise of discretionary jurisdiction for grant of a decree of specific performance of contract, as envisaged under section 20 of the Specific Relief Act, must be considered from the said angle; *Jai Narain Parasurampuria* v. *Pushpa Devi Saraf,* 2006 (133) Comp Cas 794: 2006 (8) SCALE 477: 2006 (7) SCC 756: 2006 (8) SCJ 524.

64. Discretionary Powers – The grant of specific relief is a discretionary relief and is not as a matter of right; *K.G. Arumugham* v. *K.A. Chinnappan,* 2005 (3) Cal HN 31: 2005 (1) CCC 200: JT 2005 (11) SC 29: 2005 (2) SCALE 388: 2005 (2) SCC 793.

65. Good Defense as Hardship – Law on – In a case of Specific performance, hardship is a good defense. The question as to whether the grant of relief for specific performance will cause hardship to the defendant within the meaning of clause (b) of sub section (2) of section 20 of the Specific Relief Act, 1963, being a question of fact, the first appellate court without framing such an issue ought not to have reversed the finding of the trial court while concurring with it on all other issues with regard to the appellant's entitlement to relief for specific performance of contract; *Prakash Chandra* v. *Narayan,* AIR 2012 SC 2826: JT 2012 (4) SC 349: 2012 (4) SCALE 583: 2012 (5) SCC 403.

66. Hardship on Defendant – Law on – Section 20 of the Specific Relief Act, 1963 provides that the jurisdiction to decree specific performance is discretionary and the Court is not bound to grant such relief merely because it is lawful to do so; the discretion of the Court is not arbitrary but sound and reasonable guided by judicial principles and capable of correction by a Court of appeal. Performance of the contract involving some hardship on the defendant which he did not foresee while non-performance involving no such hardship on the plaintiff is one of the circumstances in which the Court may properly exercise discretion not to decree specific performance. The doctrine of comparative hardship has been thus statutorily recognized in India. However, mere inadequacy of consideration or the mere fact that the contract is onerous to the defendant or improvident in its nature, shall not constitute an unfair advantage to the plaintiff over the defendant or unforeseeable hardship on the defendant; *K. Narendra* v. *Riviera Apartments Private Limited,* AIR 1999 SC 2309: JT 1999 (4) SC 428: 1999 (4) SCALE 22: 1999 (5) SCC 77; The principle underlying section 20 has been summed up by Apex Court in *Lourdu Mari David* v. *Louis Chinnaya Arogiaswamy,* AIR 1996 SC 2814: 1996 AIR SCW 3603 by stating that the decree for specific performance is in the discretion of the Court but the discretion should not be used arbitrarily; the discretion should be exercised on sound principles of law capable of correction by an appellate Court.

67. Identity of Land – Law on – A suit for specific performance of contract provides for a discretionary remedy. The Court in terms of section 20 of the Act may for sufficient and cogent reasons refuse to grant a decree for specific performance of contract. The Court essentially would be concerned with the identity of the land which was the subject-matter of agreement. Like any other suit, the Court in terms of Order VII, rule 7 of the Code of Civil Procedure may, however, take into consideration the subsequent events including the change in the revenue survey numbers in respect of a particular land. In other words, if the land in suit remains the same which was the subject-matter of an Agreement of Sale, a decree for specific performance can be granted; *Gurdial Kaur* v. *Piara Singh,* AIR 2008 SC 2019: 2008 (4) SCALE 695: 2008 (14) SCC 735: 2008 (4) SLT 346.

68. Ineluctability – Law on – The grant of decree for specific performance is a matter of discretion under section 20 of the Specific Relief Act, 1963. The Court is not bound to grant such relief merely because it is lawful to do so but the discretion is not required to be exercised arbitrarily. It is to be exercised on sound and settled judicial principles. One of the grounds on which the Court may decline to decree specific performance is where it would be inequitable to enforce specific performance; *Her Highness Maharani Shantadevi P. Gaekwad* v. *Savjibhai Haribhai Patel,* AIR 2001 SC 1462: JT 2001 (4) SC 43: 2001 (2) SCALE 647: 2001 (5) SCC 101.

69. Instrument of Oppression – Law on – Section 20 of the Specific Relief Act preserves judicial discretion to Courts as to decreeing specific performance. The Court should meticulously consider all facts and circumstances of the case. The Court is not bound to grant specific performance merely because it is lawful to do so. The motive behind the litigation should also enter into the judicial verdict. The Court should take care to see that it is not used as an instrument of oppression to have an unfair advantage to the plaintiff; *Parakunnan Veetill Josephs Son Mathew* v. *Nedumbara Kuruvilas Son*, AIR 1987 SC 2328: 1987 (13) All LR 676: JT 1987 (3) SC 643: 1987 (2) SCALE 588.

70. Limitation – Law on – For the purpose of limitation, what is material is that the limitation begins to run from the date the parties have stipulated for performance of the contract. The suit is required to be filed within three years from the date fixed by the parties under the contract. If the application for amendment of the plaint came to be filed after the expiry of three years, certainly it changed the cause of action as required to be specified in the plaint. The suit for mandatory injunction is filed and the specific performance was sought for by way of an amendment. The cause of action is required to be stated initially in the plaint but it was not pleaded. It was sought to be amended, along with an application for specific performance which was rejected. Under these circumstances, even by the date of filing of the application, namely the suit was barred by limitation; *T.L. Muddukrishana* v. *Lalitha Ramchandra Rao*, AIR 1997 SC 772: 1997 (1) Crimes 160: JT 1997 (1) SC 540: 1997 (1) SCALE 321: 1997 (2) SCC 611.

The Court, in applying the period of limitation, would first inquire as to whether any time was fixed for performance of agreement of sale. If it is so fixed, the suit must be filed within the period of three years, failing which the same would be barred by limitation. Here, however, no time for performance was fixed. It was for the Courts to find out the date on which the plaintiff had notice that the performance was refused and on arriving at a finding in that behalf, to see whether the suit was filed within three years thereafter; *Janardhanam Prasad* v. *Ramdas*, JT 2007 (3) SC 187: 2007 (2) SCALE 442: 2007 (15) SCC 174: 2007 (3) Supreme 299.

71. Nature of Property – Proof for – In the absence of a clear indication of the nature of the property in the allotment letter, Courts may refer to the other documentary evidence on record; *Prabha Manufacturing Industrial Co-operative Society* v. *Banwari Lal*, AIR 1989 SC 1101: JT 1989 (1) SC 397: 1989 (1) SCALE 383: 1989 (2) SCC 69.

72. Personal Bars to Relief – Law on – In a suit for specific performance on an agreement to sell, the grant of relief is discretionary. The court after consideration of all relevant circumstances must be persuaded to exercise its equitable and discretionary jurisdiction in favour of specific enforcement. The jurisdiction is subject to all the conditions to which all discretionary jurisdictions are subject. There are certain personal bars to relief; *Om Prakash* v. *Amarjit Singh*, JT 1988 (3) SC 555: 1988 (2) SCALE 567: 1988 (Supp 1) SCC 780.

73. Jurisdiction – Law on – Where there is no express exclusion the examination of the remedies and the scheme of the particular Act to find out the intendment becomes necessary and the result of the inquiry may be decisive. In the latter case, it is necessary to see if the statute creates a special right or a liability and provides for the determination of the right or liability and further lays down that all questions about the said right and liability shall be determined by the tribunals so constituted, and whether remedies normally associated with actions in civil courts are prescribed by the said statute or not. It is therefore clear that the scheme of the Industrial Disputes Act clearly excludes the jurisdiction of the civil court by implication in respect of remedies which are available under this Act and for which a complete procedure and machinery has been provided in this Act; *Jitendra Nath Biswas* v. *Empire of India and Ceylone Tea Co.*, AIR 1990 SC 255: JT 1989 (3) SC 310: 1989 (2) SCALE 158: 1989 (3) SCC 582.

74. Powers – Nature of – As per section 20(1) of the Specific Relief Act, 1963 it is only discretionary relief depending upon various factual aspects to be established by the party(s) approaching the Court; *Vasanti Bhat* v. *Premlata A. Agarwal*, 2012 (11) SCALE 261: JT 2012 (11) SC 424: 2012 (8) Supreme 221: 2012 (10) SCR 1148.

75. Principle of Justice, Equity and Good Conscience – Law on – It is the settled position of law that grants of a decree for specific performance of contract is not automatic and is one of discretion of the Court and the Court has to consider whether it will be fair, just and equitable. Court is guided by principle of justice, equity and good conscience; *Gobind Ram* v. *Gian Chand*, AIR 2000 SC 3106: 2000 (6) SCALE 522: 2000 (7) SCC 548.

76. Rise in Price – Effect of – Rise in the price of an immovable property by itself is not a ground for refusal to enforce a lawful agreement of sale; *P.S. Ranakrishna Reddy* v. *M.K. Bhagyalakshmi*, AIR 2007 SC 1256: JT 2007 (4) SC 223: 2007 (3) SCALE 409: 2007 (10) SCC 231.

77. Suit for Specific Performance – Proof for – It is again well-settled that, in a suit for specific performance, the evidence and proof of the agreement must be absolutely clear and certain; *Ganesh Shet* v. *C.S.G.K. Setty*, AIR 1998 SC 2216: 1998 (3) SCALE 643: 1998 (5) SCC 381: 1998 (2) SCJ 502.

78. Time – Enlargement of Time – Section 148 Civil Procedure Code gives power to the court to enlarge the time for complying with the orders of the court from time to time; *Yeshoda* v. *K. Nagarajan*, 1996 (7) SCALE 408: 1996 (11) SCC 228: 1996 (Supp 7) SCR 4: 1996 (7) Supreme 378.

79. Void Contract – Law on – By virtue of section 20 of the Act, the relief for specific performance lies in the discretion of the court and the court is not bound to grant such relief merely because it is lawful to do so. The exercise of the discretion to order specific performance would require the court to satisfy itself that the circumstances are such that it is equitable to grant decree for specific performance of the contract. While exercising the discretion, the court would take into consideration the circumstances of the case, the conduct of parties, and their respective interests under the contract. No specific performance of a contract, though it is not vitiated by fraud or misrepresentation, can be granted if it would give an unfair advantage to the plaintiff and where the performance of the contract would involve some hardship on the defendant, which he did not foresee. In other words, the court's discretion to grant specific performance is not exercised if the contract is not equal and fair, although the contract is not void; *Bal Krishna* v. *Bhagwan Das (Dead)*, AIR 2008 SC 1786: 2008 (4) SCALE 805: 2008 (12) SCC 145: 2008 (7) SCJ 742.

80. Law on Possession – Possession is an incidence of ownership and can be transferred by the owner of an immovable property to an other such as in a mortgage or lease. A licensee holds possession on behalf of the owner. Possession is important when there are no title documents and other relevant records before the Court, but, once the documents and records of title come before the Court, it is the title which has to be looked at first and due weightage be given to it. Possession cannot be considered in vacuum. There is a presumption that possession of a person, other than the owner, if at all it is to be called possession, is permissive on behalf of the title-holder. Further, possession of the past is one thing, and the right to remain or continue in future is another thing. It is the latter which is usually more in controversy than the former, and it is the latter which has seen much abuse and misuse before the Courts. A suit can be filed by the title holder for recovery of possession or it can be one for ejectment of an ex-lessee or for mandatory injunction requiring a person to remove himself or it can be a suit under section 6 of the Specific Relief Act to recover possession. A title suit for possession has two parts - *first*, adjudication of title, and *second*, adjudication of possession. If the title dispute is removed and the title is established in one or the other, then, in effect, it becomes a suit for ejectment where the defendant must plead and prove why he must not be ejected; *Maria Margarita Sequeria Fernandes* v. *Erasmo Jack De Sequeria*, AIR 2012 SC 1727: JT 2012 (3) SC 451: 2012 (3) SCALE 550: 2012 (5) SCC 370.

81. Appellate Court's Power to Interfere with the Discretion Exercised by Trial Court.—Normally when the trial court exercises its direction after appreciation of entire evidence and materials on record, the appellate court should not interfere unless it is established that the discretion has been exercised perversely, arbitrarily or against judicial principles. The appellate court should also not exercise its discretion against that grant of specific performance on extraneous considerations or sympathetic considerations; *K. Prakash* v. *B.R. Sampath Kumar*, AIR 2015 SC 9.

21. Power to award compensation in certain cases.—(1) In a suit for specific performance of a contract, the plaintiff may also claim compensation for its breach, either in addition to, or in substitution of, such performance.

(2) If, in any such suit, the court decides that specific performance ought not to be granted, but that there is a contract between the parties which has been broken by the defendant, and that the plaintiff is entitled to compensation for that breach, it shall award him such compensation accordingly.

(3) If, in any such suit, the court decides that specific performance ought to be granted, but that it is not sufficient to satisfy the justice of the case, and that some compensation for breach of the contract should also be made to the plaintiff, it shall award him such compensation accordingly.

(4) In determining the amount of any compensation awarded under this section, the court shall be guided by the principles specified in section 73 of the Indian Contract Act, 1872 (9 of 1872).

(5) No compensation shall be awarded under this section unless the plaintiff has claimed such compensation in his plaint:

Provided that where the plaintiff has not claimed any such compensation in the plaint, the court shall, at any stage of the proceeding, allow him to amend the plaint on such terms as may be just, for including a claim for such compensation.

Explanation.—The circumstance that the contract has become incapable of specific performance does not preclude the court from exercising the jurisdiction conferred by this section.

SYNOPSIS

1. Amount of Compensation – Determination of
2. Compensation – Amendment for
3. Compensation – Balancing of Equities for
4. Compensation – Law on
5. Compensation a Matter of Guess Work – Law on
6. Damages – Law on
7. Granting Alternative Decree for Damages – Law on
8. Industrial Dispute – Law on
9. Limited Relief to Plaintiff – Law on
10. Quantification and Assessment of Compensation – Principles of
11. Term Public Policy – Law on
12. Trial of Suit – Law on
13. Specific Performance of Agreement – Law on

COMMENTS

1. Amount of Compensation – Determination of – Section 21 corresponds to section 19 of the Specific Relief Act, 1877. Sub-section (1) re-enacts the law as contained in clause (1) of the repealed section 19 with suitable variations. The words "any person suing" have been substituted by the words "in a suit". The word "claim" has been substituted for the words "ask for" and the word "plaintiff" has been inserted before the words "performance of a contract". Sub-clause (2) reproduces verbatim the language of clause 2 of the repealed section 19 with the alteration that the word "such" has been prefixed before the word "compensation". Sub-section (3) corresponds to clause (3) of the section 19 of the repealed Act. There is no modification in this sub-section. Clause (4) of section 19 of repealed Act has been substituted by the new sub-section (4) of section 21. It provides the mode and manner of determining the amount of compensation under this section. It lays down the principle which would govern the determination of the award of compensation and provides that the Court shall be guided by the principles specified in section 73 of the Contract Act, 1872 while determining the amount of compensation. Sub-section (5) of this section is new. It provides that the compensation under this section shall not be awarded unless the plaintiff has claimed it in the plaint. An important rider has been attached to this sub-clause which is to the effect that the court shall, at any stage of the proceedings, permit the amendment of the plaint to enable the plaintiff to include his claim for compensation on such terms, as the Court may deem fit. Explanation to this sub-section re-enacts the language of the old explanation without any change. Illustrations under section 19 have been deleted. Reasons for recommending the changes have been given by the Law Commission of India in its Ninth Report on the Specific relief Act, 1877. Since in the present case, we are considering whether the compensation could be awarded in a suit for specific performance without making a claim of compensation either in the original plaint or by amending the plaint during the course of the proceedings, we would refer to the suggestions made by the Law Commission for the enactment of such clause (5) only; *Shamsu Suhara Beevi* v. *G. Alex*, JT 2004 (8) SC 457: 2004 (7) SCALE 265: 2004 (8) SCC 569: 2004 (6) Supreme 331.

2. Compensation – Amendment for – Sub-sections (4) and (5) of section 21 seem to resolve certain divergence of opinion in the High Courts on some aspects of jurisdiction to the award of compensation. The Law Commission in its 9th Law Commission Report dated 19th July, 1958 (pages 18 and 19) observed that there has been a difference of judicial opinion as to whether the Court has the power to award compensation in a suit for specific performance, where the plaintiff has not specifically prayed for it in the plaint. The Commission accordingly recommended that in no case should compensation be decreed unless it is claimed by a proper pleading. However, it should be open to the plaintiff to have an amendment, at any stage of the proceeding, in order to introduce a prayer for compensation, whether in lieu of or in addition to specific performance. Legislature accepted the suggestions made by the Law Commission of India and accepted the view expressed by the High Court of Madras to the effect that the Court cannot award compensation in addition to specific performance in the absence of a specific claim for damages and a proper pleading stating why the relief of specific performance would be insufficient to satisfy the justice of the case and the plaintiff would not be entitled to compensation; *Shamsu Suhara Beevi* v. *G. Alex*, JT 2004 (8) SC 457: 2004 (7) SCALE 265: 2004 (8) SCC 569: 2004 (6) Supreme 331.

3. Compensation – Balancing of Equities for – Balancing of equities is a difficult task. It is now well-settled that compensation can be awarded in lieu of grant of decree of specific performance of contract. The courts are now evolving separate principles in regard to the remedy of compensation; *Jai Narain Parasurampuria* v. *Pushpa Devi Saraf*, 2006 (8) SCALE 477: 2006 (7) SCC 756: 2006 (8) SCJ 524: 2006 (7) Supreme 707.

4. Compensation – Law on – There was an alternative plea for damages, on the facts of the case it would have been appropriate for the Special Court to have computed and awarded the damages in addition to ordering refund rather than requiring the vendee to purchase the units and give the same to the Vendor. In other words, a decree for specific performance was probably not appropriate especially when the Vendee could be compensated with the return of money and award of reasonable damages; *State Bank of Saurashtra* v. *P.N.B.*, AIR 2001 SC 2412: 2001 (5) SCC 751: 2001 (4) Supreme 42: 2001 (4) SCALE 102: 2001 (3) SCR 236.

5. Compensation a Matter of Guess Work – Law on – Section 21 of the Specific Relief Act provides for award of compensation either in addition to or in substitution of such performance. The explanation appended to the section expressly enacts that the Court is not precluded from exercising jurisdiction to award compensation even in a case where the contract has been rendered incapable of specific performance. Compensation to some extent is a matter of guess work; *K. Narendra* v. *Riviera Apartments Private Limited*, AIR 1999 SC 2309: JT 1999 (4) SC 428: 1999 (4) SCALE 22: 1999 (5) SCC 77: 1999 (3) SCR 777.

6. Damages – Law on – In terms of Order II, rule 2 of the Code, all the reliefs which could be claimed in the suit should be prayed for. Order II, rule 3 provides for joinder of causes of action. Order II, rule 4 is an exception thereto. For joining causes of action in respect of matters covered by clauses (a), (b) and (c) of Order II, rule 4, no leave of the court is required to be taken. Even without taking leave of the court, a prayer in that behalf can be made. A suit for recovery of possession on declaration of one's title and/or injunction and a suit for *mesne profit* or damages may involve different cause of action. For a suit for possession, there may be one cause of action; and for claiming a decree for *mesne profit,* there may be another. In terms of Order II, rule 4 of the Code, however, such causes of action can be joined and therefor no leave of the court is required to be taken. If no leave has been taken, a separate suit may or may not be maintainable but even a suit wherefor a prayer for grant of damages by way of *mesne profit* or otherwise is claimed, must be instituted within the prescribed period of limitation. Damages cannot be granted without payment of court fee. In a case where damages are required to be calculated, a fixed court fee is to be paid but on the quantum determined by the court and the balance court fee is to be paid when a final decree is to be prepared; *Shiv Kumar Sharma* v. *Santosh Kumari,* AIR 2008 SC 171: JT 2007 (11) SC 260: 2007 (11) SCALE 303: 2007 (8) SCC 600.

7. Granting Alternative Decree for Damages – Law on – It is true that the rise in prices of the property during the pendency of the suit may not be the sole consideration for refusing to decree the suit for specific performance. But it is equally settled law that granting decree for specific performance of a contract of immovable property is not automatic. It is one of discretion to be exercised on sound principles. When the Court gets into equity jurisdiction, it would be guided by justice, equity, good conscience and fairness to both the parties. Courts would have been well justified in granting alternative decree for damages, instead of ordering specific performance which would be unrealistic and unfair. Courts can hold that the decree for specific performance is inequitable and unjust to; *Kanshi Ram* v. *Om Prakash Jawal,* AIR 1996 SC 2150: JT 1996 (4) SC 733: 1996 (4) SCALE 194: 1996 (4) SCC 593.

8. Industrial Dispute – Law on – It is well-settled that Industrial Tribunal or authority adjudicating an industrial dispute, who may conveniently be referred as an industrial arbitrator, is unlike a civil Court not fettered by the agreement between the parties. He is required to decide the matter not according to the agreement of contract between the parties but according to contract what, having regard to all circumstances of reconsider to be judge and fair. In order that the workers get a proper wage that they victimized or unfairly treated and that their terms of employment generally are such as arbitrator has the power and the authority to radically modify or alter the agreed terms of the employment and to impose new contract for the parties. No authority is necessary in support of these propositions; *Rambhau Jairam Dhamange* v. *President, Vinkar Co-operative Society Ltd., Chanda,* 1966 (1) LLJ 90: AIR 1966 Bom 187: 1966 Mh LJ 1: 1967 (30) FJR 56.

9. Limited Relief to Plaintiff – Law on – It is clear that mere establishment of the facts that the agreement for sale had been entered into is not sufficient to grant a decree for specific performance and if the circumstances as indicated in section 20 of the Act, exist in a particular suit, the court ought to certainly exercise its discretion in favour of the defendant and give lesser or limited relief to the plaintiff as indicated in section 21 of the Act; *Veluyudhan Sathyadas* v. *Govindan Dakshyani,* JT 2002 (5) SC 357: 2003 (1) RCR (Civ) 28: 2003 (2) ICC 507.

10. Quantification and Assessment of Compensation – Principles of – So far as the proviso to sub-section (5) of section 21 is concerned, two positions must be kept clearly distinguished. If the amendment relates to the relief of compensation in lieu of or in addition to specific performance where the plaintiff has not abandoned his relief of specific performance the Court will allow the amendment at any stage of the proceeding. That is a claim for compensation falling under section 21 of the Specific Relief Act, 1963 and the amendment is one under the proviso to sub-section (5). But different and less liberal standards apply if what is sought by the amendment is the conversion of a suit for specific performance into one for damages for breach of contract in which case section 73 of the Contract Act is invoked. This amendment is under the discipline of rule 17, Order VI, C.P.C. The fact that sub-section (4), in turn, invokes section 73 of the Contract Act for the principles of quantification and assessment of compensation does not obliterate this distinction. The provisions of section 21 seem to resolve certain divergencies of judicial opinion in the High Courts on some aspects of the jurisdiction to award of compensation. Sub-section (5) seeks to set at rest the divergence of judicial opinion between High Courts whether a specific claim in the plaint is necessary to grant the compensation; *Jagdish Singh* v. *Natthu Singh*, AIR 1992 SC 1604: JT 1991 (5) SC 400: 1991 (2) SCALE 1363: 1992 (1) SCC 647.

11. Term Public Policy – Law on – Section 23 of the Contract Act lays down that the object of an agreement becomes unlawful if it was of such a nature that, if permitted, it would defeat the provisions of any law. The term public policy has an entirely different and more extensive meaning from the policy of the law. Winfield defined it as a principle of judicial legislation or interpretation founded on the current needs of the community. It does not remain static in any given community and varies from generation to generation. Judges, as trusted interpreters of the law, have to interpret it. While doing so precedents will also guide them to a substantial extent. The doctrine of public policy may be summarized thus: Public policy or the policy of the law is an illusive concept: it has been described as "untrustworthy guide". "Variable quality", "uncertain one", "unruly house", etc., the primary duty of a Court of a law is to enforce a promise which the parties have made and to uphold the sanctity of contract which form the basis of society, but in certain cases, the Court may relieve them of their duty on a rule founded on what is called the public policy, but the doctrine is extended not only to harmful cases but also to harmful tendencies. This doctrine of public policy is only a branch of common law, and just like any other branch of common law it is governed by precedents. The principles have been crystallized under different heads and though it is permissible for Courts to expound and apply them to different situations, it should only be invoked in clear and incontestable cases of harm to the public; *India Financial Assn. Seventh Day Adventists* v. *M.A. Unneerikutty*, JT 2006 (6) SC 578: 2006 (7) SCALE 302: 2006 (6) SCC 351: 2006 (7) SCJ 549.

12. Trial of Suit – Law on – A suit is ordinarily tried on the issues raised by the parties. The plaintiff respondent did not ask for payment of any damages. No prayer for payment of damages by way of *mesne profit* or otherwise was also made by the plaintiff. If the plaintiff was to ask for a decree, he was required to pay requisite court fees on the amount claimed. In such a situation, having regard to Order XX, rule 12 of the Code, a preliminary decree was required to be passed. A proceeding for determination of the actual damages was required to be gone into; *Shiv Kumar Sharma* v. *Santosh Kumari*, AIR 2008 SC 171: JT 2007 (11) SC 260: 2007 (11) SCALE 303: 2007 (8) SCC 600.

13. Specific Performance of Agreement – Law on – In a suit seeking specific performance of an agreement to sell governed by the provisions of the Specific Relief Act, 1963 the Court has discretion to decree specific performance of the agreement. The plaintiff may also claim compensation under section 21 or any other relief to which he may be entitled including the refund of money or deposit paid or made by him in case his claim for specific performance is refused. No compensation or any other relief including the relief of refund shall be granted by the Court unless it has been specifically claimed in the plaint by the plaintiff. Certainly the relief of specific performance is a larger relief for the plaintiff and more onerous to the defendant compared with the relief for compensation or refund of money. The relief of compensation or refund of money is a relief smaller than the relief of specific performance. A plaintiff who files a suit for specific performance claiming compensation in lieu of or in addition to the relief of specific performance or any other relief including the refund of any money has a right, to file an appeal against the original decree if the relief of specific performance is refused and other relief is granted. The plaintiff would be a person aggrieved by the decree in spite of one of the alternative reliefs having been allowed to him because what has been allowed to him is the smaller relief and the larger relief has been denied to him. A defendant against whom a suit for specific performance has been decreed may file an appeal seeking relief of specific performance being denied to the plaintiff and instead a decree of smaller relief such as that of compensation or refund of money or any other relief being granted to the plaintiff for the former is larger relief and the latter is smaller relief. The defendant would be the person aggrieved to that extent. In an appeal filed by the defendant laying challenge to the relief of compensation or refund of money or any other relief while decree for specific performance was denied to the plaintiff, the plaintiff as a respondent cannot seek the relief of specific performance of contract or modification of the impugned decree except by filing an appeal of his own or by taking cross-objection; *Banarsi* v. *Ram Phal,* AIR 2003 SC 1989: JT 2003 (5) SC 224: 2003 (2) SCALE 183: 2003 (9) SCC 606: 2003 (2) SCR 22.

22. Power to grant relief for possession, partition, refund of earnest money, etc.—(1) Notwithstanding anything to the contrary contained in the Code of Civil Procedure, 1908 (5 of 1908), any person suing for the specific performance of a contract for the transfer of immovable property may, in an appropriate case, ask for—

(a) possession, or partition and separate possession, of the property, in addition to such performance; or

(b) any other relief to which he may be entitled, including the refund of any earnest money or deposit paid or [1][made by] him, in case his claim for specific performance is refused.

(2) No relief under clause (a) or clause (b) of sub-section (1) shall be granted by the court unless it has been specifically claimed:

Provided that where the plaintiff has not claimed any such relief in the plaint, the court shall, at any stage of the proceeding, allow him to amend the plaint on such terms as may be just for including a claim for such relief.

(3) The power of the court to grant relief under clause (b) of sub-section (1) shall be without prejudice to its powers to award compensation under section 21.

SYNOPSIS

1. Multiplicity of Proceedings – Law on
2. Provision – Comments on
3. Relief of Possession of Land or Other Immovable Property – Law on
4. Substantial Question of Law – Law on
5. Word 'Proceeding' – Comments on

COMMENTS

1. Multiplicity of Proceedings – Law on – Section 22 enacts a rule of pleading. The Legislature thought it will be, useful to introduce a rule that in order to avoid multiplicity of proceedings the plaintiff may claim a decree for possession in a suit for specific performance, even though strictly speaking, the right to possession accrues only when suit for specific performance is decreed. The Legislature has now made a statutory provision enabling the plaintiff to ask for possession in the suit for specific performance and empowering the Court to provide in the decree itself that upon payment by the plaintiff of the consideration money within the given time, the defendant should execute the deed and put the plaintiff in possession; *Babu Lal* v. *Hazari Lal Kishori Lal,* AIR 1982 SC 818: 1982 (1) SCALE 79: 1982 (1) SCC 525: 1982 (3) SCR 94.

1. Subs. by Act 52 of 1964, Sch. II, for "made to" (w.e.f. 29-12-1964).

2. Provision – Comments on – Section 22(1) of the Specific Relief Act, 1963 is procedural in nature and the use of the expression "further relief in sub-section (3) of section 28 of the said Act is a clear pointer that reliefs by way of delivery of possession or partition and separate possession of property mentioned in section 22(1)(a) and in clause (b) of sub-section (3) of section 28 of the Specific Relief Act, 1963 are ancillary or consequential to the passing of a decree for specific performance of a contract to transfer immovable property. In other words, sub-sections (1) and (2) of section 22 of the Specific Relief Act, 1963 prescribe the procedure or the manner in which the Court may grant such further relief by way of delivery of possession or partition and separate possession of the property on execution of such conveyance. Till the execution and registration of the conveyance, the vendee does not acquire title, but he is granted reliefs under section 22(1)(a) of the Specific Relief Act, 1963 by enforcing the vendor's agreement to sell or to grant lease to him. In other words, at this stage, when he has not yet acquired title, the vendee's claim for possession etc. is derived from and founded upon the agreement which is specifically enforced. Thus, possessory reliefs mentioned in clause (a) of sub-section (1) of section 22 of the Specific Relief Act are dependent upon and flows from passing of a decree for specific performance of an agreement to transfer an immovable property. Even before the enactment of the said section 22(1), it was almost settled by judicial decisions that the Court could grant such possessory reliefs in favour of a successful plaintiff in a suit for specific performance. The legislature by enacting section 22 of the Specific Relief Act, 1963 has given statutory recognition to the said, power of the Court to grant delivery of possession and has also prescribed the procedure for obtaining such relief; *S.M. Dhiraj Bala Karia* v. *Jethia Estate Pvt. Limited,* AIR 1983 Cal 166: 1983 (88) Cal WN 131 **[Hon'ble Judges:** Ramendra Mohan Datta, Pradyot Kumar Banerjee, Chittatosh Mookerji].

Section 22(1) of the Specific Relief Act, 1963 is procedural in nature and the use of the expression "further relief" in sub-section (3) of section 28 is a clear pointer that reliefs by way of delivery of possession or partition and separate possession of property mentioned in section 22 (1) (a) and in clause (b) of sub-section (3) of section 28 of the Specific Relief Act, 1963 are ancillary or consequential to the passing of a decree for Specific Relief Act, 1963 are ancillary or consequential to the passing of a decree for Specific Performance of a contract to transfer immovable property. In other words, sub-sections (1) and (2) of section 22 of the Specific Relief Act, 1963 prescribe the procedure or the manner in which the court may grant such further relief by way of delivery of possession or partition and separate possession of the property on execution of such conveyance. Till the execution and registration of the conveyance, the vendee does not acquire title, but he is granted reliefs under section 22(1)(a) of the Specific Relief Act, 1963 by enforcing the vendors' agreement to sell or grant lease to him. In other words, at this stage, when he has not yet acquired title, the vendee's claim for possession etc., is derived from and founded upon the agreement which is specifically enforced. Thus, possessory reliefs mentioned in clause (a) of sub-section (1) of section 22 of the Specific Relief Act are dependent upon and flows from passing of a decree for specific performance of an agreement to transfer an immovable property. Even before the enactment of the said section 22(1), it was almost settled by judicial decisions that the court could grant such possessory reliefs in favour of a successful plaintiff in a suit for specific performance. The legislature by enacting section 22 of the Specific Relief Act, 1963 has given statutory recognition to the said power of the court to grant delivery of possession and has also prescribed the procedure for obtaining such reliefs; *Jathia Estate Pvt. Ltd.* v. *Dhiraj Bala Karia,* 1982 (1) Cal LT 252 **[Hon'ble Judges:** Ramendra Mohan Datta, Pabitra Kumar Banerjee, Chittatosh Mookerji].

3. Relief of Possession of Land or Other Immovable Property – Law on – A "suit for land" is a suit in which the relief claimed relates to title to or delivery of possession of land or immovable property. Whether a suit as a "suit for land" or not has to be determined on the averments in the plaint with reference to the reliefs claimed therein;

where the relief relates to adjudication of title to land or immovable property or delivery of possession of the land or immovable property, it will be a "suit for land." In a suit for specific performance of contract for sale of immovable property containing stipulation that on execution of the sale deed the possession of the immovable property will be handed over to the purchaser, it is implied that delivery of possession of the immovable property is a part of the decree of specific performance of contract. But in this connection it is necessary to refer to section 22 of the Specific Relief Act, 1963. It may be seen that sub-section (1) is an enabling provision. A plaintiff in a suit of specific performance may ask for further reliefs mentioned in clauses (a) and (b) thereof. Clause (a) contains reliefs of possession and partition and separate possession of the property, in addition to specific performance. The mandate of sub-section (2) of section 22 is that no relief under clauses (a) and (b) of sub-section (1) shall be granted by the Court unless it has been specifically claimed. Thus it follows that no Court can grant the relief of possession of land or other immovable property, subject-matter of the agreement for sale in regard to which specific performance is claimed, unless the possession of the immovable property is specifically prayed for; *Adcon Electronics Pvt. Ltd.* v. *Daulat*, AIR 2001 SC 3712: JT 2001 (7) SC 580: 2001 (6) SCALE 252: 2001 (7) SCC 698.

4. Substantial Question of Law – Law on – Substantial question of law should admittedly be formulated relying on or on the basis of findings of fact arrived at by the Trial Court and the First Appellate Court; *Abdul Raheem* v. *Karnataka Electricity Board*, AIR 2008 SC 956: JT 2007 (13) SC 63: 2007 (13) SCALE 326: 2007 (14) SCC 138.

5. Word 'Proceeding' – Comments on – The word 'proceeding' is not defined in the Act. Shorter Oxford Dictionary defines it as "carrying on of an action at law, a legal action or process; any act done by authority of a Court of law; any step taken in a cause by either party". The term 'proceeding' is a very comprehensive term and generally speaking, means a prescribed course of action for enforcing a legal right. It is not a technical expression with a definite meaning attached to it, but one the ambit of whose meaning will be governed by the statute. It indicates a prescribed mode in which judicial business is conducted. The word 'proceeding' in section 22 includes execution proceedings also. It is a term giving the widest freedom to a Court of law so that it may do justice to the parties in the case. Execution is a stage in the legal proceedings. It is a step in the judicial process. It marks a stage in litigation. It is a step in the ladder. In the journey of litigation there are various stages. One of them is execution; *Babu Lal* v. *Hazari Lal Kishori Lal*, AIR 1982 SC 818: 1982 GLH 954: 1982 (1) SCALE 79: 1982 (1) SCC 525: 1982 (3) SCR 94; *Rameshwar Nath* v. *Uttar Pradesh Union Bank Ltd.*, AIR 1956 All 586.

23. Liquidation of damages not a bar to specific performance.—(1) A contract, otherwise proper to be specifically enforced, may be so enforced, though a sum be named in it as the amount to be paid in case of its breach and the party in default is willing to pay the same, if the court, having regard to the terms of the contract and other attending circumstances, is satisfied that the sum was named only for the purpose of securing performance of the contract and not for the purpose of giving to the party in default an option of paying money in lieu of specific performance.

(2) When enforcing specific performance under this section, the court shall not also decree payment of the sum so named in the contract.

SYNOPSIS

COMMENTS

1. Distinction between a Contract of Sale of Immovable Property and a Contract of Re-sale or Reconveyance – Law on – There is a distinction between a contract of sale of immovable property and a contract of re-sale or reconveyance of immovable property. An agreement to reconvey property, after the vendor has transferred it by sale to the vendee is in the nature of a concession and, as such, has to be exercised according to the strict requirements of the agreement of reconveyance. In *Halsbury's Laws of England*, 3rd Edn., Vol. 14, para 1151, reads as follows: 'Where under a contract, conveyance or will a beneficial right is to arise upon the parties by the beneficiary of some act in a stated manner, or at a stated time, the act must be performed accordingly in order to obtain the enjoyment of the right, and in the absence of fraud, accident or surprise, equity will not relieve against a breach of the terms"; *Munawwar Husen* v. *Zakir Husen*, 1984 AWC 1 **[Hon'ble Judges:** K.C. Agrawal, S.D. Agarwala, O.P. Saxena] *See* Also: *Simrathmull* v. *Nanjalingiah*, AIR 1963 SC 1182. In *Shanmugam Pillai* v. *Annalkhshmi Ammal*, AIR 1950 SC 38, the Federal Court also held that the option given under a deed of reconveyance is in the nature of a concession or privilege.

2. Payment – Law on – Reference to section 22 of the old Act, (the corresponding provision is section 20 of the Act of 1963), would show that the jurisdiction of the Court to decree specific relief is discretionary and must be exercised on sound and reasonable grounds "guided by judicial principles and capable of correction by a Court of appeal". This Jurisdiction cannot be curtailed or taken away by merely fixing a sum even as liquidated damages. We think that this is made perfectly clear by the provisions of section 20 of the old Act (corresponding to section 23 of the Act of 1963) so that the Courts has to determine, on the facts and circumstances of each case before it whether specific performance of a contract to convey a property ought to be granted. Section 23 of the Act of 1963 contains a comprehensive statement of the principles on which, even before the Act of 1963, the presence of a term in a contract specifying a sum of money to be paid for a breach of the contract has to be construed. Where payment is an alternative to carrying out the other terms of the contract, it would exclude, by the terms of the contract itself, specific performance of the contract to convey a property; *M.L. Devender Singh* v. *Syed Khaja*, AIR 1973 SC 2457: 1973 (2) SCC 515: 1974 (1) SCR 312.

24. Bar of suit for compensation for breach after dismissal of suit for specific performance.—The dismissal of a suit for specific performance of a contract or part thereof shall bar the plaintiff's right to sue for compensation for the breach of such contract or part, as the case may be, but shall not bar his right to sue for any other relief to which he may be entitled, by reason of such breach.

COMMENTS

Void Agreement – Law on – Section 24 provides that if any part of a single consideration for one or more objects, or any one or any part of any one of several considerations for a single object is unlawful, the agreement is void; *India Financial Assn., Seventh Day Adventists* v. *M.A. Unneerikutty*, JT 2006 (6) SC 578: 2006 (7) SCALE 302: 2006 (6) SCC 351: 2006 (7) SCJ 549.

Enforcement of awards and directions to execute settlements

25. Application of preceding sections to certain awards and testamentary directions to execute settlements.—The provisions of this Chapter as to contracts shall apply to awards to which the Arbitration Act, 1940 (10 of 1940), does not apply and to directions in a will or codicil to execute a particular settlement.

SYNOPSIS

1. Application to Arbitration Awards
2. Application to Directions in a Will or Codicil to a Particular Settlement

COMMENTS

1. Application to Arbitration Awards – Section 24 provides that the provisions of Chapter II of Part II of the Specific Relief Act, 1963 as to contract shall apply to awards other than those to which the Arbitration Act, 1940 applies. The Arbitration Act, 1940 has now been replaced by the Arbitration and Conciliation Act, 1996 and this new Act applies to all arbitrations including arbitrations under a statute.

2. Application to Directions in a Will or Codicil to a Particular Settlement – The provisions of Chapter II, Part II of the Specific Relief Act, 1963 apply to directions in a will or codicil to execute a particular settlement.

CHAPTER III

RECTIFICATION OF INSTRUMENTS

26. When instrument may be rectified.—(1) When, through fraud or a mutual mistake of the parties, a contract or other instrument in writing [not being the articles of association of a company to which the Companies Act, 1956 (1 of 1956) applies] does not express their real intention, then—

(a) either party or his representative in interest may institute a suit to have the instrument rectified; or

(b) the plaintiff may, in any suit in which any right arising under the instrument is in issue, claim in his pleading that the instrument be rectified; or

(c) a defendant in any such suit as is referred to in clause (b), may, in addition to any other defence open to him, ask for rectification of the instrument.

(2) If, in any suit in which a contract or other instrument is sought to be rectified under sub-section (1), the court finds that the instrument, through fraud or mistake, does not express the real intention of the parties, the court may, in its discretion, direct rectification of the instrument so as to express that intention, so far as this can be done without prejudice to rights acquired by third persons in good faith and for value.

(3) A contract in writing may first be rectified, and then if the party claiming rectification has so prayed in his pleading and the court thinks fit, may be specifically enforced.

(4) No relief for the rectification of an instrument shall be granted to any party under this section unless it has been specifically claimed:

Provided that where a party has not claimed any such relief in his pleading, the court shall, at any stage of the proceeding, allow him to amend the pleading on such terms as may be just for including such claim.

SYNOPSIS

1. Rectification – Parties for
2. Rectification of Instrument – Law on
3. Rectification – Specific Pleadings and Claim for
4. Doctrine on Undue Influence – Ambit of
5. Relief of Rectification
6. "Other Instrument in Writing"
7. Fraud or Mutual Mistake
8. Parties who can Seek Rectification
9. Agreement of Sale in favour of Two Persons
10. Policy of Government
11. Without Prejudice to the Rights of the Third Parties
12. Rectification when Refused
13. Rectification of Deed During Pendency of Suit hit by Section 52, the T.P.A.

COMMENTS

1. Rectification – Parties for – Section 26 of the Act has a limited application, and is applicable only where it is pleaded and proved that through fraud or mutual mistake of the parties, the real intention of the parties is not expressed in relation to an instrument. Such rectification is permissible only by the parties to the instrument and by none else; *Joseph John Peter Sandy* v. *Veronica Thomas Rajkumar*, 2013 (3) SCC 801: JT 2013 (4) SC 9: 2013 (3) SCALE 328.

2. Rectification of Instrument – Law on – In a suit for specific performance of contract for sale, it is permissible to amend a part of the description of the suit property not only in the plaint but also in the agreement. Section 26 clearly says as to when a contract or other instrument can be rectified and provides that when through fraud or a mutual mistake of the parties, the agreement in writing does not express their real intention, it is open to the parties to apply for amendment of the instrument. It provides that when such a situation arises, then—

(a) Either party or his representative in interest may institute a suit to have the instrument rectified, or

(b) The plaintiff may, in any suit in which any right arising under the instrument is in issue, claim in his pleading that the instrument be rectified.

A reading of these two conditions made under section 26 of the Act would amply show that either party may institute a suit to have the instrument rectified or a party who has already filed a suit in which any right arising under the instrument is in issue may claim in his pleading that the instrument be rectified. It cannot be doubted that the main issue in the suit for specific performance of the contract for sale was relating to the agreement for sale in which a part of the description of the suit property was wrongly given by mutual mistake and therefore, needed to be amended. Section 26, of course, says that it would be open to a party to institute a suit for correcting the description of the suit property, but the proviso to section 26 clearly permits that where a party has not claimed any such relief in his pleading, the court shall at any stage of the proceeding allow him to amend the plaint on such terms as may be just for including such claim; *Puran Ram* v. *Bhaguram*, AIR 2008 SC 1960: JT 2008 (4) SC 37: 2008 (4) SCALE 40: 2008 (4) SCC 102.

3. Rectification – Specific Pleadings and Claim for – The provisions of section 26 of the Act would be attracted in limited cases. The provisions of this section do not have a general application. These provisions can be attracted in the cases only where the ingredients stated in the section are satisfied. The relief of rectification can be claimed where it is through fraud or a mutual mistake of the parties that real intention of the parties is not expressed in relation to an instrument. Even then the party claiming will have to make specific pleadings and claim an issue in that behalf; *Subhadra* v. *Thankam*, AIR 2010 SC 3031: JT 2010 (7) SC 374: 2010 (11) SCC 514: 2010 (5) SCJ 949.

4. Doctrine on Undue Influence – Ambit of – Executor was an educated woman and was serving as a teacher, her allegation of undue influence to sign on blank non-judicial stamp papers, cannot be relied upon and, so it was a document executed by her voluntarily and by free will and, hence, it was binding on her and it was not permissible for her to say that it was a forged document. Even though the document may be admissible, still its contents have to be proved and, as the appellant did not examine either the attesting witnesses of the document, nor proved its contents, no fault can be found with the judgment impugned before us. Section 26 provides for rectification of a document if the parties feel that they have committed any mistake. Also, it was only, the father of the parties who could have sought rectification of the deed. Mere rectification by parties does not take the case within the ambit of section 26 of the Act. Taking note of the statutory provisions of section 16 of the Contract Act and the parameters laid down by Apex Court for application of doctrine on undue influence; *Joseph John Peter Sandy* v. *Veronica Thomas Rajkumar*, 2013 (3) SCC 801: JT 2013 (4) SC 9: 2013 (3) SCALE 328: 2013 (2) SCR 368.

5. Relief of Rectification – The relief of rectification is discretionary. This has been made clear in sub-section (2) of section 26. The relief of rectification is granted by the court when the contract or other instrument in writing when such contract or other instrument does not express real intention of the parties due to fraud or mutual mistake An oral evidence may be adduced to show the real intention of the parties. Rectification of may be allowed only when fraud or mutual mistake is proved; *Ariat-ullah* v. *Sadat Ullah*, AIR 1915 Cal 727.

Where the plaintiff for rectification of instrument filed a suit for declaration, the plaintiff claimed that sale-deed in question covered only 600 square yards and not 1600 square yards, it was necessary for him to plead that figure of 1600 square yards was mentioned in deed wrongfully; *Akkiraju Saraswathi* v. *Mohd. Jahangir Pasha*, AIR 2007 (NOC) 502 (AP).

6. "Other Instrument in Writing" – The relief of rectification is not confined to written contracts. Other instruments in writing may also be rectified. In *Commissioner of Income-tax* v. *Kamala Town Trust*, AIR 1996 SC 620: (1996) 7 SCC 349 one of the main question for the conservation before the Apex Court was whether the instrument of trust can be rectified because in the strict sense it is not a contract. The Supreme Court held the words "other instrument" have been in section 26 and these words will include the instrument of trust. Therefore, the Court has jurisdiction to rectify the trust deed. The Supreme Court observed, so far as the jurisdiction of the Civil Court to grant rectification of the Trust Deed is concerned, the relevant provision finds mention in section 26 of the Specific Relief Act, 1963 which had succeeded the prior Specific Relief Act, 1877. Under the earlier Act, an analogous provision was contained in section 31 of the Act. As per these provisions a suit could be filed before the competent Civil Court for rectification of an instrument when through fraud or mutual mistake a contract or other instrument in writing does not express their real intention. It is obvious that a trust deed is not a contract in the strict sense of the term but it would certainly be covered by the expression "other instrument in writing". It could not be urged with any emphasis that competent Civil Court which was approached, was not having requisite jurisdiction to entertain such proceedings"; *Commissioner of Income-tax, Kanpur* v. *Kamla Town Trust*, AIR 1996 SC 620 (627): (1996) SCC 349: 1995 AIR SCW 4597: JT 1995 (8) SC 364.

In this case the settlor company namely, M/s J&K Spinning and Weaving Mills Ltd., Kanpur averred that the actual intention was to create a Public Charitable Trust and this intention was not clearly expressed in the words of the original Trust Deed, and therefore, there was need to rectify the instrument, as neither the settler company nor the trustees who assumed the legal ownership of the property settled in trust would have agreed to the transaction in question if it had purported not to create a public charitable trust. It was this mutual trust on the part of both the parties that required rectification of the instrument to make what was the latest intention a patent one. The Supreme Court observed that it cannot be said that the two parties to the trust are not there. Settlor company is one of the parties which gives the property for the beneficiaries and the trustees to whom the property has been transferred are the second party. Moreover, the third or other parties are beneficiaries though they are not direct parties. Thus trust is a tripartite transaction; *Commissioner of Income-tax, Kanpur* v. *Kamla Town Trust*, AIR 1996 SC 620 (630-633): (1996) SCC 349: 1995 AIR SCW 4597: JT 1995 (8) SC 364.

7. Fraud or Mutual Mistake – Thus under section 26(1) of the Specific Relief Act, 1963, if due to mistake the instrument does not express the real intention of the parties. either party or his representative may institute a suit to have the instrument rectified so as to express the real intention of the parties. But the mistake is unilateral, then the relief under section 26 cannot be obtained. Relief can be granted when the intention of both the parties is same. For example *Wallington* v. *Townsend*, (1939) 2 All ER 225, *A*, the owner of two adjoining bunglows, conveyed the East bunglows to *B* keeping the west bunglow with himself. The plan accompanying the conveyance showed a straight line boundary. But in fact to the east of the line there were bathroom and other domestic offices of the West bunglow. *A's* claim for rectification because it was not the intention of both the parties while *A* did not intend to sell the disputed strip, *B* intended to buy it.

Similarly, in *Haji Abdul Rahman* v. *P.S.N. Company*, ILR (1892) 16 Bom 561 some pilgrims wanted to go for Haj. The plaintiff therefore chartered a ship for taking him and others from Jeddah to Bombay on 10th August, 1892. He entered into this agreement under a mistaken calculation that the said day would fall on the 15th day after during Haj. But in fact the said fifteenth day fell on 19th July, 1892. After realizing his mistake, he sued the respondent company for rectification of the instrument. It was clear from the facts of the case that the mistake was only from the side of the appellant. That is to say, the mistake unilateral. As a matter of the fact, the appellant had asked for the ship on 18th August, 1892 and the respondent agreed to provide the ship for the said date. That is why, the court rejected the prayer for rectification. The court observed that in matters of unilateral mistake the relief of rectification cannot be granted but in appropriate cases, the court may cancel the instrument. In this case, the parties mutually agreed to have the instrument cancelled. The court, therefore, passed orders for cancellation of the instrument.

Rectification of the instrument can also be ordered on the ground of mistake of law. For example, in *Jervis* v. *Howle*, (1937) Ch 67 the contract was relating to giving of royalty on coal. The instrument showed that 3 Pence of royalty free of taxes on every ton of coal was payable. The parties intended that on every ton of coal net 3 Pence of royalty was to be paid. But this agreement was void under the statute. With a view to validate the court ordered the rectification of the agreement and directed that in place of the said word, after deducting the income tax in force from time to time royalty on per ton of coal would be 3 Pence, be substituted.

Where in a suit for rectification of sale deed, the plaintiff claimed that the suit land was described in the sale-deed in his favour by wrong patta and dag numbers although the boundaries were given correctly but the sale deed contained identity of property by sufficient particulars and boundaries of land were given as additional description and there was clear evidence that following the contract for sale the proposed purchaser was put into physical possession and he continued to do so uninterruptedly till execution of the sale deed and formal delivery, and the vendor was ready to rectify deed by substituting boundaries, the court ordered rectification to be done by substituting with correct and proper boundaries to identity and mean part of land covered by the concerned dag number and patta number; *Bhabani Sarma* v. *Narayan Sarma*, AIR 2003 Gau 171 (175-176).

8. Parties who can Seek Rectification – The repealed Specific Relief Act, 1877 referred to only suit, for rectification but in a number of decisions it was held that in a suit for rectification, the defendant would also be entitled to make a claim for the rectification of the instrument; *William Charles Binns* v. *W & T Avery Ltd.*, AIR 1934 Cal 778.

9. Agreement of Sale in favour of Two Persons – Where the agreement to sell was executed by the uncle in favour of his two nephews, plaintiff and defendant 1, the sale-deed could not be executed by him in favour of defendant 1 only. Since sale-deed was found to be the result of misrepresentation and fraud acted upon the uncle, the suit for rectification of sale-deed was maintainable; *Sheo Murat* v. *Ram Murat*, AIR 2004 All 263 (267): 2004 All LJ 2764: (2004) 55 All LR 505: (2004) 2 All WC 1320.

10. Policy of Government – A contract was entered into between the State and the plaintiffs awarding right to vend arrack to the plaintiff on payment of bid amount in monthly instalments but there was no term incorporated in contract regarding enforcement of ban on trade of toddy to the public. There was no plea of any mutual mistake in matter of setting down terms of the contract or about any fraud on part of the State in entering into contract. The plaintiffs entered into contract on their belief that the policy of prohibition of sale of toddy to the public would be implemented by State as per budget speech of concerned Minister and they were under expectation that they would get more profit from the sale of arrack. Held—The decree to the effect that the State was estopped from claiming kist amounts as per bids of plaintiffs in view of non-implementation of policy of State to ban sale on toddy, purporting to rectify part of contract only as regards payment of kist would be unsustainable. Further, the estoppel does not apart at the level of government policy; *State of Karnataka* v. *K.K. Mohandas,* AIR 2007 SC 2917 (2922, 23): 2007 AIR SCW 5311: (2007) 6 SCC 484: (2007) 9 SCALE 531.

11. Without Prejudice to the Rights of the Third Parties – Such a third party having acquired interest in good faith, for value and without notice may be a party in a suit for rectification of the instrument and may also be impleaded in a suit for rectification; *Ram Suchit* v. *1st Additional District Judge, Gorakhpur,* AIR 1986 All 149: 1984 All WC (Supp) 664.

12. Rectification when Refused – Rectification is an equitable relief and depends on the discretion of the court. A person who sues for rectification must file his suit within reasonable time otherwise the court may refuse the relief on account of delay; *Marappuredigari Sayamma* v. *R. Venkata Reddy,* AIR 1931 Mad 785.

But in India mere delay may not be the sole ground for refusal of relief. But where because of delay third party has acquired rights, relief may be refused on account of delay; *Rajaram* v. *Manik,* AIR 1952 Nag 90: 1954 NLJ 12.

The court may also refuse the relief of rectification if rectification will not change its effectt; *Gardner* v. *Knight,* 124 Alabama 273 will make the instrument inoperative; *Mecrazy* v. *Williams,* 127 Alabama 251.

The court will rectify an agreement which has been construed and performance under the orders of a competent court; *Gaird* v. *Moss,* (1866) 33 Ch D 22.

Rectification of an instrument in writing is granted when because of the fraud or mutual mistake. It does not express the real intention of the parties but where no fraud or mutual mistake is proved, the claim for rectification will be refused; *Anant Bibi* v. *Lachman Prasad,* ILR 14 Cal 308 (PC): 141 A 18.

13. Rectification of Deed During Pendency of Suit hit by Section 52, the T.P.A. – In a suit for restoration of land on the ground that the land purchased by the plaintiff was encroached upon by the defendant but the defendant's plea was that he had purchased suit land from the owner of it and the land mentioned in the sale-deed in favour of the plaintiff did not relate to the suit land. During the pendency of the suit, the plaintiff obtained rectification deed showing land as part of relevant patta number. The rectification was got done without leave of the court. Since the rectification deed was executed during the pendency of the suit without leave of the court and its contents if accepted would adversely affect the plea of the defendant-respondent, the document was, therefore, clearly hit under section 52 of the Transfer Property Act. The finding by the courts below as to title and possession in favour of the defendant was without any legal error and was not interfered with in the second appeal; *Khalil Nahak* v. *Hadu Nahak (dead),* AIR 2006 Ori 131 (134-135): 2007 (3) Civ LJ 759: 2007 (3) Cur CC 298: (2007) 103 Cut LT 118.

CHAPTER IV

RESCISSION OF CONTRACTS

27. Where rescission may be adjudged or refused.—(1) Any person interested in a contract may sue to have it rescinded, and such rescission may be adjudged by the court in any of the following cases, namely:—

(a) where the contract is voidable or terminable by the plaintiff;

(b) where the contract is unlawful for causes not apparent on its face and the defendant is more to blame than the plaintiff.

(2) Notwithstanding anything contained in sub-section (1), the court may refuse to rescind the contract—

(a) where the plaintiff has expressly or impliedly ratified the contract; or

(b) where, owing to the change of circumstances which has taken place since the making of the contract (not being due to any act of the defendant himself), the parties cannot be substantially restored to the position in which they stood when the contract was made; or

(c) where third parties have, during the subsistence of the contract, acquired rights in good faith without notice and for value; or

(d) where only a part of the contract is sought to be rescinded and such part is not severable from the rest of the contract.

Explanation.—In this section "contract", in relation to the territories to which the Transfer of Property Act, 1882 (4 of 1882), does not extend, means a contract in writing.

SYNOPSIS

1. Rescission when Refused
   (a) On Contract Being Voidable
   (b) On Contract Being Terminable
   (c) Contract Being Unlawful
2. Who can Sue for Rescission
3. Grounds of Refusal of Rescission
   (a) Rectification by Plaintiff
   (b) Third Parties Having Acquired Rights

COMMENTS

1. Rescission when Refused – ***(a) On Contract Being Voidable*** – Sub-section (1) of section 27 provides that any person interested in a contract where the contract is voidable by the plaintiff, where a contract is induced by actual fraud, it will be voidable and the court may set it aside on the ground of fraud. But where the defendant has misrepresentated though he is innocent and has no knowledge of actual facts, it cannot be got rescinded by the purchaser; *Wide* v. *Gibson*, (1848) 1 HLC 605 (632-633).

Where the corporation sought to avoid the contract of allotment of plots by issuing show cause notice on the ground that it had acted without jurisdiction while the other party expended huge money in construction work on the plot, it was not open to the corporation to take a unilateral decision to cancel the allotment after the appellants had acted on the basis thereof. Further, the allotment done on individual application was neither prohibited by law nor opposed to the public policy; *Sunil Pannalal Banthia* v. *City & Industrial Development Corporation of Maharashtra Ltd.*, (2007) 10 SCC 674 (683): AIR 2007 SC 1529: 2007 AIR SCW 2117: (2007) 4 SCALE 216.

A person who sues for rescission of contract cannot claim alternative relief of specific enforcement but a person who files the suit for specific enforcement can alternatively claim for rescission of contract; *Prem Raj* v. *D.L.F. Housing and Construction Co. Ltd.*, AIR 1968 SC 1355: (1968) 3 SCR 648.

(b) On Contract Being Terminable – It may be noted that where a party has an option to rescind a contract aid of court is not necessary. The court simply adjudges the rights of the parties which already exist. Thus by adjudging the rescission the court does not create a right in favour of the party, at simply declares the antecedent right of the parties; *Hungerford Investment Trust Ltd.* v. *Haridas Mundra*, AIR 1972 SC 1826: (1972) 3 SCC 684.

(c) Contract Being Unlawful – But where the parties are equally at fault (*pari delictio*), the provisions of clause 1(b) of section 27 will not apply; *Hari* v. *Naro,* (1894) 18 Bom 342.

2. Who can Sue for Rescission – Where the purchaser had put only half of the consideration amount and was put into possession of the land but he failed to pay balance consideration and get the sale-deed executed, the owner *i.e.,* the vendor was entitled to cancellation of agreement and to be put in possession on refund of earnest money; *Damodar Namdeo Sase* v. *Namdeo Baburao Sase,* AIR 2009 (NOC) 851 (Bom): 2008 (6) AIR Bom R 663.

Where the vendee fails to pay balance consideration within a reasonable time, rescission of contract by the vendor is proper; *Ram Prasad Chandulal Brahman* v. *Syed Hussain,* AIR 2009 (NOC) 2446 (Bom): (2009) 4 AIR Bom R 128 (Aurangabad Bench).

3. Grounds of Refusal of Rescission – ***(a) Ratification by Plaintiff*** – The court may refuse to rescind the contract where the plaintiff has expressly or impliedly ratified the contract; *Rangaswami Gowden* v. *Nachiappa Gowden,* AIR 1918 PC 196: 42 Mad 523.

(b) Third Parties Having Acquired Rights – The court may refuse to rescind a contract where third parties have, during the subsistence of the good faith without notice and for value. This provision has been enacted because law protects a party to a contract who has performed his part of the contract and is innocent against the party who has committed fraud or other wrong. But the law also protects who enters into a contract in good faith for vale and without notice. That is why, the court will refuse to rescind where third parties have acquired rights in good faith, for value and without notice. But where the third parties have acquired rights, the burden for proving that they have acquired such rights in good faith, without notice and for value; *Nirmal Singh (deceased by LRs.)* v. *Gejo d/o Mihan Singh,* AIR 1997 P&H 260: 1997 (1) ICC 616: 1998 (2) Land LR 200: (1997) 115 Punj LR 301.

It is the subsequent purchaser who has to prove that he has paid full value for which he purchased the property and he must have paid it in good faith and without notice of the prior contract; *Begum Seeni Pichai Ammal* v. *Janab K. Madhu Muthu Mohamed,* (2003) 3 LW 535 (546) Mad (DB).

28. Rescission in certain circumstances of contracts for the sale or lease of immovable property, the specific performance of which has been decreed.—(1) Where in any suit a decree for specific performance of a contract for the sale or lease of immovable property has been made and the purchaser or lessee does not, within the period allowed by the decree or such further period as the court may allow, pay the purchase money or other sum which the court has ordered him to pay, the vendor or lessor may apply in the same suit in which the decree is made, to have the contract rescinded and on such application the court may, by order, rescind the contract either so far as regards the party in default or altogether, as the justice of the case may require.

(2) Where a contract is rescinded under sub-section (1), the court—

(a) shall direct the purchaser or the lessee, if he has obtained possession of the property under the contract, to restore such possession to the vendor or lessor, and

(b) may direct payment to the vendor or lessor of all the rents and profits which have accrued in respect of the property from the date on which possession was so obtained by the purchaser or lessee until restoration of possession to the vendor or lessor, and if the justice of the case so requires, the refund of any sum paid by the vendee or lessee as earnest money or deposit in connection with the contract.

(3) If the purchaser or lessee pays the purchase money or other sum which he is ordered to pay under the decree within the period referred to in sub-section (1), the court may, on application made in the same suit, award the purchaser or lessee such further relief as he may be entitled to, including in appropriate cases all or any of the following reliefs, namely:—

(a) the execution of a proper conveyance or lease by the vendor or lessor;

(b) the delivery of possession, or partition and separate possession, of the property on the execution of such conveyance or lease.

(4) No separate suit in respect of any relief which may be claimed under this section shall lie at the instance of a vendor, purchaser, lessor or lessee, as the case may be.

(5) The costs of any proceedings under this section shall be in the discretion of the court.

SYNOPSIS

1. Execution of Decree of Specific Performance – Law on
2. Extension of Time – Law on
3. Separate Suit – Law on
4. Suit Filed within Prescribed Period of Limitation – Law on
5. Trial Court – Power and Jurisdiction of
6. Provision – Comments on
7. Refusal by Registrar – Suit for

COMMENTS

1. Execution of Decree of Specific Performance – Law on – The execution of a decree of specific performance can only be in the manner prescribed by this rule; sub-rule (1) of the rule says that if a decree for specific performance is not obeyed, the decree is to be enforced by the detention of the party in default in the civil prison or by attachment of his property or by both. The detention in the civil prison of the party who failed to obey the decree and the attachment of his property are simply the means to compel him to obey the decree. That is made clear by sub-rule (3), which says that if the judgment-debtor has failed to obey the decree when the attachment has remained in force for one year, the property attachment may be sold and out of the proceeds the decree-holder may be awarded such compensation as the Court thinks fit. Sub-rule (5) which provide that the Court may direct the act required to be done may be done by the decree-holder or some other person appointed by the Court can only refer to an act other than an act of payment of money; *Hungerford Investment Trust Ltd. (In Voluntary Liquidation)* v. *Haridas Mundhra*, AIR 1972 SC 1826: 1972 (3) SCC 684: 1972 (3) SCR 690.

2. Extension of Time – Law on – In a suit a decree for specific performance of a contract for the sale of immovable property has been made and time has been prescribed for performance, it should be complied within time. On its default, power has been given to the Court that passed the decree to further extend the time as the Court may allow and the purchase money or any other sum be paid within the extended time. It was open to the court to exercise the power under section 28(1) of the Act either for extension of time or for rescinding the contract as claimed for; *Ramankutty Guptan* v. *Avara*, AIR 1994 SC 1699: JT 1994 (1) SC 342: 1994 (1) SCALE 390: 1994 (2) SCC 642.

It is perfectly open to the court in control of a suit for specific performance to extend the time for deposit, and this court may do so even now to enable the plaintiff to get the advantage of the agreement to sell in her favour. Even so, specific performance is an equitable relief and he who seeks equity can be put on terms to ensure that equity is done to the opposite party even while granting the relief. The final end of law is justice, and so the means to it too should be informed by equity. That is why he who seeks equity shall do equity; *K. Kalpana Saraswathi* v. *P.S.S. Somasundaram Chettiar*, AIR 1980 SC 512: 1980 (1) SCC 630: 1980 (2) SCR 293.

3. Separate Suit – Law on – Sub-section (3) of section 28 clearly contemplates that if the purchaser or lessee pays the purchase money or other sum which he is ordered to pay under the decree. The Court may on application made in the same suit, award the purchaser or lessee such further relief as he may be entitled to. Sub-clause (b) of sub-section (3) of section 28 contemplates the delivery of possession or partition and separate possession of the property on the execution of such conveyance or lease. Sub-section (4) of section 28 bars the filing of a separate suit for any relief which may be claimed under this section. Procedure is meant to advance the cause of justice and not to retard it. The difficulty of the decree-holder starts in getting possession in pursuance of the decree obtained by him. The judgment-debtor tries to thwart the execution by all possible objections; *Babu Lal* v. *Hazari Lal Kishori Lal*, AIR 1982 SC 818: 1982 (1) SCALE 79: 1982 (1) SCC 525: 1982 (3) SCR 94; *Rameshwar Nath* v. *Uttar Pradesh Union Bank Ltd.*, AIR 1956 All 586.

4. Suit Filed within Prescribed Period of Limitation – Law on – Under article 54 of the Limitation Act, 3 years period is prescribed for filing the suit for specific performance of contract of sale from the date of the agreement or when the cause of action arises. Merely because a suit is filed within the prescribed period of limitation does not absolve the vendee-plaintiff from showing as to whether he was ready and willing to perform his part of agreement and if there was non-performance was that on account of any obstacle put by the vendor or otherwise. Provisions to grant specific performance of an agreement are quite stringent. Equitable considerations come into play. Court has to see all the attendant circumstances including if the vendee has conducted himself in a reasonable manner under the contract of sale; *V.S. Palanichamy Chettiar Firm* v. *C. Alagappan*, AIR 1999 SC 918: JT 1999 (1) SC 216: 1999 (1) SCALE 219: 1999 (4) SCC 702.

5. Trial Court – Power and Jurisdiction of – Section 28 gives power to grant order of rescission of the decree would indicate that till the sale deed is executed in execution of the decree, the trial court retains its power and jurisdiction to deal with the decree of specific performance. It would also be clear that the court has power to enlarge the time in favour of the judgment-debtor to pay the amount or to perform the conditions mentioned in the decree for specific performance, in spite of an application for rescission of the decree having been filed by the judgment-debtor and rejected. In other words, the court has the discretion to extend time for compliance of the conditional decree as mentioned in the decree for specific performance; *Sardar Mohar Singh Through Power of Attorney Holder, Manjit Singh* v. *Mangilal* alias *Mangtya*, 1997 ACJ 281: JT 1997 (2) SC 94: 1997 (2) RCR (Civ) 296: 1997 (9) SCC 217: 1997 (1) Supreme 846.

6. Provision – Comments on – The decree for specific performance has been described as a preliminary decree. The power under section 28 of the Act is discretionary and the Court cannot ordinarily annul the decree once passed by it. Although the power to annul the decree exists yet section 28 of the Act provides for complete relief to both the parties in terms of the decree. The Court does not cease to have the power to extend the time even though the trial Court had earlier directed in the decree that payment of balance price to be made by certain date and on failure suit to stand dismissed. The power exercisable under this section is discretionary; *Chanda* v. *Rattni*, AIR 2007 SC 1514: JT 2007 (5) SC 28: 2007 (5) SCALE 53: 2007 (14) SCC 26: 2007 (4) SCR 402.

7. Refusal by Registrar – Suit for – When the Registrar declined to register the sale deed presented by the plaintiffs, the plaintiffs were under no obligation to bring suit within thirty days of such refusal as contemplated under section 77 of the Registration Act. Section 77 of the Registration Act gives option to a vendee either to file suit under section 77 of the Act or bring a suit for specific performance of an agreement for sale of the property. If plaintiff has chosen to bring the suit for specific performance of the agreement for sale of the property within the period of limitation, in such a situation the plaintiff's suit cannot be dismissed on the ground of limitation, having not filed within thirty days of refusal by the Registrar to register the sale deed as contemplated under section 77 of the Registration Act; *Chandeshwar Yadav* v. *Radha Devi*, 2001 (5) ALT (SC) 60: 2002 (Supp 1) BCR 589: 2001 (5) Supreme 598: 2001 (2) Apex CJ 96: 2001 (3) PLJR (SC) 72.

29. Alternative prayer for rescission in suit for specific performance.—A plaintiff instituting a suit for the specific performance of a contract in writing may pray in the alternative that, if the contract cannot be specifically enforced, it may be rescinded and delivered up to be cancelled; and the court, if it refuses to enforce the contract specifically, may direct it to be rescinded and delivered up accordingly.

COMMENTS

Alternative Prayer for Rescission in Suit for Specific Performance – Section 29 of the Specific Relief Act, 1963 provides that a plaintiff suing for specific performance of the contract can alternatively sue for the rescission of the contract but the converse is not provided. It is, therefore not open to a plaintiff to sue for rescission of the agreement and in the alternative sue for specific performance; *Prem Raj* v. *D.L.F. Housing and Construction (P) Ltd.*, AIR 1968 SC 1355: (1968) 3 SCR 648.

Where a party is guilty of anticipatory breach, the other party becomes entitled to treat the contract as repudiated or ended but in that situation he cannot claim specific performance of the contract; *Jawaharlal Wadhawa* v. *Haripad Chakrobarty*, AIR 1989 SC 609 (610): 1988 Supp SCC 552.

But where alongwith a suit for declaration that agreement for development of plot and construction thereof was void as the plaintiff had been deceived to accept for lessor consideration an alternative prayer for decree of specific performance of said agreement in full was made but the defendants made submission that they were ready and willing to perform and complete the transaction knowing full well that as an alternative relief for specific performance was sought after seeking a declaration that the agreement was void, it was held that the alternative plea was maintainable. This has been held by the Bombay High Court in *Krishnabai C. Kadam* v. *Wellworth Developers*, AIR 2001 Bom 9 (17-18): (2000) 4 Bom CR 757: 2001 (1) Civ LJ 443: (2000) 4 Mah LJ 532.

This was in fact the chamber summons taken out by the defendants (Nos. 1 to 4) in the suit striking out a part of the plaint and also seeking a direction to the plaintiff to elect between some of the prayers made in the plaint. The High Court dismissed the summons. Distinguishing *Prem Raj* v. *D.L.F. Housing and Construction (P) Ltd.*, AIR 1968 SC 1355: (1968) 3 SCR 648 the High Court observed that the proposition laid down in that judgment very much stands that a plaintiff cannot be permitted to take such inconsistent pleas where each of them is not maintainable. At the same time it cannot be lost sight of that in that matter the objection to the grant of alternative relief was raised at the outset. In a case where the defendant himself agrees specifically in clear terms to the alternative plea taken by the plaintiff, the facts will stand on a different footing. The present is a case wherein the defendants themselves are saying that they are ready and willing for specific performance knowing fully well that the relief of specific performance is sought as an alternative relief after initially contending in the plaint that the agreement was bad in law and bad; *Krishnabai C. Kadam* v. *Wellworth Developers*, AIR 2001 Bom 9 (17): (2000) 4 Bom CR 757: 2001 (1) Civ LJ 443: (2000) 4 Mah LJ 532.

Further, as held by the Privy Council in *Mohan Manucha* v. *Manzoor Ahmad*, AIR 1943 PC 29: 70 IA 1 quoted with approval in the case of *Firm Sriniwas Ram Kumar* v. *Mahabir Prasad*, AIR 1951 SC 177: 1951 SCR 277 even when the alternative relief was otherwise available to the plaintiff, it could be granted by the court even in the absence of pleadings by the plaintiff. This is because as held by the Apex Court "in such circumstances, when no injustice can possibly result to the defendant, it may not be proper to derive the plaintiff to a separate suit." The Apex Court did look into the written statement in the case of *Firm Srinivas Ram Kumar* to decide whether a particular inconsistent relief could be granted. Surely in the present case the replies of the defendants would have to be looked into far that purpose. The court cannot shut its eyes to the specific averments of the defendants, apart from the improper conduct on the part of the defendants equitable reliefs; *Krishnabai C. Kadam* v. *Wellworth Developers*, AIR 2001 Bom 9 (18): (2000) 4 Bom CR 757: 2001 (1) Civ LJ 443: (2000) 4 Mah LJ 532.

Where the plaintiff who had sold his property to the defendant for a sum of Rs. 45,000 due to his property being put to sale in execution proceeding and he being devoid of money to pay the liability towards his creditors, which he was entitled to be reconveyed after 7 years and before 9 years for the same consideration without any interest, the relief of specific performance of contract could not be denied, when there were a proper averments as to readiness and willingness to perform his part of contract in the plaint. Merely because alternative relief under the Maharashtra Debt Relief Act was sought by the plaintiff consequent to finding of document as a mortgage, the document could not be construed as a mortgage under section 58(C) of the Contract Act. There were no inconsistent pleas and the plaintiff could not be saddled with dire consequences of wrong legal advice in a suit validly instituted for specific performance; *Nilkanth Dhondiba Chavan (D) by LRs.* v. *Sou. Umabai,* AIR 2005 Bom 98 (103): (2005) 2 Bom CR 220: (2005) 2 Mah LJ 8 (DB).

30. Court may require parties rescinding to do equity.—On adjudging the rescission of a contract, the court may require the party to whom such relief is granted to restore, so far as may be, any benefit which he may have received from the other party and to make any compensation to him which justice may require.

COMMENTS

Court may Require Parties to do Equity – Section 30 is based on English equitable rules. From the point of view of equity and justice, the party who gets rescinded is bound to restore the benefit he has taken from the other party. However, the party who claims restoration of the benefit has to prove the value of that benefit; *Govindram Saksaria* v. *Edward Radbone,* (1947) 74 IA 295.

Where third parties have purchased the property with the notice of the agreement and who undertake the obligation to repay the amount paid by the plaintiff to the vendor, the court may order such third parties as well as vendor to pay or refund the purchase price; *Vasudeo Harchand Kolhe* v. *Bhaulal Nadarsingh Rajput,* AIR 1994 Bom 124: 1995 (1) Bank Cas 251: (1994) 1 Mah LR 579.

CHAPTER V

CANCELLATION OF INSTRUMENTS

31. When cancellation may be ordered.—(1) Any person against whom a written instrument is void or voidable, and who has reasonable apprehension that such instrument, if left outstanding may cause him serious injury, may sue to have it adjudged void or voidable; and the court may, in its discretion, so adjudge it and order it to be delivered up and cancelled.

(2) If the instrument has been registered under the Indian Registration Act, 1908 (16 of 1908), the court shall also send a copy of its decree to the officer in

whose office the instrument has been so registered; and such officer shall note on the copy of the instrument contained in his books the fact of its cancellation.

SYNOPSIS

COMMENTS

1. Cancellation of an Instrument – Limitation for – Article 59 of the Schedule to the Limitation Act, 1908 had provided *inter alia* for suits to set aside decree obtained by fraud. There was no specific article to set aside a decree on any other ground. The present article 59 of the Schedule to the Act will govern any suit to set aside a decree either on fraud or any other ground. Therefore, article 59 would be applicable to any suit to set aside a decree either on fraud or any other ground. It is true that article 59 would be applicable if a person affected is a party to a decree or an instrument or a contract. There is no dispute that article 59 would apply to set aside the instrument, decree or contract between the *inter se* parties. The question is whether in case of person claiming title through the party to the decree or instrument or having knowledge of the instrument or decree or contract and seeking to avoid the decree by a specific declaration. Article 59 is a general provision. In a suit to set aside or cancel an instrument, a contract or a decree on the ground of fraud, article 59 is attracted. The starting point of limitation is the date of knowledge of the alleged fraud. When the plaintiff seeks to establish his title to the property which cannot be established without avoiding the decree or an instrument that stands as an insurmountable obstacle in his way which otherwise binds him, though not a party, the plaintiff necessarily has to seek a declaration and have that decree, instrument or contract cancelled or set aside or rescinded; *Noorul Hoda* v. *Bibi Raifunnisa,* 1996 (1) Cut LT 192: JT 1995 (9) SC 256: 1995 (7) SCALE 326: 1996 (7) SCC 767.

2. Dispossession – Law on – The limitation starts running from the date when the cause of action had arisen, *viz.,* when dispossession was sought to be made. Therefore, the suit should rightly be filed within three years under article 58 of the Schedule to the Act; *Rameshwer Dubey* v. *Masomat Asha Kaur,* 1996 (6) AD (SC) 514: 1996 (6) SCALE 141: 1996 (11) SCC 160: 1996 (6) Supreme 492.

3. Material Defect in Property – Law on – Section 55(1) of the Transfer of Property Act, 1882 regulates rights and liabilities of the buyer and seller. The seller is bound to disclose to the buyer any material defect in the property or in the seller's title thereto of which the seller is, and the buyer is not, aware, and which the buyer could not with ordinary care discover. The seller is to answer, to the best of his information, all relevant questions put to him by the buyer in respect of the property or the title thereto. The seller shall be deemed to contract with the buyer that the interest which the seller professes to transfer to the buyer subsists and that he has power to transfer the same. Section 3 provides that "a person is said to have a notice of a fact when he actually knows the fact, or when but for willful abstention from an enquiry or search which he ought to have made, or gross negligence, he would have known it". *Explanation II* amplifies that "any person acquiring any immovable property or any share or interest in any such property shall be deemed to have notice of the title, if any, of any person who is for the time being in actual possession thereof". Constructive notice in equity treats a man who ought to have known a fact, as if he actually knows it. Generally speaking, constructive notice may not be inferred unless some specific circumstances can be shown as a starting point of enquiry which if pursued would have led to the discovery of the fact; *Noorul*

Hoda v. *Bibi Raifunnisa*, 1996 (1) CCC 41: 1996 (1) Cut LT 192: JT 1995 (9) SC 256: 1995 (7) SCALE 326: 1996 (7) SCC 767.

4. Transfer of Immovable Property – Law on – Any transfer of immovable property made with intent to defeat or delay the creditors of the transferors and transfer made without consideration with intent to defraud a subsequent transferee are void and at the option of the subsequent transferee is voidable; *Yanala Malleshwari* v. *Ananthula Sayamma*, 2007 AIHC 1471: AIR 2007 AP 57: 2006 (6) ALT 523: 2007 (1) Civ CC 527: 2007 (1) CTC 97: 2007 (5) RCR (Civ) 609.

Any transfer of immovable property made with intent to defeat or delay the creditors of the transferors and transfer made without consideration with intent to defraud a subsequent transferee are void and at the option of the subsequent transferee is voidable; *Yanala Malleshwari* v. *Ananthula Sayamma*, 2007 AIHC 1471: AIR 2007 AP 57: 2006 (6) ALD 623: 2006 (6) ALT 523.

5. Un-explained Delay – Effect of – One more fact which disentitles the plaintiff to the equitable relief under section 27/31 of the Specific Relief Act is the unexplained delay in filing the suit after almost three years later, the suit was filed. This inaction has its own revelation. Either the plaintiff did not stand by his declaration to rescind the contract, as held by the trial Court, or the plaintiff was sitting on the fence and waiting to see whether the turn of events would be to his advantage or disadvantage; *Lalit Kumar Jain* v. *Jaipur Traders Corporation Private Limited*, 2002 (4) SCALE 180: 2002 (5) SCC 383: 2002 (3) SCR 445: 2002 (4) Supreme 375.

6. Word 'Person' – Law on – Section 31 of the Specific Relief Act, 1963 regulates suits for cancellation of an instrument which lays down that any person against whom a written instrument is void or voidable and who has a reasonable apprehension that such instrument, if left outstanding, may cause him serious injury, can sue to have it adjudged void or voidable and the court may in its discretion so adjudge it and order it to be delivered or cancelled. It would thus be clear that the word 'person' in section 31 of the Specific Relief Act is wide enough to encompass a person seeking derivative title from his seller. It would, therefore, be clear that if he seeks avoidance of the instrument, decree or contract and seeks a declaration to have the decrees set aside or cancelled he is necessarily bound to lay the suit within three years from the date when the facts entitling the plaintiff to have the decree set aside, first became known to him; *Noorul Hoda* v. *Bibi Raifunnisa*, 1996 (81) Cut LT 192: JT 1995 (9) SC 256: 1995 (7) SCALE 326: 1996 (7) SCC 767.

7. Document – Cancellation of – Cancellation of the deed comes within the purview of section 31 of the Specific Relief Act, 1963; *Om Prakash Singh* v. *M. Lingamaiah*, AIR 2009 SC 3091: JT 2009 (6) SC 115: 2009 (6) SCALE 267: 2009 (12) SCC 613.

8. Registered Document – Presumption for – A registered document carries with it a presumption that it was validly executed. It is for the party questioning the genuineness of the transaction to show that in law the transaction was not valid; *Abdul Rahim* v. *Sk Abdul Zabar*, AIR 2010 SC 211: JT 2009 (3) SC 569: 2009 (5) SCALE 43: 2009 (6) SCC 160.

9. Suit for Cancellation of Transaction – Limitation for – A suit for cancellation of transaction whether on the ground of being void or voidable would be governed by article 59 of the Limitation Act. The suit, therefore, should have been filed within a period of three years from the date of knowledge of the fact that the transaction which according to the plaintiff was void or voidable had taken place; *Abdul Rahim* v. *Sk Abdul Zabar*, AIR 2010 SC 211: JT 2009 (3) SC 569: 2009 (5) SCALE 43: 2009 (6) SCC 160.

10. Gift under Mohammedan Law – Law on – A gift indisputably becomes complete when a person transfers with immediate effect the ownership of his movable or immovable property to another person, and that other person himself or someone else with his consent takes possession of the property gifted. Under Mohammedan Law it is a contract which takes effect through offer and acceptance. The conditions to make a valid and complete gift under the Mohammedan Law are as under:

(a) The donor should be sane and major and must be the owner of the property which he is gifting.

(b) The thing gifted should be in existence at the time of hiba.

(c) If the thing gifted is divisible, it should be separated and made distinct.

(d) The thing gifted should be such property to benefit from which is lawful under the Shariat.

(e) The thing gifted should not be accompanied by things not gifted; *i.e.* should be free from things which have not been gifted.

(f) The thing gifted should come in the possession of the donee himself, or of his representative, guardian or executor.

It is also well-settled that if by reason of a valid gift the thing gifted has gone out of the donees ownership, the same cannot be revoked. The donor may lawfully make a gift of a property in the possession of a lessee or a mortgagee. For effecting a valid gift, the delivery of constructive possession of the property to the donee would serve the purpose. Even a gift of a property in possession of trespasser is permissible in law provided the donor either obtains and gives possession of the property to the donee or does all that he can to put it within the power of the donee to obtain possession; *Abdul Rahim* v. *Sk Abdul Zabar*: AIR 2010 SC 211: JT 2009 (3) SC 569: 2009 (5) SCALE 43: 2009 (6) SCC 160.

11. Adverse Possession – Law on – For claiming title by adverse possession, it was necessary for the plaintiff to plead and prove *animus possidendi.* A peaceful, open and continuous possession being the ingredients of the principle of adverse possession as contained in the maxim *nec vi, nec clam, nec precario,* long possession by itself would not be sufficient to prove adverse possession; *Vishwanath Bapurao Sabale* v. *Shalinibai Nagappa Sabale,* AIR 2009 SCW 3592: JT 2009 (5) SC 395: 2009 (5) SCALE 74: 2009 (12) SCC 101: 2009 (4) SCR 976.

32. What instruments may be partially cancelled.—Where an instrument is evidence of different rights or different obligations, the court may, in a proper case, cancel it in part and allow it to stand for the residue.

COMMENTS

Cancellation of Part of the Instrument – For attracting section 32 is necessary that the written instrument is evidence of different obligation which can be separated so as to stand for themselves. For example, *A* executes mortgage deed in favour of *B*. *A* is able to procure form *B* by fraud and makes therein an endorsement a receipt of Rs. 1,200 appearing to have been signed by *B*. Thus signature of *B* is forged. *B* is entitled to get the endorsement cancelled and have the deed to stand in other respects; *Ram Chander* v. *Ganga Saran,* (1917) 39 All 103.

33. Power to require benefit to be restored or compensation to be made when instrument is cancelled or is successfully resisted as being void or voidable.—(1) On adjudging the cancellation of an instrument, the court may require the party to whom such relief is granted, to restore, so far as may be any benefit which he may have received from the other party and to make any compensation to him which justice may require.

(2) Where a defendant successfully resists any suit on the ground—

(a) that the instrument sought to be enforced against him in the suit is voidable, the court may if the defendant has received any benefit under the instrument from the other party, require him to restore, so far as may be, such benefit to that party or to make compensation for it;

(b) that the agreement sought to be enforced against him in the suit is void by reason of his not having been competent to contract under section 11 of the Indian Contract Act, 1872 (9 of 1872), the court may, if the defendant has received any benefit under the agreement from the other party, require him to restore, so far as may be, such benefit to that party, to the extent to which he or his estate has benefited thereby.

SYNOPSIS

1. Court's Power to Order Restoration of Benefit
2. Application of Section 33 in Respect of Minor

COMMENTS

1. Court's Power to Order Restoration of Benefit – Under sub-section (1) of section 33, where an instrument is adjudged as cancelled, the party to whom such relief is granted may be ordered by the court to restore the benefit which he has received from the other party and in case justice of the case requires he may also be asked to pay compensation. Further, under section 33(2)(a), where the defendant successfully resists the suit on the ground that the instrument sought to be enforced against him in the suit is voidable, he may require him to restore the benefit to the other party or to make compensation for it. Where an instrument is cancelled, the decree which is passed by the court is conditional that the party getting the relief has to restore the benefit which had been received from the other party or if the justice of the case so requires also to pay compensation; *Ramnath Singh* v. *Deoraj Singh,* AIR 1957 Pat 495: 1957 BLJR 181.

2. Application of Section 33 in Respect of Minors – The doctrine of equitable restitution was propounded by Lord Summer in *Leslie* v. *Sheill,* (1914) 3 KB 607.

The doctrine of equitable restitution propounded by Lord Sumner was approved by the Privy Council; *Mohd. Syedol Ariffin* v. *Yesh Ori Gark,* AIR 1916 PC 242: 43 Ind App 256.

But in *Khan Gul* v. *Lakhan Singh,* ILR (1928) 9 Lah 701 (FB): AIR 1928 Lah 609 the Full Bench of the Lahore High Court refused to follow completely the doctrine of equitable restitution as applicable to minors. In this case, the plaintiff filed the suit against the defendant for recovery of possession of land. The defendant had sold the suit land to the plaintiff for Rs. 17,500.

However, in a later Allahabad Full Bench case, namely; *Ajodhia Prasad* v. *Chandan Lall,* AIR 1937 All 610: 1937 All LJ 688 (FB).

The Law Commission of India expressed its view in favour of the view expressed by Sir Shadi Lal, C.J., in *Khan Gul* v. *Lakhan Singh,* ILR (1928) 9 Lah 701: AIR 1928 Lah 609.

CHAPTER VI

DECLARATORY DECREES

34. Discretion of court as to declaration of status or right.—Any person entitled to any legal character, or to any right as to any property, may institute a suit against any person denying, or interested to deny, his title to such character or right, and the court may in its discretion make therein a declaration that he is so entitled, and the plaintiff need not in such suit ask for any further relief:

Provided that no court shall make any such declaration where the plaintiff, being able to seek further relief than a mere declaration of title, omits to do so.

Explanation.—A trustee of property is a "person interested to deny" a title adverse to the title of some one who is not in existence, and whom, if in existence, he would be a trustee.

SYNOPSIS

1. "Acceptance" – Law on
2. "Period of Limitation" – Law on
3. "Presumption" and "Proof" – Law on
4. Admissibility of Evidence in Absence of Written Statement – Law on
5. Admission – Importance of
6. Alternative Relief – Amendment for
7. Benami Transaction – Law on
8. Declaration and Injunction Relating to Commercial Transactions – Law on
9. Endorsed Documents – Law on
10. Execution Court – Law on
11. Future Rights of an Intending Purchaser – Law on
12. High Court – Guidelines for
13. Injury of a Substantial Nature – Law on
14. Jurisdiction of Civil Court – Law on
15. Jurisdiction of High Court – Law on
16. Partition – Law on
17. Plaint – Importance of
18. Possession of Property – Effect of
19. Pre-emption Decree – Law on
20. Privileged Tenant – Law on
21. *Res Judicata* – Law on
22. Review of Judgment – Law on
23. Rights and Liabilities of Mortgagor – Law on
24. Scheme – Construction of
25. Variety of Declaratory Relief – Law on
26. Will – Law on
27. Withholding of Important Documents – Effect of
28. Bill of Exchange – Law on
29. Cancellation of Sale Deed by Third Party – Law on
30. Custom – Law on
31. Doctrine of *Lis Pendens* – Effect of
32. Jurisdiction of Civil Court – Law on
33. Jurisdiction of Civil Courts under Civil Courts – Law on
34. 'Material Facts' and 'Particulars' – Law on
35. Order of Injunction – Requirement for
36. Promissory Estoppels – Law on
37. Registrable Document – Law on
38. *Res Judicata* – Law on
39. Revenue Records – Law on
40. Second Appeal – Law on
41. Some Blanks in Schedule of Property – Effect of
42. Special Leave Petition – Law on
43. Specific Performance of Contract of Sale of Immovable Property on Basis of an Oral Agreement – Law on
44. Suit for Declaration – Maintainability of
45. Suit for Specific Performance – Nature of
46. Violation of Order of Injunction – Law on
47. Amendment in Plaint – Law on
48. Power of Review – Law on
49. Presumption of Title as Result of Possession – Law on
50. Property of Real Owner – Law on
51. Statutory Notice – Law on

COMMENTS

1. "Acceptance" – Law on – "Acceptance" in regard to a bill of exchange is a technical term. It does not mean "taking" or "receiving". Acceptance of a bill of exchange is the signification by the drawee of his assent to the order of the drawer. It is the act by which the drawee evinces his consent to comply with, and be bound by, the request contained in a bill of exchange directed to him, and is the drawee's agreement to pay the bill when it falls due. In commercial parlance acceptance of a bill of exchange is the drawee's signed engagement to honour the draft as presented. The contract of the acceptor is a new and independent one. It comes within the rules as to consideration for a contract on a negotiable instrument, and, like every contract on a negotiable instrument, is incomplete and revocable until delivery of the instrument for the purpose of giving effect thereto. Acceptance, generally speaking, is therefore, necessary to render a drawee liable upon a bill of exchange and until he accepts it the drawee is not liable on the bill. As between a drawer and a drawee, the latter is to be under an obligation to accept a bill of exchange drawn by the former. Thus it is a well-settled rule of commercial law that no one but the person upon whom it is drawn, or his duly authorised agent, can accept a bill except for need or honour. That no person except a drawee of a bill of exchange can bind himself by acceptance. The drawee of the bill of exchange, in the absence of any contract to the contrary, on acceptance is the acceptor before maturity by the bill of exchange and is bound to pay the amount thereof at maturity to the holder on demand. When the drawee does accept he undertakes that he will pay the bill according to the tenor of the acceptance and he remains primarily liable on the bill of exchange as acceptor; *American Express Bank* v. *Calcutta Steel Company*, 1992 (3) SCALE 536: 1993 (2) SCC 199: 1993 (1) SCJ 262: 1993 (1) UJ 798 [**Hon'ble Judges:** A.M. Ahmadi, M.M. Punchhi, K. Ramaswamy].

2. "Period of Limitation" – Law on – Section 3 of the Limitation Act provides that a suit, appeal or application instituted after the prescribed "period of limitation" must subject to the provisions of sections 4 to 24 be dismissed although limitation has not been set up as a defence. Section 2(j) defines the expression "period of limitation" to mean the period of limitation prescribed in the Schedule for suit, appeal or application. Section 2(j) also defines, "prescribed period" to mean the period of limitation computed in accordance with the provisions of the Act. The Court's function on the presentation of plaint is simply to examine whether, on the assumed facts, the plaintiff is within time. The Court has to find out when the "right to sue" accrued to the plaintiff. If a suit is not covered by any of the specific articles prescribing a period of limitation, it must fall within the residuary article. The purpose of the residuary article is to provide for cases which could not be covered by any other provision in the Limitation Act. The residuary article is applicable to every variety of suits not otherwise provided for. The words "right to sue" ordinarily mean the right to seek relief by means of legal proceedings. Generally, the right to sue accrues only when the cause of action arises, that is, the right to prosecute to obtain relief by legal means. The suit must be instituted when the right asserted in the suit is infringed or when there is a clear and unequivocal threat to infringe that right by the defendant against whom the suit is instituted; *State of Punjab* v. *Gurdev Singh and Ashok Kumar*, AIR 1991 SC 2219: JT 1991 (3) SC 465: 1991 (2) SCALE 365: 1991 (4) SCC 1 [See: (i) *Mt. Bolo* v. *Mt. Koklan*, AIR 1930 PC 270 and (ii) *Gannon Dunkerley and Co.* v. *Union of India*, AIR 1970 SC 1433].

3. "Presumption" and "Proof" – Law on – There is a distinction between "presumption" and "proof". A presumption has been defined as "an inference, affirmative or disaffirmative of the truth or falsehood of a doubtful fact or proposition drawn by a process of probable reasoning from something proved or taken for granted". They are rules of evidence which attempt to assist the judicial mind in the matter of weighing the probative or persuasive force or certain facts proved in relation to other facts presumed or inferred. Sometimes a discretion is left with the Court either to raise a presumption or not as in section 114 of the Evidence Act. On other occasions, no such discretion is given to the Court so that when a certain set of facts are proved, the Court is bound to raise the prescribed presumption. But that is all. The presumption may be rebutted; *M.S. Madhusoodhanan* v. *Kerala Kaumudi Pvt. Ltd.*, AIR SC 909: JT 2003 (6) SC 560: 2003 (6) SCALE 191: 2004 (9) SCC 204; *Izhar Ahmad* v. *Union of India*, AIR 1962 SC 1052.

4. Admissibility of Evidence in Absence of Written Statement – Law on – Even if the suit proceeds *ex parte* and in the absence of a written statement, unless the applicability of Order VIII, rule 10 of the C.P.C. is attracted and the Courts act thereunder, the necessity of proof by the plaintiff of his case to the satisfaction of the Court cannot be dispensed with. In the absence of denial of plaint averments the burden of proof on the plaintiff is not very heavy. A *prima facie* proof of the relevant facts constituting the cause of action would suffice and the Court would grant the plaintiff such relief as to which he may in law be found entitled. In a case which has proceeded *ex parte* the court is not bound to frame issues under Order XIV and deliver the judgment on every issue as required by Order XX, rule 5. Yet the trial Court would scrutinize the available pleadings and documents, consider the evidence adduced, and would do well to frame the 'points for determination' and proceed to construct the *ex parte* judgment dealing with the points at issue one by one. Merely because the defendant is absent the Court shall not admit evidence the admissibility whereof is excluded by law nor permit its decision being influenced by irrelevant or inadmissible evidence; *Ramesh Chand Ardawatiya* v. *Anil Panjwani*, AIR 2003 SC 2508: JT 2003 (4) SC 450: 2003 (4) SCALE 652: 2003 (7) SCC 350.

5. Admission – Importance of – In view of the admission of the plaint allegation made by the defendants in their written statement should be reliable; *Badri Prasad* v. *Chandrakantabai*, AIR 2001 SCW 2260: JT 2000 (10) SC 223: 2002 (9) SCC 580.

6. Alternative Relief – Amendment for – Granting of amendment of plaint seeking to introduce alternative relief of mandatory injunction for payment of specified amount is bad in law. The alternative relief was available to be asked for when the suit was filed but not made. Litigant cannot be permitted to amend the plaint after the suit was barred by the limitation during the pendency of the proceeding in the appellate court or the second appellate court; *Muni Lal* v. *Oriental Fire and General Insurance Company Ltd*, AIR 1996 SC 642: JT 1995 (8) SC 283: 1995 (6) SCALE 501: 1996 (1) SCC 90.

7. Benami Transaction – Law on – There is no formula or acid test uniformly applicable it is well nigh settled that the question depends predominantly upon the intention of the person who paid the purchase money. For this, the burden of proof is on the person who asserts that it is a benami transaction. However, if it is proved that the purchase money came from a person other than the recorded owner (ostensible owner) there can be a factual presumption at least in certain cases, depending on facts, that the purchase was for the benefit of the person who supplied purchase money; *Heirs of Vrajlal J. Ganatra* v. *Heirs of Parshottam S. Shah*, 1996 ACJ 399: JT 1996 (4) SC 725: 1996 (4) SCALE 53: 1996 (4) SCC 490.

8. Declaration and Injunction Relating to Commercial Transactions – Law on – Declaration of the rights or status is one of discretion of the court under section 34 of the Specific Relief Act, 1963. Equally the grant or refusal of the relief of declaration and injunction under the provision of that Act is discretionary. The plaintiff cannot claim the relief as of right. It has to be granted according to sound principles of law and *ex debito justitiae*. The court cannot convert itself into an instrument of injustice or vehicle of oppression. While exercising its discretionary power, the court must keep in its mind the well-settled principles of justice and fair play and the discretion would be exercised keeping in view the ends of justice since justice is the hallmark and it cannot be administered in vacuum. Grant of declaration and injunction relating to commercial transactions tend to aid dishonesty and perfidy. Conversely, refusal to grant relief generally encourages candour in business behaviour, facilitates free flow of capital, prompt compliance with covenants, sustained growth of commerce and above all inculcates respect for the efficacy of judicial adjudication. Before granting or refusing to grant relief of declaration or injunction court must weigh pros and cons in each case, consider the facts and circumstances in their proper perspective and exercise discretion with circumspection to further the ends of justice. The relief of declaration granted is unjust and illegal. It tended to impede free flow of capital, thwarted the growth of mercantile business and deflected the course of justice; *American Express Bank* v. *Calcutta Steel Company*, 1992 (3) SCALE 536: 1993 (2) SCC 199: 1993 (1) SCJ 262 **[Hon'ble Judges:** A.M. Ahmadi, M.M. Punchhi, K. Ramaswamy].

9. Endorsed Documents – Law on – Order XIII, rule 4 of the C.P.C. provides for every document admitted in evidence in the suit being endorsed by or on behalf of the Court, which endorsement signed or initiated by the Judge amounts to admission of the document in evidence. An objection to the admissibility of the document should be raised before such endorsement is made and the Court is obliged to form its opinion on the question of admissibility and express the same on which opinion would depend the document being endorsed as admitted or not admitted in evidence. In the latter case, the document may be returned by the Court to the person from whose custody it was produced; *R.V.E. Venkatachala Gounder* v. *Arulmigu Viswesaraswami and V.P. Temple*, AIR 2003 SC 4548: 2003 (8) SCALE 474: 2003 (8) SCC 752: 2003 (6) SLT 307.

10. Executing Court – Law on – A declaratory decree merely declares the right of the decree holder *vis-a-vis* the judgment debtor and does not in terms direct the judgment debtor to do or refrain from doing any particular act or thing. A decree holder was free to seek his remedy for arrears of salary in the suit for declaration. The executing Court has no jurisdiction to direct payment of salary or grant any other consequential relief which does not flow directly and necessarily from the declaratory decree. It is not that if in a suit for declaration where the plaintiff is able to seek further relief he must seek that relief though he may not be in need of that further relief; *State of Madhya Pradesh* v. *Mangilal Sharma*, AIR 1998 SC 743: 1997 (7) SCALE 781: 1998 (2) SCC 510.

In the absence of pleadings and directions in the judgment or decree which was under execution, it was not open to the executing court to award interest. The Execution Court is bound by the terms of the decree; it cannot add or alter the decree on its notion of fairness or justice. The right of the decree holder to obtain relief is determined in accordance with the terms of the decree. No doubt the Courts have power to award interest on the arrears of salary or pension or other amount to which a Government servant is found entitled having regard to the facts and circumstances of the case but that power cannot be exercised by the execution Court in the absence of any direction in the decree; *State of Punjab* v. *Krishan Dayal Sharma*, AIR 1990 SC 2177: 1990 Lab IC 1871.

11. Future Rights of an Intending Purchaser – Law on – Although, the mere possibility of future rights of an intending purchaser could not, by itself, be enough to entitle him to get a declaration relating to a purported lease affecting the right to possess and enjoy the property; *Supreme General Films Exchange Ltd.* v. *His Highness Maharaja Sir Brijnath Singhji Deo of Maihar*, AIR 1975 SC 1810: 1975 (2) SCC 530: 1976 (1) SCR 237.

12. High Court – Guidelines for – Since the 1976 amendment, effective from 1-2-1977, in the Code of Civil Procedure, compliance with section 100(4) is not being insisted on and such non-compliance is defeating the purpose sought to be achieved by the amendment. Ordinarily Apex Court would have set aside the judgment of the High Court and sent the matter back for rehearing and decision afresh in the appeal after compliance with section 100(4) of the C.P.C.; *Manohar Lal* v. *Maya*, AIR 2003 SC 2362: 2003 (3) SCALE 569: 2003 (9) SCC 478: 2003 (3) SLT 39.

13. Injury of a Substantial Nature – Law on – The concept of an "injury of a substantial nature" does not much differ in content from the concept of "substantial prejudice". In *Chamber's Twentieth Century Dictionary* one of the meanings of the word 'prejudice' is given as "injury or hurt". An order issued in exercise of non existent power or, in other words, an order which is entirely without jurisdiction must in terms be deemed to result in an injury of a substantial nature; *Shantilal Ambalal Mehta* v. *M.A. Rangaswamy*, 1977 BLR 633: 1977 MhLJ 587.

14. Jurisdiction of Civil Court – Law on – If a special procedure is contemplated and a special remedy is provided to approach a particular forum in a particular manner and in a particular way either by the statute or by the statutory instructions through the Government orders as an alternative remedy which can be challenged, the said remedy has to be sought for only through the said special provisions in the appropriate forum and in appropriate manner and, if the party is further aggrieved, it can approach the High Court under article 226 and then the Supreme Court under article 136 and, in those circumstances, the Civil Court's jurisdiction is impliedly barred; *P. Maragathamani; V. Ramasamy; K. Thangavelu* v. *General Manager (In-charge), Bharat Heavy Electricals Limited*, 2006 (1) CTC 497: 2007 (1) JCR 283: 2006 (1) Mad LJ 480.

15. Jurisdiction of High Court – Law on – It is important to note that the writs which are contemplated by article 226 include a writ of prohibition and if any illegality in the nature of the wrongful assumption of jurisdiction by the inferior tribunal or the authority is complained of, then in a given case, in our view, it would be possible for a person to approach the High Court invoking the writ of prohibition without waiting for the completion of the proceedings, if there is no other bar which stands in his way, to seek the writ of prohibition. Illegality may, therefore, have different facets including wrongful assumption of jurisdiction, which in a given case fall even under clause (b). To a certain extent, therefore, it appears to be unavoidable that within a small area the remedies provided by clauses (b) and (c) may overlap. The fact, however, remains that now the area of jurisdiction of the High Court under new article 226 stands limited to clauses (b) and (c) in cases which do not deal with the enforcement of fundamental rights. Clause (2) of article 226 is identical to the original article 226(1A) and no change is made in respect of jurisdiction of the High Court to issue writs in respect of Government or authority or a person where the cause of action wholly or in part arises for the exercise of such power within the jurisdiction of the High Court notwithstanding that the seat of such Government or authority or the residence of such person is not within those territories; *Shantilal Ambalal Mehta* v. *M.A. Rangaswamy*, 1977 BLR 633: 1977 Mah LJ 587.

16. Partition – Law on – The partition having remained unquestioned for a long period of time by any of the parties to the deed, it does not lie in the mouth of a third party to impeach the nature of the transaction recorded in the said document when opposing party himself had not questioned the partition deed; *Padmini Chandrasekharan* v. *R. Rajagopal Reddy*, JT 1996 (12) SC 618: 1996 (Supp 1) JT 618: 1996 (1) Rent LR 763: 1996 (2) SCALE 766: 1996 (8) SCC 632.

17. Plaint – Importance of – It is well-established that for deciding the nature of a suit the entire plaint has to be read and not merely the relief portion. The court-fee payable on the plaint has also to be assessed accordingly; *Corporation of City of Bangalore* v. *M. Papaiah*, AIR 1989 SC 1809: 1989 (2) GLH 524: JT 1989 (3) SC 294: 1989 (2) SCALE 182: 1989 (3) SCC 612.

18. Possession of Property – Effect of – The plaintiff can on the strength of his possession resist interference from persons who have no better title than himself to the suit property. Once it is accepted that the plaintiff was in possession of the property ever since 1947 then his possession has to be protected as against interference by someone who is not proved to have a better title than himself to the suit property. On the findings arrived at by the fact finding courts as regards possession, the plaintiff was entitled to the second relief asked for by him even if he had failed to prove his title satisfactorily; *M. Kallappa Setty* v. *M.V. Lakshminarayana Rao*, AIR 1972 SC 2299: 1973 (2) SCC 358: 1973 UJ 50.

19. Pre-emption Decree – Law on – A plain reading of the rule 14(1) of Order XX, Code of Civil Procedure shows that the title to the decree-holder accrues from the date of the payment required to be made under a pre-emption decree. In view of the deposit by the original plaintiff of the pre-emption amount in terms of the pre-emption decree, the dismissal of the execution petition was inconsequential since the plaintiff was in joint possession of the land, which was part of joint khata; *Reshmu* v. *Rajinder Singh*, AIR 2000 SC 1064: JT 2000 (2) SC 151: 2000 (1) SCALE 583: 2000 (3) SCC 47.

20. Privileged Tenant – Law on – Once the defendant claimed title as a privileged tenant in terms of the provisions of the Bihar Privileged Persons Homestead Tenancy Act, 1947, the relationship of landlord and tenant came to an end. It was, therefore, obligatory on the part of the plaintiff-landlord to file a suit in terms of section 18 of the Act, 1947. In absence of a decree passed in such a suit would lie only a limited ground for want of jurisdiction or fraud, the plaintiff was not entitled to have a decree in his favour in a suit of the nature instituted by him and for the reliefs sought for by him;

Mehar Chand Das v. *Lal Babu Siddique*, AIR 2007 SC 1499: 2007 (2) SCALE 539: 2007 (14) SCC 253.

21. *Res Judicata* – Law on – It is well neigh settled that a decision on an issue raised in a writ petition under article 226 or article 32 of the Constitution would also operate as *res judicata* between the same parties in subsequent judicial proceedings. The only exception is that the rule of *res judicata* would not operate to the detriment or impairment of a fundamental right; *Ashok Kumar Srivastav* v. *National Insurance Company Limited*, AIR 1998 SC 2046: JT 1998 (3) SC 519: 1998 (3) SCALE 265: 1998 (4) SCC 361.

22. Review of Judgment – Law on – Though the Plenary jurisdiction of Apex Court in review is not very much circumscribed there are definitive limits. Apex Court can exercise the powers on a wider canvass on any analogous ground; still the scope for review has its own restrictions and may not be exercised in the manner in which the powers can be exercised in an appeal. A review of a judgment is a serious step and reluctant resort to it is proper only where a glaring omission or patent mistake or like grave error has crept in earlier by judicial fallibility. A mere repetition through different counsel of old and overruled arguments cannot create a ground for 'review'; *Gujarat University* v. *Miss Sonal P. Shah*, AIR 1982 Guj 58: 1982 (1) GLR 171 **[Hon'ble Judges:** N.H. Bhatt, A.M. Ahmadi, V.V. Bedarkar]; *Sow Chandra Kanta* v. *Sheik Habib*, AIR 1975 SC 1500 (V.R. Krishna Iyer); *Shivdeo Singh* v. *State of Punjab*, AIR 1963 SC 1909.

23. Rights and Liabilities of Mortgagor – Law on – The rights and liabilities of Mortgagor are dealt with in section 60 of the Transfer of Property Act. It is true that at any time after the principal money has become due, the mortgagor has a right, on payment or tender, at a proper time and place of the mortgage-money, to require the mortgagee (a) to deliver to the mortgagor the mortgage-deed and all documents relating to the mortgaged property which are in the possession or power of the mortgagee, (b) where the mortgagee is in possession of the mortgaged property to deliver possession thereof to the mortgagor and (c) at the cost of the mortgaged either to re-transfer the mortgaged property to him or to such third person as he may direct, or to execute and to have registered an acknowledgment in writing that any right in derogation of his interest transferred to the mortgagee has been extinguished. There is a proviso that the right conferred by this section has not been extinguished by the act of the parties or by decree of a Court. The right conferred by section 60 of the Transfer of Property Act is called a right to redeem. Therefore, the said section 60 provides for a right of redemption provided that the right has not been extinguished by the act of parties. Section 69 of the Transfer of Property Act deals with mortgagee's power of sale. Under the said section 69(1)(c), a mortgagee has power of sale without the intervention of the Court where power is conferred by the mortgage deed and the mortgaged property or any part thereof was on the date of the execution of the mortgage deed, situate within the towns of Calcutta, Madras, Bombay or in any other town or area which the State Government may, by notification in the official Gazette specify; *Narandas Karsondas* v. *S.A. Kamtam*, AIR 1977 SC 774: 1977 (3) SCC 247: 1977 (2) SCR 341.

24. Scheme – Construction of – In view of the settled legal position that while construing any Scheme in connection with the question of providing compassionate appointments to the heirs of deceased employee who was the bread-winner and whose exit had left his heirs in the lurch and in precarious and vulnerable economic position a construction which fructifies such a welfare measure has to be preferred as compared to another construction which stultifies such a benevolent welfare measure; *Indian Bank* v. *K. Usha*, AIR 1998 SC 866: JT 1998 (1) SC 265: 1998 (1) SCALE 226: 1998 (2) SCC 663.

25. Variety of Declaratory Relief – Law on – Chapter II contains a fasciculus of rules relating to specific performance of contracts. Section 14 falls within that Chapter and it points to contracts which are not specifically enforceable. Powers of the Court to grant declaratory relief are adumbrated in section 34 of the Act which falls under Chapter VI of the Act. It is well to remember that even the wide language contained in section 34 did not exhaust the powers of the Court to grant declaratory relief. Mere fact that a suit which is not maintainable under section 14 of the Act is not to persist with its disability of non admission to Civil Courts even outside the contours of Chapter II of the Act. Section 34 is enough to open the corridors of Civil Courts to admit suits filed for a variety of declaratory relief; *Ashok Kumar Srivastav* v. *National Insurance Company Limited,* AIR 1998 SC 2046: JT 1998 (3) SC 519: 1998 (3) SCALE 265: 1998 (4) SCC 361.

26. Will – Law on – Even if it is assumed that the property in question was bequeathed by executing the Will, the title to the suit property cannot be declared in favour of the plaintiff unless the title of the executor of the Will is fully established; *Ram Das* v. *Salim Ahmed,* JT 1998 (9) SC 534: 1998 (9) SCC 719.

27. Withholding of Important Documents – Effect of – Even if the burden of proof does not lie on a party, the Court may draw an adverse inference if such party withholds important documents in his possession which can throw light on the facts in issue. Even if adverse inference is drawn against the Municipality for not producing the documents in its possession, the plaintiff cannot succeed unless the plaintiff establishes the plaintiff's title to the suit property and also possession in respect of the same; *Shakir Hussain* v. *Administrator, Nagar Palika, Mandsaur,* AIR 1999 SC 2872: AIR 1999 SCW 2478: JT 1998 (9) SC 49: 1998 (9) SCC 613.

28. Bill of Exchange – Law on – It would thus be clear that the maker of a bill of exchange is the drawer; the person thereby directed to pay is called the drawee; after the drawee had signed his assent upon the bill he is called the acceptor. In the absence of any contract to the contrary, the acceptor, before maturity of a bill of exchange, is bound to pay the amount thereof at maturity according to the acceptance to the holder on demand. No person except the drawee of the bill of exchange, in case of numerical drawees one or all drawees or the person named thereon as a drawee in case of need or for honour can bind himself by an acceptance; *American Express Bank* v. *Calcutta Steel Company,* 1992 (3) SCALE 536: 1993 (2) SCC 199: 1993 (1) SCJ 262: 1993 (1) UJ 798 **[Hon'ble Judges:** A.M. Ahmadi, M.M. Punchhi, K. Ramaswamy].

29. Cancellation of Sale Deed by Third Party – Law on – There is no dispute that a third party can claim title to the property against the purchaser who purchased the property for valuable consideration and came into possession of the same. But it is the Civil Court of competent jurisdiction to give such declaration in favor of the third party or a stranger. It can also not be overlooked or ignored that a unilateral cancellation of a sale deed by registered instrument at the instance of the vendor only encourages fraud and is against public policy. But there are circumstances where a deed of cancellation presented by both the vendor and the purchaser for registration has to be accepted by the Registrar if other mandatory requirements are complied with. Hence, the vendor by the unilateral execution of the cancellation deed cannot annul a registered document duly executed by him as such an act of the vendor is opposed to public policy; *Latif Estate Line India Ltd., Habib Abdul Latif and Mohideen Abdul Latif* v. *Hadeeja Ammal; Syeda Aamina Raheem,* AIR 2011 Mad 66: 2011 (2) CTC 1: 2011 (2) JCR 1: 2011 (2) RCR (Civ) 531.

30. Custom – Law on – It is a settled law by a catena of decisions of Apex Court and also of the other High Courts that a custom must be pleaded and proved; *Ram Swarup: Ram Swaroop* v. *Mahindru,* JT 2003 (10) SC 422: 2003 (10) SCALE 921: 2003 (12) SCC 436.

31. Doctrine of *Lis Pendens* – Effect of – It is well-settled that the doctrine of *lis pendens* is a doctrine based on the ground that it is necessary for the administration of justice that the decision of a court in a suit should be binding not only on the litigating parties but on those who derive title *pendente lite.* The provision of this section does not indeed annul the conveyance or the transfer otherwise, but to render it subservient to the rights of the parties to litigation; *Thomson Press (India) Ltd.* v. *Nanak Builders & Investors P. Ltd.,* 2013 (3) SCALE 26: JT 2013 (3) SC 289: 2013 (5) SCC 397: AIR 2013 SC 2389.

32. Jurisdiction of Civil Court – Law on – There cannot be any doubt that the suit was under section 34 of the Specific Relief Act, 1963. It is rather doubtful as to how the suit for mere declaration without any consequential relief was maintainable. Be that as it may whether jurisdiction of the Civil Court to issue a declaration that a person belongs to a particular caste, which comes under Scheduled Tribe, is ousted by reason of section 9 of the Code of Civil Procedure, 1908? Section 9 of the C.P.C. lays down that a Civil Court shall have jurisdiction to try all suits of a civil nature "excepting suits of which cognizance is either expressly or impliedly barred". The law is well-settled that unless the suit is expressly or impliedly barred, the doctrine of *ubi jus ibi remedium* (where there is a right there is a remedy) is attracted; *Andhra Pradesh Scheduled Tribes Employees Association* v. *Aditya Pratap Bhanj Dev*, 2001 (6) ALD 582: 2001 (6) ALT 433.

33. Jurisdiction of Civil Courts under Civil Courts – Law on – Service Rules, neither expressly nor by implication have taken away the jurisdiction of the Civil Courts to deal with service matter; *Ramendra Kishore Biswas* v. *State of Tripura*, AIR 1999 SC 294: 1998 (6) SCALE 454: 1999 (1) SCC 472: 1999 (1) ACJ 126.

34. 'Material Facts' and 'Particulars' – Law on – There is distinction between 'material facts' and 'particulars'. The words 'material facts' show that the facts necessary to formulate a complete cause of action must be stated. Omission of a single material fact leads to an incomplete cause of action and the statement or plaint becomes bad; *Sopan Sukhdeo Sable* v. *Assistant Charity Commissioner*, 2004 (1) SCR 1004: AIR 2004 SC 1801: 2004 (2) SCALE 82: 2004 (3) SCC 137.

35. Order of Injunction – Requirement for – A court of law before passing an order of injunction must take into consideration three relevant factors, *viz., prima facie* case, balance of convenience and irreparable injury; *Sonu Babu Bhambid* v. *Dream Developers*, JT 2009 (13) SC 397: 2009 (17) SCC 124: 2009 (8) SCJ 382.

36. Promissory Estoppels – Law on – Promissory estoppel is based on equity or obligations. It is not based on vested right. In equity the court has to strike a balance between individual rights on one hand and the larger public interest on the other hand. Freedom to contract is a common law civil liberty enjoyed by all persons. But when the Government is contracting with private parties this common law freedom is circumscribed by the principles of administrative law which requires larger public interest to be taken into account. Larger public interest is not only for accommodating retiree workmen but also to accommodate in-service workmen. Even applying the principles enshrined in article 39(b) and (c) of the Constitution, egalitarian equality requires the Government to strike a balance between competing claims. Even in the realm of social justice, on which our Constitution is founded, the administration has to strike a balance between the competing claims. DTC which is a public sector undertaking had to act in public interest; *M.P. Mathur* v. *D.T.C.*, AIR 2007 SC 414: 2006 (12) SCALE 446: 2006 (13) SCC 706.

37. Registrable Document – Law on – The registering officers being public authorities have to act within the ambit of registration law and if a document does not fall under any of the categories in sections 17 and 18 of the Registration Act, the registering officer is bound to refuse to admit the document for registration. A deed of cancellation (of sale deed) is one such species of the document, which ought to have been refused by the registering officer for registration. If the cancellation deed is considered to be a registrable document and the registering officer is permitted to register the cancellation deed, the same would be contrary to public policy. After insertion of section 32A by the Registration and Other Related Laws (Amendment), 2001 (Act No. 48 of 2001), whenever a document relating to transfer of ownership is presented for registration, the passport size photograph and finger print of the vendor and vendee shall have to be affixed to the document. If the vendor desires to avoid the sale transaction, the remedy is only to seek by filing a suit for cancellation of deed as contemplated under section 31 of the Specific Relief Act, in which event, the Court adjudicating the case shall send a copy of its decree to the Registering Officer, who registered the document, whereupon the Registering Officer shall note on the copy of the instrument contained in his books the fact of its cancellation; *Yanala Malleshwari* v. *Ananthula Sayamma*, 2007 AIHC 1471: AIR 2007 AP 57: 2007 (1) CTC 97: 2007 (5) RCR (Civ) 609.

38. *Res Judicata* – Law on – It is not possible to accept that the principle of *res judicata* will apply to bar the appeal. Section 11 of the C.P.C. would bar the Court from trying any suit or issue in which the matter "directly and substantially in issue" between the same parties or between the parties under whom they or any of them claim, litigating under the same title in a Court competent to try such subsequent suit or suit in which such issue has been subsequently raised, has been "heard and finally decided by such Court"; *Bajranglal Shivchandrai Ruia* v. *Shashikant N. Ruia*, AIR 2004 SC 2546: 2004 (3) SCALE 580: 2004 (5) SCC 272: 2004 (3) SLT 434.

39. Revenue Records – Law on – It is true that in some of the documents produced by the Mr. X, is shown as the cultivator of these properties. This is not sufficient to prove that the occupancy right or the title of the suit property vested in Mr. X. These revenue records are quite consistent with the fact that Mr. X must have been in possession of this property as an employee or manager of the Gurdwara. The entries in the revenue records by itself cannot prove the title to the property unless it is supported by other evidence; *Dalip Singh* v. *Sikh Gurdwara Prabandak Committee*, AIR 2004 SC 137: JT 2005 (6) SC 182: 2003 (8) SCALE 637: 2003 (10) SCC 352.

40. Second Appeal – Law on – No question of law much less a substantial question of law arose in the case worth being gone into by the High Court in exercise of its second appellate jurisdiction under section 100 of the C.P.C. The High Court was bound by the findings of fact arrived at by the two Courts below and should not have entered into the exercise of re-appreciating and evaluating the evidence; *R.V.E. Venkatachala Gounder* v. *Arulmigu Viswesaraswami and V.P. Temple*, AIR 2003 SC 4548: 2003 (8) SCALE 474: 2003 (8) SCC 752: 2003 (6) SLT 307.

41. Some Blanks in Schedule of Property – Effect of – It is now well-settled that the pleadings of the parties are to be read in their entirety. They are to be construed liberally and not in a pedantic manner. It is also not a case where by reason of an amendment, one property is being substituted by the other. If the Court has the requisite power to make an amendment of the decree, the same would not mean that it had gone beyond the decree or passing any decree. The statements contained in the body of the plaint have sufficiently described the suit lands. Only because some blanks in the schedule of the property have been left, the same, by itself, may not be a ground to deprive the plaintiff from the fruit of the decree; *Niyamat Ali Molla* v. *Sonargon Housing Co-operative Society Ltd.*, AIR 2008 SC 225: JT 2007 (12) SC 367: 2007 (12) SCALE 374: 2007 (13) SCC 421: 2007 (11) SCR 346.

42. Special Leave Petition – Law on – This is not the function of this Court, in a special leave petition under article 136 of the Constitution, to reappraise the evidence unless the findings are shown to be perverse or they are vitiated by any error of law resulting in miscarriage of justice; *Prabhakar Adsule* v. *State of Madhya Pradesh*, AIR 2004 SC 3557: JT 2004 (5) SC 187: 2004 (5) SCALE 790: 2004 (11) SCC 249.

43. Specific Performance of Contract of Sale of Immovable Property on Basis of an Oral Agreement – Law on – In a case where the plaintiffs come forward to seek a decree for specific performance of contract of sale of immovable property on the basis of an oral agreement alone, heavy burden lies on the plaintiffs to prove that there was consensus ad idem between the parties for a concluded oral agreement for sale of immovable property. Whether there was such a concluded oral contract or not would be a question of fact to be determined in the facts and circumstances of each individual case. It has to be established by the plaintiffs that vital and fundamental terms for sale of immovable property were concluded between the parties orally and a written agreement if any to be executed subsequently would only be a formal agreement incorporating such terms which had already been settled and concluded in the oral agreement; *Brij Mohan* v. *Sugra Begum*, 1990 (2) CCC 688: JT 1990 (3) SC 255: 1990 (2) SCALE 125: 1990 (4) SCC 147: 1990 (3) SCR 413.

44. Suit for Declaration – Maintainability of – If it appears, *prima facie*, that apart from making a prayer for declaration there is also a consequential prayer for a decree for permanent injunction restraining the defendant from alienating the suit property or interfering in peaceful possession of plaintiff therein and there is an alternative prayer for decree for possession also; *Gian Kaur* v. *Raghubir Singh*, JT 2011 (7) SC 44: 2011 (3) SCALE 241: 2011 (4) SCC 567: 2011 (2) SCR 486.

45. Suit for Specific Performance – Nature of – The suit for specific performance is in the nature of discretionary remedy and on equity. The court has power and discretion to extend the time for fulfillment of the contract; *Bhupinder Kumar* v. *Angrej Singh*, 2009 (6) All MR 464: 2009 (8) SCC 766: 2009 (8) SCJ 578: 2009 (4) Civ CC 195.

46. Violation of Order of Injunction – Law on – Section 151 confers wide powers on the court to make such orders as may be necessary for the ends of justice or to prevent abuse of the process of the court. The power of section 151 to pass order of injunction in the form of restoration of possession of the code is not *res integra* now. At the same time, it is also well-settled that when parties violate order of injunction or stay order or act in violation of the said order the court can, by exercising its inherent power, put back the parties in the same position as they stood prior to issuance of the injunction order or give appropriate direction to the police authority to render aid to the aggrieved parties for the due and proper implementation of the orders passed in the suit and also order police protection for implementation of such order. It is also well-settled that when in the event of utter violation of the injunction order, the party forcibly dispossesses the other, the court can order restoration of possession to the party wronged. For exercising of power under section 151 of Code of Civil Procedure; *Meera Chauhan* v. *Harsh Bishnoi*, JT 2007 (1) SC 458: 2006 (13) SCALE 581: 2007 (12) SCC 201: 2007 (2) Supreme 772; *Manohar* v. *Hira Lal*, AIR 1962 SC 527.

47. Amendment in Plaint – Law on – The very purpose of the proviso to section 34 of the Act 1963 is to avoid the multiplicity of the proceedings, and also the loss of revenue of court fees. When the Specific Relief Act, 1877 was in force, the 9th Report of the Law Commission of India, 1958, had suggested certain amendments in the proviso, according to which, the plaintiff could seek declaratory relief without seeking any consequential relief, if he sought permission of the court to make his subsequent claim in another suit/ proceedings. However, such an amendment was not accepted. There is no provision analogous to such suggestion in the Act 1963. A mere declaratory decree remains non-executable in most cases generally. However, there is no prohibition upon a party from seeking an amendment in the plaint to include the unsought relief, provided that it is saved by limitation. However, it is obligatory on the part of the defendants to raise the issue at the earliest; *Venkataraja* v. *Vidyane Doureradjaperumal*, JT 2013 (4) SC 505: 2013 (5) SCALE 511: AIR 2013 SCW 3063: 2013 (125) All Ind Cas 19.

48. Power of Review – Law on – Section 114 of the Code of Civil Procedure provides for a substantive power of review by a Civil Court and consequently by the appellate courts. The words "subject as aforesaid" occurring in section 114 of the Code means subject to such conditions and limitations as may be prescribed as appearing in section 113 thereof and for the said purpose, the procedural conditions contained in Order XLVII of the Code must be taken into *consideration; Inderchand Jain (D) through LRs.* v. *Motilal (D) through LRs.*, AIR 2009 SCW 5364: JT 2009 (9) SC 537: 2009 (9) SCALE 777: 2009 (14) SCC 663: 2009 (11) SCR 252.

49. Presumption of Title as Result of Possession – Law on – The principle enshrined in section 110 of the Evidence Act, is based on public policy with the object of preventing persons from committing breach of peace by taking law into their own hands, however good their title over the land in question may be. It is for this purpose, that the provisions of section 6 of the Specific Relief Act, 1963, section 145 of Code of Criminal Procedure, 1973, and sections 154 and 158 of Indian Penal Code, 1860, were enacted. All the aforesaid provisions have the same object. The said presumption is read under section 114 of the Evidence Act, and applies only in a case where there is either no proof, or very little proof of ownership on either side. The maxim "possession follows title" is applicable in cases where proof of actual possession cannot reasonably be expected, for instance, in the case of waste lands, or where nothing is known about possession one-way or another. Presumption of title as a result of possession can arise only where facts disclose that no title vests in any party. Possession of the plaintiff is not *prima facie* wrongful, and title of the plaintiff is not proved. It certainly does not mean that because a man has title over some land, he is necessarily in possession of it. It in fact means, that if at any time a man with title was in possession of the said property, the law allows the presumption that such possession was in continuation of the title vested in him. A person must establish that he has continued possession of the suit property, while the other side claiming title, must make out a case of trespass/encroachment etc. Where the apparent title is with the plaintiffs, it is incumbent upon the defendant, that in order to displace this claim of apparent title and to establish beneficial title in him, he must establish by way of satisfactory evidence, circumstances that favour his version. Even, a revenue record is not a document of title. It merely raises a presumption in regard to possession. Presumption of possession and/or continuity thereof, both forward and backward, can also be raised under section 110 of the Evidence Act; *State of Andhra Pradesh* v. *Star Bone Mill & Fertiliser Co.*, 2013 (2) SCALE 728: JT 2013 (3) SC 401: AIR 2013 SCW 1454: 2013 (9) SCC 319.

50. Property of Real Owner – Law on – The property of the real owner would be protected, and *bona fide* purchaser will be entitled to get back his money along with interest and costs etc. from his vendor; *Niranjan Kaur* v. *Financial Commissioner*, AIR 2011 P&H 1: 2011 (161) Pun LR 110: 2010 (4) RCR (Civ) 610.

51. Statutory Notice – Law on – There can be no dispute to the proposition that a notice under section 80 can be waived. If a new cause of action is being introduced a fresh notice under section 80, C.P.C. would be required to be given. If the same not having been given, the suit on this cause of action was not maintainable; *Bishandayal and Sons* v. *State of Orissa*, AIR 2001 SC 544: JT 2001 (1) SC 58: 2000 (8) SCALE 172: 2001 (1) SCC 555.

35. Effect of declaration.—A declaration made under this Chapter is binding only on the parties to the suit, persons claiming through them respectively, and, where any of the parties are trustees, on the persons for whom, if in existence at the date of declaration, such parties would be trustees.

SYNOPSIS

COMMENTS

1. Person Drawing Benefit from a Transaction – Law on – In any case the compromise decree having become final it was binding between the parties. In equity a person drawing benefit from a transaction is not permitted to escape from the disadvantage if any flowing from it; *Bakshi Ram* v. *Brij Lal*, AIR 1995 SC 395: JT 1994 (5) SC 422: 1994 (3) SCALE 352: 1995 (1) SCJ 64.

2. Section 21 of the Limitation Act – Attraction of – Section 21 of the Limitation Act provides that wherever on institution of a suit a new plaintiff or defendant is substituted or added, the suit shall, as regards him, be deemed to have been instituted when he is so made a party. However, if court is satisfied that omission to include a new plaintiff or defendant was due to a mistake made in good faith it may direct that the suit as regards such plaintiff or defendant shall be deemed to have been instituted on any earlier date. Sub-section (2) thereof makes it very clear that these provisions would not apply to a case where a party is added or substituted owing to assignment or devolution of any interest during the pendency of the suit or where plaintiff is made a defendant or a defendant is made a plaintiff. Section 21 has no application to cases of transposition of parties. Since transposition also involves addition of a plaintiff or a defendant as the case may be, into the suit as originally filed, sub-section (2) of section 21 of the Limitation Act applies only to those cases where the claim of the person transposed as plaintiff can be sustained on the plaintiff as originally filed or where person remaining as a plaintiff after the said transposition can sustain his claim against the transposed defendant on the basis of the plaint as originally filed. For sub-section (2) to apply all that is necessary is that suit as filed originally should remain the same after the transposition of the plaintiff and there should be no addition to its subject-matter. Where a suit as originally filed is properly framed with the proper parties on record the mere change of a party from array of defendants to that of plaintiff under Order I, rule 10 of the Civil Procedure Code will not make him a new plaintiff and will not bring the case within this section and in such a case sub-section (2) will not apply. For instance, where one of the plaintiffs refusing to join as plaintiff was first made a defendant and thereafter transposed as a plaintiff, he is not a new plaintiff; *Mukesh Kumar* v. *Col. Harbans Waraiah*, AIR 2000 SC 172: JT 1999 (8) SC 563: 1999 (6) SCALE 644: 1999 (9) SCC 380.

PART III

PREVENTIVE RELIEF

CHAPTER VII

INJUNCTIONS GENERALLY

36. Preventive relief how granted.—Preventive relief is granted at the discretion of the court by injunction, temporary or perpetual.

SYNOPSIS

1. Preventive Relief – Law on
2. Injunction – Law on
3. Question of Possession – Law on

COMMENTS

1. Preventive Relief – Law on – Section 36 postulates that "Preventive relief is granted at the discretion of the Court by injunction, temporary or perpetual". Temporary or perpetual injunctions are regulated by section 37; *Agriculture Produce Market Committee, Gondal* v. *Girdharbhai Ramjibhai Chhaniyara*, AIR 1997 SC 2674: JT 1997 (5) SC 591: 1997 (4) SCALE 298: 1997 (5) SCC 468.

2. Injunction – Law on – Section 36 provides that preventive relief is granted at the discretion of the Court by injunction. Section 37 specifies the nature and character of temporary and perpetual injunctions. Temporary injunctions are such as are to continue until a specified time, or until the further order of the Court, and they may be granted at any stage of a suit, and are regulated by the Code of Civil Procedure, 1908. Permanent injunctions can only be granted by the decree made at the hearing and upon merits of the suit and thereby defendant in the suit is perpetually enjoined from assertion of a right or from commission of an act, which would be contrary to the rights of the plaintiffs. Section 38 sets out situations in which the court can grant a perpetual injunction to the plaintiff to prevent the breach of an obligation existing in its favour, whether expressly or by implication. Section 38 is thus an enabling section which confers power on the court to grant perpetual injunction in situations and circumstances therein enumerated.

Section 41 caters to the opposite situation. It provides that an injunction cannot be granted in the situation and circumstances therein set out; *Export Credit Guarantee Corporation of India Ltd.* v. *Annamma Philips*, AIR 2011 Bom 18: 2010 (6) All MR 50: 2010 (5) BCR 823: 2010 (112) BLR 4118.

3. Question of Possession – Law on – The question of possession of the suit land is essentially one of fact. There was hardly any scope for the High Court to interfere with the finding of possession concurrently recorded by the Courts below within the limited parameters of section 100 of the Civil Procedure Code; *Mohan Lal* v. *Nihal Singh*, AIR 2001 SC 2942: JT 2001 (9) SC 58: 2001 (7) SCALE 328: 2001 (8) SCC 584.

37. Temporary and perpetual injunctions.—(1) Temporary injunctions are such as are to continue until a specified time, or until the further order of the court, and they may be granted at any stage of a suit, and are regulated by the Code of Civil Procedure, 1908 (5 of 1908).

(2) A perpetual injunction can only be granted by the decree made at the hearing and upon the merits of the suit; the defendant is thereby perpetually enjoined from the assertion of a right, or from the commission of an act, which would be contrary to the rights of the plaintiff.

SYNOPSIS

1. Derivative Title-Holder – Right of
2. Perpetual Injunction – Law on
3. Revenue Court – Powers of
4. Order of Injunction – Procedure for
5. Temporary Injunction
6. Permanent Injunction
7. Plaintiff to Establish this Right
8. Case – *Prima Facie* Wrong
9. Suit to Disturb the Transaction
10. Assignee in Actual Possession
11. Suit for not Determination on Merit
12. Revocation of Power-of-Attorney
13. Consequential Relief
14. Suit for Injunction Simpliciter
15. Insufficient Stamp-Agreement
16. Time Essence
17. Necessary Party to be Pleaded
18. Plaintiff's Failure to Prove his Case
19. Want of Prayer for Declaration of Title
20. Prayer in Interlocutory Application
21. Law Summarised by Supreme Court on Prohibitory Injunction

COMMENTS

1. Derivative Title-Holder – Right of – The person being a derivative title-holder is bound by the decree as judgment-debtor. He cannot seek any declaration of his independent title thereof. He can no longer avail of his tenancy rights which stood merged in his title held under pre-emption 90; *Jangli* v. *Bhagwati*, 1995 (3) CCC 480: JT 1995 (6) SC 679: 1995 (5) SCALE 469.

2. Perpetual Injunction – Law on – The perpetual injunction can be granted by the High Court in the second appeal; 1997 (1) AD (Cri) 165: 1997 (1) Cut LT 213: JT 1996 (12) SC 266: 1996 (9) SCALE 276: 1997 (1) SCC 749: 1997 (1) Supreme 210: 1997 (1) ICC 802.

3. Revenue Court – Powers of – In case the revenue court makes any interim order regarding possession, the same shall be given effect to; otherwise the interim arrangement under the receiver shall be continued till the disposal of the dispute in the revenue court; *Padam Ravinder Jeet Singh* v. *Jagat Singh*, 1988 (25) All Cri C 136: JT 1988 (1) SC 25.

4. Order of Injunction – Procedure for – Section 37 of the said Act makes it clear that temporary injunctions are to be regulated by the C.P.C. and not by the provisions of the Specific Relief Act, 1963. That it is well established that while passing an interim order of injunction under Order XXXIX, rules 1 and 2 C.P.C., the Court is required to consider (i) whether there is a *prima facie* case in favour of the plaintiff; (ii) whether the balance of convenience is in favour of passing the order of injunction; and (iii) whether the plaintiff will suffer irreparable injury if an order of injunction would not be passed as prayed for; *Best Sellers Retail (India) Pvt. Ltd.* v. *Aditya Birla Nuvo Ltd.*, AIR 2012 SC 2448: JT 2012 (5) SC 357: 2012 (5) SCALE 437: 2012 (6) SCC 792.

5. Temporary Injunction – A temporary Injunction is granted for a specific time or until the further order of the court. It can be granted at any stage of the suit. It is granted on the *prima facie* case of the plaintiff. A temporary injunction automatically ends with the finalization or finality of suit. Moreover, temporary injunctions are regulated by the Code of Civil Procedure, 1908 (5 of 1908). While exercising its discretion to grant a temporary injunction the courts first ascertains whether the plaintiff has a *prima facie* case, whether the balance of convenience is in favour of the plaintiff, and whether irreparable injury would be suffered by the plaintiff if temporary injunction is not granted to him; *Gujarat Botting Co.* v. *Coca Cola Co.*, AIR 1995 SC 2372 (2388): (1995) 5 SCC 545.

When the petitioner-original plaintiff had alleged, averred and proved that there was no other way to reach the petitioner's field and that he had been using the suit way in question regularly and uninterruptedly and continuously for a period of more than 20 years, the aspect of balance of convenience and irreparable loss and injury was automatically proved and it was not correct to state that all the three celebrated principles of granting an injunction had not been satisfied by the petitioner; *Ganesh Kesha Hanath* v. *Kantaben Lakhman Hanath*, AIR 2007 Guj 165 (170): 2007 AIHC 504 (NOC): 2008 (61) All Ind Cas 493: (2007) 2 Guj LR 1590.

Thus irreparable injury, comparable mischief and inconvenience are consideration for temporary injunction; *Dilkush Dessai* v. *Don Bosco Farmers Rehabilitation Society, Sulcorna*, AIR 1981 Goa 34.

It is well-established that while passing an interim order of injunction under Order XXXIX, rules 1 and 2 of the CPC, the court is required to consider three basic principles—(i) *prima facie* case, (ii) balance of convenience and inconvenience; and (iii) irreparable loss and injury. So where the respondent remained slept over its rights for more than 19 years, it will be inequitable on its prayer to restrain the owners of the property from dealing with the same, having particular regard to the fact that a large portion of land had already been conveyed to as may as 280 purchasers; *Kishorasinh Ratansinh Jadeja* v. *Maruti Corporation*, (2009) 11 SCC 229 (238-239).

6. Permanent Injunction – A permanent injunction is granted for perpetuity or for ever. A permanent injunction is granted at the hearing and upon the merits of the suit. A permanent injunction merges into the decree, when issued by the Court. A permanent injunction restring landlord from evicting him permanently cannot be granted by the court at the suit of the tenant because it is an embargo on the right of the landlord to enjoy the property; *Saraswathi Ammal* v. *Viveka Primary School*, AIR 2001 Mad 417 (418).

7. Plaintiff to Establish this Right – The question of granting an injunction only after the plaintiff first establishes his right. A person filing a suit for injunction can succeed only when he is in possession of the property. If he is not in possession of the property or adverse possession has not been confirmed an injunction cannot be issued in his favour; *Bruce* v. *Silva Raj*, (1987) Supp SCC 161.

But where the plaintiff is in possession of the property and the possession is not illegal and there is no evidence that the possession before the suit has been obtained by unfair means, injunction without declaration can be granted; *Kallappa Rama Londa* v. *Shivappa Nagappa Aparaj*, AIR 1995 Kant 238 (243): 1995 (2) Cur CC 386: (1995) 1 Kant LJ 351.

The plaintiff was out of possession of land in question. The O.P. who was initially made a party purchased the shares of the plaintiff in the property. The possession of flats constructed on the land was transferred to different purchasers. The plaintiff failed to establish *prima facie* case. The refusal of injunction in favour of plaintiff was not perverse or without jurisdiction, there being no balance of convenience and inconvenience with the plaintiff; *Chandana Karmakar* v. *Amit Kumar Ghosh*, AIR 2008 (NOC) 1398 (Cal).

8. Case – *Prima Facie* Wrong – While deciding interim injunction, the trial judge is under a duty to find out from documentary evidence on record whether any *prima facie* case is made out or not. There is no legal requirement to grant automatically *status quo* or interim protection on the mere filing of injunction application in a suit. In case of a suit *prima facie* appearing to be false and vexations, the interim injunction cannot be granted; *Vishnu Ramtaji Thakore* v. *Amit Pransukhlal Patel,* AIR 2007 Guj 133 (135-136): 2007 AIHC 419 (NOC): 2007 (4) AKAR (NOC) 547.

9. Suit to Disturb the Transaction – Where the agreement of sale in favour of plaintiff *prima facie* does not inspire confidence and the defendants claimed themselves the *bona fide* purchaser for value and there was a registered sale-deed in favour of the defendants and the original owner joined hands with the plaintiff to disturb the transaction, it was held that the interim injunction could not be granted; *Jayantibhai Mafatbhai Patel* v. *Dilipbhai Becharbhai Patel,* AIR 2007 Guj 136: 2007 AIHC 420 (NOC): 2007 (1) Cur CC 476: (2007) 1 Guj LR 79.

The suit was filed by the plaintiff-appellant for permanent injunction for a direction to the defendant-respondent from interfering with peaceful possession and enjoyment over suit schedule property. The Trial Court dismissed the suit but the first appellate court allowed the appeal. In the Second Appeal, the High Court dismissed the appeal, but directed the plaintiff to return the money along with interest, taken from the defendant under an agreement to sell the property to the defendant of which the defendant was in possession and the injunction would come into operation only after payment of the said amount by the appellant to the defendant. It was not the case of the plaintiff that there was an agreement for sale but of the defendant. The High Court, in the Second Appeal, held that there was a valid agreement found to be by the First Appellate Court and it was the duty of the plaintiff to return the amount. On the contrary, the First Appellate Court's holding was that the alleged existence of an agreement for sale was not established. The plaintiff had also denied the execution of any document. The review petition was also rejected by the High Court. Since there was complete non-application of mind and the High Court proceeded totally on untenable premises and recorded findings which were contrary to materials on record and findings recorded, the direction for refund of money was clearly indefensible and set aside; *Ramakrishna Rao (Dead) by LRs.* v. *Rai Murari,* AIR 2008 SC 1182 (1183): 2008 AIR SCW 1134: (2008) 3 SCC 175: (2008) 1 SCALE 558.

The co-sharers in exclusive possession cannot be prevented from raising any construction over the land possessed by them and if the property has been partitioned, the members in possession of their separate shares are entitled to raise construction; *Surjeet* v. *Raj Hans,* AIR 2008 (NOC) 553 P&H.

Where from the averments of the plaint and prayer clause of the same, it was clear that the respondent plaintiff was in possession of the shop but the attempt was made by the petitioner to dispossess but could not succeed and plaintiff was in possession on the date of filing of suit and it was prayed that permanent injunction be issued in their favour restraining the petitioner without following the due process of law either by himself or through his agents but during the pendency of the suit, the respondent was dispossessed forcibly from the shop, it was held that the civil suit for permanent injunction was maintainable; *Mohammad Salim* v. *Shahin Sah,* AIR 2006 Raj 200 (202): 2007 AIHC 1 (NOC): (2006) 1 Raj LR 371: (2006) 1 Raj LW 643.

10. Assignee in Actual Possession – Where the respondent was assignee of contractor and was in actual possession of mining area carrying on the activities of extracting, lifting and transporting of the ore with active knowledge/concurrence of the owner of mining property and had invested huge amount for carrying out work, he could not be considered as a trespasser and could not be evicted without due process of law and injunction against the respondent to restrain him from carrying out mining activities could not be granted; *Balaji Produce Co.* v. *Selvaraj,* AIR 2007 (NOC) 716 (Kant): 2007 (1) AIR Kant R 635.

11. Suit for not Determination on Merit – Where the suit is filed for mere injunction of enforcement of bank-guarantee and it is not laid for determination upon merits of terms and conditions of bank-guarantee and its validity, non-valuation of it on the basis of bank-guarantee will render it not maintainable; *South India Wire Ropes Ltd.* v. *Usha Martin Industries Ltd.,* AIR 2007 Kant 59 (70): 2007 AIHC 709: 2007 (3) ALJ (NOC) 421: 2007 (1) AIR Kant R 267.

12. Revocation of Power-of-Attorney – The developer filed a suit for specific performance of contract and also consequential prayer of permanent injunction restraining the owner of the property who had executed irrevocable power-of-attorney in favour of developer to enter into agreement with any third party for development of the suit property. The suit for specific performance by the developer was barred under the provisions contained in section 14(3)(c). It was held that the developer could not get a decree for permanent injunction simply on the basis of revocation of said power-of-attorney. If a person has granted irrevocable power-of-attorney in favour of another for acting as his agent and on the basis of such power-of-attorney, the agent incurs expenditure, the agent is entitled to get damages if the power-of-attorney is revoked without just reason; *Vipin Bhimani* v. *Sunanda Das,* AIR 2006 Cal 209 (213): 2006 AIHC 311 (NOC): (2006) 2 Cal HN 396: (2006) 2 Cal LT 157 (DB).

Where the execution of sale deed in favour of the plaintiff was contingent upon sale in favour of the defendant from the original owners within the stipulated period but the said event did not happen within that period, the parties would be released from the promise and the contract would become unenforceable in view of section 35 of the Contract Act, the injunction restraining the defendant to alienate the suit property pending suit could not be granted; *S.B. Sharma* v. *Suresh C. Sharma,* AIR 2008 (NOC) 1622 (P&H).

13. Consequential Relief – A suit for bare injunction without claiming consequential relief, even where title of the plaintiff is disputed, is maintainable; *Sivakumar* v. *M. Sengodan,* AIR 2009 (NOC) 265 (Mad).

In a suit for perpetual injunction of enforcement of bank-guarantee where no declaration is sought by the plaintiff regarding his compliance of obligations under the main contract, restraint order cannot be sought either against the principal-debtor or the guarantor bank because liability of the guarantor is co-extensive with principal-debtor. Such suit is also not maintainable in view of section 41(h) of the Specific Relief Act; *South India Wire Ropes Ltd.* v. *Usha Martin Industries Ltd.,* AIR 2007 Kant 59 (70): 2007 AIHC 709: 2007 (3) ALJ (NOC) 421: 2007 (1) AIR Kant R 267.

14. Suit for Injunction Simpliciter – Suit for injunction simpliciter without claiming possession is not maintainable; *Davender Lal Mehta* v. *Dharmender Mehta,* AIR 2009 Del 189 (191): 2009 (81) All Ind Cas 376: 2009 (160) DLT 22.

Suit for declaration simpliciter where plaintiff is already in possession of property is maintainable; *Lal Chand* v. *Kali Bai,* AIR 2004 P&H 173 (174): 2005 (1) Civ LJ 45: 2005 (2) Land LR 396: (2004) 2 Punj LR 312.

15. Insufficient Stamp-Agreement – In a suit for specific performance of contract, rejection application for grant of temporary injunction on the sole ground that the agreement sought to be enforced was on insufficient stamp-paper was held to be not proper as the provisions in the Stamp Act are applicable for the purpose of impounding agreement; *Sekh Nurmat Ali* v. *Dhanindra Kumar Sil,* AIR 2008 (NOC) 1617 Cal (DB).

16. Time Essence – In a suit for specific performance of contract, application was given for injunction restraining the defendant-vendor from alienating property. The defendant took the plea of breach of contract and time being essence of contract. Held—It was a matter which could be answered finally only after the parties were permitted to lead evidence; *Avdel Tools & Services* v. *Trust Fasteners Pvt. Ltd.,* AIR 2009 (NOC) 1054 Bom (DB).

17. Necessary Party to be Pleaded – Where the corporation was not impleaded as a party in the suit for alleged construction in deviation of sanctioned building plan so as to interfere with air and light of the plaintiff, the order of the court directing demolition of compound wall in excess of 4′ height and leaving set back space of 3′ between the compound and wall was set aside; *Rohini Bai* v. *B.L. Rajashri,* AIR 2005 Kant 115 (116): 2005 AIR Kant HCR 29: (2005) 1 Kant LJ 500.

Where the defendant purchased property adjacent to the property of plaintiff and the dispute was regarding a small price of land between the two properties and the sale-deed under which property was purchased by the defendant included property in dispute also and the Commissioners' report, also showed that the property was in possession and enjoyment of the defendant and the plaintiff failed to prove that the property after partition fell in his share, the refusal of injunction was proper; *K.S. Lakxmi* v. *Venkateswaran,* AIR 2004 (NOC) 438 (Mad): (2004) AIHC 2679.

In a suit for permanent injunction, the defendant resisted the suit on the ground that he was in possession of property in part-performance of contract as per agreement of sale entered into with the plaintiff. There was an unregistered agreement which was held to be admissible in evidence and further fact that the defendant did not reside in suit property would not itself prove possession of the plaintiff since it was a case of the defendant that the suit property had been leased. Injunction passed was set aside; *Velu* v. *Nagappa,* AIR 2008 (NOC) 530 (Kant): 2006 (2) AIR Kant R 9.

18. Plaintiff's Failure to Prove his Case – The plaintiff sought permanent injunction against the defendant from raising any structure on his plot of land on the ground that the plot of the defendant adjoining the plot of the plaintiff had been acquired to widen the road and the plaintiff had legal right of road frontage to his plot. The plaintiff and defendant both had purchased their plots from the unauthorised layouts. The plaintiff also failed to show any sanctioned layout or sanctioned building plan or that construction made by him on his plot was legal. Subsequently, the High Court quashed proceedings for acquisition of land for construction of road. The plaintiff also failed to show any town planning scheme in force for public road on the side of his plot. Held—The plaintiff was not entitled to relief; *Narendra Chirkutrao Balpande* v. *Atulkumar Pundalikrao Atkar,* AIR 2008 (NOC) 2148 (Bom) (Nag Bench).

19. Want of Prayer for Declaration of Title – A suit for injunction is not bad for want of prayer for declaration of title. The prayer for declaration of title can be added by the plaintiff. The aspect of title can be gone into question whether *prima facie* title buttresses plea of possession; *Ramasamy* v. *Kasinathan,* AIR 2009 (NOC) 2289 (Mad).

20. Prayer in Interlocutory Application – In a suit for permanent injunction to restrain the defendants from interfering with peaceful possession of the plaintiffs, the direction was sought for the deposit of Rs. 92,000 (as part of sale consideration) by the defendants. It was held that the prayer in interlocutory application being not in consonance with main relief sought for in suit, such direction by the Trial Court was in excess of its authority; *D.K. Sriramulu* v. *P. Malika,* AIR 2007 (NOC) 1317 (Mad).

When there were no specific pleadings that flour mill in the shop in question was definitely in possession of plaintiffs, interlocutory mandatory injunction to open lock of shop in question could not be granted; *Abdul Karim* v. *Abdul Sattar,* AIR 2008 (NOC) 2651 (Raj).

The grant of an interlocutory injunction during the pendency of legal proceedings is a matter requiring the exercise of discretion of the court. While exercising the discretion, the court applies the three tests—(i) whether the plaintiff has a *prima facie* case; (ii) whether the balance of convenience is in favour of the plaintiff; and (iii) whether the plaintiff would suffer an irreparable injury if the prayer for interlocutory injunction is disallowed; *Farinni* v. *Dream Food Products,* 2008 (2) CHN 689 (694).

21. Law Summarised by Supreme Court on Prohibitory Injunction – The Supreme Court in *Anathula Sudhakar* v. *P. Buchi Reddy*, AIR 2008 SC 2033 has summarised the law regarding prohibitory injunction relating to immovable property as follows:

(a) Where a cloud is raised over plaintiff's title and he does not have possession, a suit for declaration and possession, with or without a consequential injunction, is the remedy. Where the plaintiff's title is not in dispute or under a cloud, but he is out of possession, he has tc sue for possession with a consequential injunction. Where there is merely an interference with plaintiff's lawful possession or threat of dispossession, it is sufficient to sue for an injunction simpliciter.

(b) As a suit for injunction simpliciter is concerned only with possession, normally the issue of title will not be directly and substantially in issue. The prayer for injunction will be decided with reference to the finding on possession. But in cases where *de jure* possession has to be established on the basis of title to the property, as in the case of vacant sites, the issue of title may directly and substantially arise for consideration, as without a finding hereon, it will not be possible to decide the issue of possession.

(c) But a finding on title cannot be recorded in a suit for injunction, unless there are necessary pleadings and appropriate issue regarding title [either specific, or implied as noticed in *Annaimuthu Thevar* (supra)]. Where the averments regarding title are absent in a plaint and where there is no issue relating to title, the court will not investigate or examine or render a finding on a question of title, in a suit for injunction. Even where there are necessary pleadings and issue, if the matter involves complicated questions of fact and law relating to title, the court will relegate the parties to the remedy by way of comprehensive suit for declaration of title, instead of deciding the issue in a suit for mere injunction.

(d) Where there are necessary pleadings regarding title, and appropriate issue relating to title on which parties lead evidence, if the matter involved is simple and straight-forward, the court may decide upon the issue regarding title, even in a suit for injunction. But such cases, are the exception to the normal rule that question of title will not be decided in suits for injunction. But persons having clear title and possession suing for injunction, should not be driven to the costlier and more cumbersome remedy of a suit for declaration, merely because some meddler vexatiously or wrongfully makes a claim or tries to encroach upon his property. The court should use its discretion carefully to identify cases where it will enquire into title and cases where it will refer to plaintiff to a more comprehensive declaratory suit, depending upon the facts of the case.

CHAPTER VIII

PERPETUAL INJUNCTIONS

38. Perpetual injunction when granted.—(1) Subject to the other provisions contained in or referred to by this Chapter, a perpetual injunction may be granted to the plaintiff to prevent the breach of an obligation existing in his favour, whether expressly or by implication.

(2) When any such obligation arises from contract, the court shall be guided by the rules and provisions contained in Chapter II.

(3) When the defendant invades or threatens to invade the plaintiff's right to, or enjoyment of, property, the court may grant a perpetual injunction in the following cases, namely:—

(a) where the defendant is trustee of the property for the plaintiff;

(b) where there exists no standard for ascertaining the actual damage caused, or likely to be caused, by the invasion;

(c) where the invasion is such that compensation in money would not afford adequate relief;

(d) where the injunction is necessary to prevent a multiplicity of judicial proceedings.

SYNOPSIS

1. Auction Purchaser – Rights of
2. Cause of Action and Jurisdiction – Law on
3. Common Land and Common Channel – Law on
4. Court – Duties of
5. Courts – Powers of
6. Educational Institutions – Injunction Against
7. Grant of Injunction – Law on
8. High Court – Powers of
9. Injunction against Transfer Order – Law on
10. Negative Covenant – Law on
11. Permanent Injunction by a Coparcener against Father or Manager of Joint Hindu Family Property – Law on
12. Permissive Possession – Law on
13. Person in Physical Control or *De Facto* Possession – Law on
14. Plaintiff – Intention of
15. Possession – Significance of
16. Separate Fresh Suit – Law on
17. Settled Possession – Concept of
18. Settled Possession – Law on
19. Trade Practice – Law on
20. Trespasser – Injunction Against
21. True Owner – Injunction Against
22. Unilateral Possession – Law on
23. Will – Law on
24. Amendment of Decree – Law on
25. Injunction – Law on
26. Law on Possession – View on
27. Possession – Determination of
28. Writ Jurisdiction – Law on
29. 'Cause of Action' – Law on
30. Possession – *Explanation* for
31. Grant of Permanent Injunction Restraining Daughter-in-law to Interfere with the Peaceful Living of Father-in-law in his Self Acquired House

COMMENTS

1. Auction Purchaser – Rights of – The court auction cannot be of an interest which was more than what the previous owner had in the property. If attached to the property was a right which was given to Mr. X and his successors to use the said door and there was a prohibition on auction purchaser and his successors from interfering with this right, then it is with this restriction that the right of auction purchaser which could be sold. As a result of the purchase by the auction purchaser, he stepped into the shoes of the erstwhile owner and such a sale could not bring to an end a right in the property of use of the said door which existed in favour of the others; *Kanhaiya Lal* v. *Babu Ram*, AIR 2000 SC 350: 2000 (3) ICC 743: JT 2000 (1) SC 124: 2000 (1) Ori LR 188: 1999 (8) SCC 529.

2. Cause of Action and Jurisdiction – Law on – It is settled law that cause of action consists of bundle of facts which give cause to enforce the legal injury for redress in a court of law. The cause of action means, therefore, every fact, which if traversed, it would be necessary for the plaintiff to prove in order to support his right to a judgment of the court. In other words, it is a bundle of facts, which taken with the law applicable to them, gives the plaintiff a right to claim relief against the defendant. It must include some act done by the defendant since in the absence of such an act no cause of action would possibly accrue or would arise. In view of the admitted position that contract was executed in Bombay, *i.e.*, within the jurisdiction of the High court of Bombay, performance of the contract was also to be done within the jurisdiction of the Bombay High court; merely because bank guarantee was executed at Delhi and transmitted for performance to Bombay, it does not constitute a cause of action to give rise to the respondent to lay the suit on the original side of the Delhi High court. Since the bank guarantee was executed and liability was enforced from the bank at Delhi, the court cannot get jurisdiction; *South East Asia Shipping Company Limited* v. *Nav Bharat Enterprises Private Limited*, 1996 (3) AD (SC) 453: JT 1996 (3) SC 656: 1996 (3) SCALE 190: 1996 (3) SCC 443: 1996 (3) SCR 405.

3. Common Land and Common Channel – Law on – Plaintiff filed a suit for declaration of their right to take water from their exclusive well. In the absence of any specific pleading regarding prejudice or detriment to the defendants the plaintiffs have every right to use the common land and the common channel under Easements Act, 1882; *Ayyaswami Gounder* v. *Munnuswamy Gounder*, AIR 1984 SC 1789: 1984 (2) SCALE 437: 1984 (4) SCC 376: 1985 (1) SCR 808.

4. Court – Duties of – Court should satisfy the *prima facie* case put forward by the parties and should also be satisfied that the refusal of interim order will result in irreparable injury to the parties seeking interim order. Balance of convenience and other materials to be considered by the court in passing an interlocutory order should weigh with the Court. But, when an interim order is issued and the other party appears, unless circumstances compel, court should not go on passing interlocutory orders affecting the rights of parties without disposing of the main application. If both parties appear, court has to decide the question of transfer or withdrawal of the case and leaving the matter to be adjudicated according to law in the proper court; *Balan* v. *Sivagiri Sree Narayana Dharma Sanghom Trust*, AIR 2006 Ker 58: 2006 (4) CTC 273: 2006 (2) JCR 94: 2005 (4) Ker LT 865.

5. Courts – Powers of – It is well-known that a court will not issue directions over the compliance of which it has no control; *Suresh Jindal* v. *Rizsoli Corriere Della Sera Prodzioni TVSPA*, AIR 1991 SC 2092: JT 1992 (1) SC 33: 1991 (2) SCALE 124 [**Hon'ble Judges:** S. Ranganathan, M. Fathima Beevi, N.D. Ojha].

6. Educational Institutions – Injunction Against – In a matter touching either the discipline or the administration of the internal affairs of a University, Courts should be most reluctant to interfere. They should refuse to grant an injunction unless a fairly good *prima facie* case is made out for interference with the internal affairs of educational institutions; *Varanasaya Sanskrit Vishwavidyalaya* v. *Rajkishore Tripathi*, AIR 1977 SC 615: 1977 Lab IC 290: 1977 (1) SCC 279: 1977 (2) SCR 213.

7. Grant of Injunction – Law on – The Consolidation Authorities are not therefore, devoid of the jurisdiction to decide the title nor have power to consolidate and allot plots of the lands among the parties thereto. The abadi lands are not subject to the consolidation proceedings. Though the grant of injunction is discretionary, the same must be exercised on settled principles of law to advance the cause of justice. It is subject to correction by the appellate court; *Surya Nath Singh* v. *Khedu Singh*, 1994 (Supp 3) SCC 561.

8. High Court – Powers of – The High Court can fell into error in ignoring the concurrent findings of the Courts below and accepting the appeal on an issue which was neither raised nor argued before the Courts below; *Gitarani Paul* v. *Dibyendra Kundu*, AIR 1991 SC 395: JT 1990 (4) SC 702: 1990 (2) SCALE 1198.

9. Injunction against Transfer Order – Law on – In the absence of a term prohibiting transfer of the employee, *prima facie* the transfer order cannot be called in question. Non-compliance of the transfer order amounts to refusal to obey the orders passed by superiors for which the employer can reasonably be expected to take appropriate action against the concerned employee. Even though it is a case of private employment, the management proposed to hold an enquiry against the delinquent officer, that is, the plaintiff. In case of such insubordination, termination of service would be a possibility. Such a decision purely rests within the discretion of the management. An injunction against a transfer order or against holding a departmental enquiry in the facts would clearly amount to imposing an employee on an employer, or to enforcement of a contract of personal service, which is not permissible under the law. An employer cannot be forced to take an employee with whom relations have reached a point of complete loss of faith between the two; *Pearlite Liners Pvt. Ltd.* v. *Manorama Sirsi*, AIR 2004 SC 1373: JT 2004 (1) SC 58: 2004 (1) SCALE 280: 2004 (3) SCC 172.

10. Negative Covenant – Law on – The next question is where the injunction in the terms in which it is framed should have been granted. There is no doubt that the courts have a wide discretion to enforce by injunction a negative covenant; *Niranjan Shankar Golikari* v. *Century Spinning and Manufacturing Co. Ltd.*, AIR 1967 SC 1098: 1967 (69) BLR 535: 1967 (2) SCR 378.

11. Permanent Injunction by a Coparcener against Father or Manager of Joint Hindu Family Property – Law on – In a suit for permanent injunction under section 38 of the Specific Relief Act by a coparcener against the father or Manager of the Joint Hindu family property, an injunction cannot be granted as the coparcener has got equally efficacious remedy to get the sale set aside and recover possession of the property. Sub-section (h) of section 38 of Specific Relief Act bars the grant of such an injunction in the suit. The grant of such a relief will have the effect of preventing the father permanently from selling or transferring the suit property belonging to the joint Hindu undivided family even if there is a genuine legal necessity for such transfer. If such a suit for injunction is held maintainable the effect will be that whenever the father as *Karta* of the Joint Hindu coparcenary property will propose to sell such property owing to a *bona fide* legal necessity, any coparcener may come up with such a suit for permanent injunction and the father will not be able to sell the property for legal necessity until and unless that suit is decided; *Sunil Kumar* v. *Ram Parkash*, AIR 1988 SC 576: JT 1988 (1) SC 387: 1988 (1) SCALE 80: 1988 (2) SCC 77.

12. Permissive Possession – Law on – The proposition of law that permissive possession cannot be converted into an adverse possession unless it is proved that the person in possession asserted an adverse title to the property to the knowledge of the true owners for a period of 12 years or more, cannot be disputed; *Pt. Shamboo Nath Tikoo* v. *S. Gian Singh*, JT 1995 (5) SC 107: 1995 (4) SCALE 232: 1995 (Supp 3) SCC 266.

13. Person in Physical Control or *De Facto* Possession – Law on – Litigious and lawful possession are concepts of varying legal shades deriving their colour from the setting in which they emerge. Epithet used itself indicates the field in which they operate. The one pertains to dispute in which possession may be conterminous with physical or *de facto* control, only, whereas the domain of other is control with some legal basis. The former may be uncertain in character and may even be without any basis or interest but the latter is founded on some rule, sanction or excuse. Dictionarily 'litigious' means "disputed" or "disputable" or "marked by intention to quarrel", "inviting controversy"4, "relating to or marked by litigation", "that which is the subject of law suit". Lawful on the other hand is defined as, "legal, warranted or authorised by the law. "Jurisprudentially a person in physical control or *de facto* possession may have an interest but no right to continue whereas a person in possession, *de jure*, actually or constructively has the right to use, enjoy, destroy or alienate property. "Rights are interest protected or recognised by law. But every interest may not be so. Its violation may not be wrong. Many interests exist *de facto* and not *de jure;* they receive no recognition or protection from any rule or right"; *Krishna Kishore Firm* v. *Government of Andhra Pradesh*, AIR 1990 SC 2292: JT 1990 (4) SC 241: 1990 (2) SCALE 709: 1991 (1) SCC 184.

14. Plaintiff – Intention of – No one could have known the intention better than plaintiff who was a party to the contract; *Tarapore and Company, Madras* v. *V/o Tractoroexport Moscow*, AIR 1970 SC 891: 1970 (40) Comp Cas 447: 1969 (1) SCC 233: 1969 (2) SCR 920.

15. Possession – Significance of – In order to succeed in the suit, it is sufficient for the plaintiffs to show that the land was in possession of the plaintiffs; *Kishanlal Biharilal Maheshwari* v. *Ramrao Hanumant Rao Patil*, AIR 1981 SC 1183: 1981 (3) SCC 20: 1981 UJ 313.

16. Separate Fresh Suit – Law on — If the decree-holder makes any construction clubbing the other adjacent property, property which is part of the subject-matter in the earlier suit, a party cannot and should not, by his action, be permitted to drive the decree for another round of adjudication of the rights in the second suit to be settled afresh. In other words, giving such a liberty will amount to encouraging persons to take the law into their own hands and drive the decree-holder to another suit. It can never be facilitated to circumvent the law and relegate the party for tardy process of the civil action. What is needed is an opportunity to obey the injunction. Non-compliance is a continuing disobedience entailing penal consequences. A separate fresh suit is barred under section 49 of the C.P.C.; *Walter Louis Franklin* v. *George Singh*, 1996 (9) SCALE 252: 1997 (3) SCC 503: 1996 (8) Supreme 754: 1997 (1) UJ 260.

17. Settled Possession – Concept of – The person in peaceful possession is entitled to retain his possession and in order to protect such possession he may even use reasonable force to keep out a trespasser. A rightful owner who has been wrongfully dispossessed of land may retake possession if he can do so peacefully and without the use of unreasonable force. If the trespasser is in settled possession of the property belonging to the rightful owner, the rightful owner shall have to take recourse to law; he cannot take the law in his own hands and evict the trespasser or interfere with his possession. The law will come to the aid of a person in peaceful and settled possession by injunction even a rightful owner from using force or taking law in his own hands, and also by restoring him in possession even from the rightful owner (of course subject to the law of limitation), if the latter has dispossessed the prior possessor by use of force. In the absence of proof of better title, possession or prior peaceful settled possession is itself evidence of title. Law presumes the possession to go with the title unless rebutted. The owner of any property may prevent even by using reasonable force a trespasser from an attempted trespass, when it is in the process of being committed, or is of a flimsy character, or recurring, intermittent, stray or casual in nature or has just been committed, while the rightful owner did not have enough time to have recourse to law. It is the settled possession or effective possession of a person without title which would entitle him to protect his possession even as against the true owner. The concept of settled possession and the right of the possessor to protect his possession against the owner has come to be settled by a catena of decisions; *Rame Gowda* v. *M. Varadappa Naidu*, AIR 2004 SC 4609: 2003 (10) SCALE 950: 2004 (1) SCC 769.

18. Settled Possession – Law on – Law respects possession even if there is no title to support it. No one is permitted to take law in one's own hands and to dispossess the person in actual settled possession without due course of law. No person can be allowed to become a judge in his own case. The object of section 6 is to discourage people to act in self-help, however good their title may be. The licensee in possession of well over 15 years is in settled possession and is entitled to remain in possession and make use of the premises for the purpose for which it was demised until he is ejected in due course of law. The acquiescence of the landlord in this context would be to the initial unlawful entry into possession and continuation thereafter but not to the continuance in possession of the licensee after the expiry or termination of the licence. That was what this court appears to have meant in the previous decisions. Take for instance that when a licence was granted for a couple of years and after its expiry by efflux of time, or on termination, if the possession of the licensee, though unlawful and unjust is not protected, the aggressor or mighty would trample upon the rights of the weak and meek and denial of relief under section 6 would put a premium upon the aggression or treachery or tricks. No doubt long delay in disposal of cases due to docket explosion became a ruse to unscrupulous litigant to abuse the due course of law to protract litigation and remain in unjust or wrongful possession of the property. Landlord could be suitably compensated by award of damages. It cannot, by any stretch of imagination, be said that a person in settled possession, though unlawful, is not entitled to the protection under section 6 of the Act. Maintenance of law and order, and enthusing confidence in the efficacy of rule of law are condition precedent for orderly society. Therefore, giving primacy, legitimacy or legality to the conduct or acts of the landlord to take possession of the property in derogation of the due course of law would be deleterious to rule of law and a pat on high-handedness or self-help; *East India Hotels Limited* v. *Syndicate Bank*, 1992 (1) Bank Cas 1: 1993 (1) Comp LJ 1: JT 1991 (6) SC 112: 1991 (2) SCALE 638.

19. Trade Practice – Law on — By virtue of section 38(1)(h), the restrictive trade practice would not be treated as contrary to public interest if "the restrictive trade practice does not directly or indirectly restrict or discourage competition to any material degree in the relevant trade or industry and is not likely to do so; *Peico Electronics and Electricals Limited* v. *Union of India*, AIR 2004 SC 2669: 2004 (2) Comp LJ 193: 2004 (3) SCALE 175: 2004 (3) SCC 658.

20. Trespasser – Injunction Against – It is equally settled law that injunction would not be issued against the true owner. Even assuming that they had any possession, their possession is wholly unlawful possession of a trespasser and an injunction cannot be issued in favour of a trespasser or a person who gained unlawful possession, as against the owner. Pretext of dispute of identity of the land should not be an excuse to claim injunction against true owner; *Premji Ratansey Shah* v. *Union of India*, JT 1994 (6) SC 585: 1994 (3) SCALE 562: 1994 (5) SCC 547: AIR 1994 SC 376.

21. True Owner – Injunction Against — It is settled law by series of judgment of Apex Court that one of the accepted modes of taking possession of the acquired land is recording of a memorandum or *Panchanama* by the Land Acquisition Officer in the presence of witnesses signed by him/them and that would constitute taking possession of the land as it would be impossible to take physical possession of the acquired land. It is common knowledge that in some cases the owner/interested person may not co-operate in taking possession of the land. The injunction cannot be issued against the true owner, namely, the Housing Board in whom the land ultimately stood vested and then stood transferred to Municipal Corporation. A trespasser cannot claim injunction against the owner nor can the Court to issue the same; *T.N. Housing Board* v. *A. Viswam*, AIR 1996 SC 3377: JT 1996 (2) SC 549: 1996 (2) SCALE 418: 1996 (8) SCC 259.

22. Unilateral Possession – Law on – If no agreement existed between the parties, the question of unilateral possession does not arise; *Gail (I) Ltd.* v. *Bal Kishan Agarwal Glass Industries Ltd.*, JT 2008 (9) SC 57: 2008 (11) SCALE 223: 2008 (8) SCC 161: 2008 (7) SCJ 87.

23. Will – Law on – The mere suit for injunction cannot be converted into a suit for probation of a will where ever the will is to be proved. If the will is to be proved according to law, it has to be by way of probate in the Court having competency and jurisdiction according to the procedure provided under the Indian Succession Act. That procedure cannot be converted in a suit for mere injunction as a probate suit and direct the parties to adduce as the circumstances may warrant; *T. Venkata Narayana* v. *Venkata Subbamma*, AIR 1996 SC 1807: 1996 (3) SCALE 689: 1996 (4) SCC 457: 1996 (3) SCR 1042.

24. Amendment of Decree – Law on – Code of Civil Procedure recognises the inherent power of the court. It is not only confined to the amendment of the judgment or decree as envisaged under section 152 of the Code but also inherent power in general. The courts also have duty to see that the records are true and present the correct state of affair. There cannot, however, be any doubt whatsoever that the court cannot exercise the said jurisdiction so as to review its judgment. It cannot also exercise its jurisdiction when no mistake or slip occurred in the decree or order. This provision should, however, not be construed in a pedantic manner. A decree may, therefore, be corrected by the Court both in exercise of its power under section 152 as also under section 151 of the Code of Civil Procedure. Such a power of the court is well recognized; *Niyamat Ali Molla* v. *Sonargon Housing Co-operative Society Ltd.*, AIR 2008 SC 225: JT 2007 (12) SC 367: 2007 (12) SCALE 374: 2007 (13) SCC 421.

25. Injunction – Law on – As far as this country is concerned the general law relating to injunctions is contained in sections 36 to section 42 of the Specific Relief Act, 1963. Although these provisions may not limit the powers of this Court under article 131 nevertheless they provide valuable guidelines as to the nature of this form of equitable relief. An injunction may be permanent (perpetual) or temporary (Specific Relief Act, 1963, section 36). A permanent injunction is final and conclusive of the facts in the context of which the injunction is granted. A temporary injunction by contrast is granted on a *prima facie* view of the facts and, as the word 'temporary' itself indicates, is an interim order pending a final adjudication of the rights of the parties. This distinction is not to be confused with the distinction between a prohibitory or preventive injunction on the one hand and a mandatory injunction on the other. In the first case a party is prevented from doing a particular thing or continuing with a particular action. A mandatory injunction on the other hand commands an act to be done and is provided for under section 39 of the Specific Relief Act, 1963; *State of Haryana* v. *State of Punjab and Haryana*, JT 2004 (5) SC 72: 2004 (6) SCALE 75: 2004 (12) SCC 673.

26. Law on Possession – View on – Court should have dismissed the suit only on the ground that the Plaintiff had failed to prove that they were in possession of the disputed lands. Under section 38 of the Specific Relief Act, 1963 an injunction restraining disturbance of possession will not be granted in favour of the plaintiff who is not found to be in possession. In the case of a permanent injunction based on protection of possessory title in which the plaintiff alleges that he is in possession, and that his possession is being threatened by the defendant, the plaintiff is entitled to sue for mere injunction without adding a prayer for declaration of his rights; *Ramji Rai* v. *Jagdish Mallah*, AIR 2007 SC 900: 2006 (13) SCALE 328: 2007 (14) SCC 200.

27. Possession – Determination of – Courts should formulate a definite point relating to possession and then analyse the evidence on record with reference to that question and decide the case; *Thimmaiah* v. *Shabira*, AIR 2008 SC 1275: JT 2008 (2) SC 277: 2008 (2) SCALE 252: 2008 (4) SCC 182: 2008 (2) SCR 506.

28. Writ Jurisdiction – Law on – Writ jurisdiction of the high Court is very limited. Although the High Court has the requisite jurisdiction, the same must be exercised having regard to the scope and ambit of article 227 of the Constitution of India; *Yeshwant Sakhalkar* v. *Hirabat Kamat Mhamai*, AIR 2004 SCW 7449: 2004 (2) All CJ 1688: 2004 (9) SCALE 38: 2004 (6) SCC 71: 2004 (7) SLT 587.

29. 'Cause of Action' – Law on – The 'cause of action' under Order XXIII, rule 6(a) is this 'sole condition' which is required to be satisfied before the jurisdiction of Apex Court can be invoked under article 131. If the plaint does not *ex facie* show the fulfilment of that condition, it would not be maintainable. This follows from the language of article 131 itself. Therefore merely because the phrase "cause of action" has been used in Order XXIII, rule 6(a) does not mean that principles enunciated in the context of section 20 of the Code of Civil Procedure are imported. Order XXIII, rule 6(a) only gives effect to limitations implicit in article 131 itself. It follows that it does not violate article 131 or any other provision of the Constitution; *State of Haryana* v. *State of Punjab and Haryana*, JT 2004 (5) SC 72: 2004 (6) SCALE 75: 2004 (12) SCC 673.

30. Possession – Explanation for – Salmond on jurisprudence explains that the word "possession" is a word of 'open texture'. Its legal meaning has to be ascertained from the context. Such property is possessed by a person who has control over the same. This 'control' over the property means 'power to exclude all others'. The test then for determining whether a man is in possession of anything is whether he is in 'general control' of it - maybe that he is not in actual and physical possession or using the same; *Ashan Devi* v. *Phulwasi Devi*, 2004 (1) CTC 55: 2004 (1) DNJ 221: 2004 (1) PLJR 132 (SC).

31. Grant of Permanent Injunction Restraining Daughter-in-law to Interfere with the Peaceful Living of Father-in-law in his Self Acquired House – Where the issue relates to the grant of permanent injunction restraining daughter-in-law from interfering in peaceful living of father-in-law along with his wife, it was held that the house being self acquired house of father-in-law, the daughter-in-law has got no legal right to claim to live in the house, especially when her husband was not living in the said house. It was further held that father-in-law being old age retired person had every right to live peacefully during the remaining part of his life; *Smt. Chanchal Agrawal* v. *Jagdish Prasad Gupta*, AIR 2015 All 28.

39. Mandatory injunctions.—When, to prevent the breach of an obligation, it is necessary to compel the performance of certain acts which the court is capable of enforcing, the court may in its discretion grant an injunction to prevent the breach complained of, and also to compel performance of the requisite acts.

SYNOPSIS

1. Discretionary Relief
2. Mandatory Injunction when Granted
3. Encroachment by Defendant
4. Sections 36 to 39 of the Specific Relief Act and Section 9 of the Arbitration and Conciliation Act, 1996
5. Privity of Contract
6. Court not to Act Like an Allotting Authority
7. Award of Damages instead of Permanent Injunction
8. Compensation not Adequate Relief

COMMENTS

1. Discretionary Relief – Mandatory injunction can be issued only when claim of the plaintiff is very strong so as to show that the injunction has been rightly granted. The granting of a mandatory injunction depends on the discretion of the court. Since the granting injunction is discretionary the conduct of the plaintiff should be good and fair and he himself ought not to be guilty of some error or violation of law. Moreover, if he delays the seeking of the relief of injunction, the court may refuse to grant the relief of mandatory injunction; *Kothapalli Satyanarayana* v. *Koganti Ramaiyya*, AIR 1983 SC 452: (1984) 2 SCC 439.

Thus discretion to be exercised by the court under section 39 should not be exercised in favour of the person who comes with unclean fingers; *National Auto Impex* v. *Auto Cap (India) Pvt. Ltd.*, (2001) 93 DLT 74.

2. Mandatory Injunction when Granted – Where decree of mandatory and perpetual injunction in respect of obstructing the way of the plaintiff by the defendant becomes final, it becomes the obligation of the defendant to comply. It is not proper on the part of the High Court to set aside such a decree on the ground of non-compliance of section 32 of the Easement Act. After the decree of mandatory and perpetual injunction becomes final, it will not be justified to compel re-adjudication of the case; *Jai Dayal* v. *Krishanlal Garg*, AIR 1997 SC 3765 (3766-3767): (1966) 11 SCC 588.

When the question of granting injunction against public authorities, not only the three ingredients for the grant of injunction should be considered, but in addition to it, the public interest and/or public policy also is to be considered, otherwise, if the public interest or public policy is not considered, it will bring chaos to the society and cause distress to the public in general. The court cannot be used as an instrument to cause injury to the society or loss to the community, the requirement of the society, the demand of the society must be considered, the court must be coutious as its order affects a large chunk of the society. By exercising equitable jurisdiction to give benefit to somebody, larger interest of the society cannot be scarified. If injunction is granted affecting the right of the community in general, it will be a dangerous precedent and court should not easily succumb to such a prayer. This was held by Gauhati High Court in *State of Assam* v. *M.S. Associates*, AIR 1994 Gau 105 (108): 1994 (3) Civ LJ 281: 1994 (2) Gau LR 104.

This case was regarding the law on lotteries. On the basis of the complaints of the people that lotteries especially single digit daily lotteries were adversely affecting the people, the Government of Assam decided to ban lotteries. In respect of the management of lotteries, the State Government had entered into an agreement with the defendants on terminating the said agreement with the Government, the defendants challenged the said order through a suit and the Additional District Magistrate II granted injunction against the Government. In view of the above observation, the Gauhati High Court allowed the appeal of the State Government and set aside the order; *State of Assam* v. *M.S. Associates*, AIR 1994 Gau 105 (109): 1994 (3) Civ LJ 281: 1994 (2) Gau LR 104.

The High Court observed that the suit itself was for permanent injunction and in such suit temporary injunction must be granted in a cautious manner because by granting temporary injunction relief in the suit is being granted. That should not be adopted as a general and normal course; *State of Assam* v. *M.S. Associates*, AIR 1994 Gau 105: 1994 (3) Civ LJ 281: 1994 (2) Gau LR 104.

In a suit for mandatory injunction burden of proof lies on the plaintiff. If he fails to discharge the burden, he will not be entitled to the relief of injunction. He cannot get the relief of injunction on the ground that the defendant has failed to prove his case; *Sankar Kumar* v. *Mohanlal Sharma*, AIR 1998 Ori 117 (118).

Where the plaintiff files a suit for mandatory injunction for ejectment of a trespasser stating that he entered into an agreement to sell suit properly to the defendant, the defendant paid only part consideration and failed to pay the balance thereof but despite this the defendant and his men entered into the suit property and claimed in his written statement that he was permitted to occupy building after mediation talk since plaintiff was not willing to execute the sale deed but the facts of the case showed that the defendant was not keen in enforcing agreement as he had obtained the decree for the return of the amount paid, the suit for mandatory injunction in favour of the plaintiff would be sustainable and the fact that the plaintiff had not sought relief of recovery of possession was immaterial; *Paramu* v. *Balan*, AIR 2002 Ker 97: 2002 (1) ICC 938: 2001 (2) Ker LJ 603: 2001 (3) Ker LT 803.

In a suit by the plaintiff, partnership firm, for grant of mandatory injunction against a retired partner who claimed ownership over the suit property whereas the evidence on record showed that ownership of the suit property was that of the firm and the defendant partner instigated tenants of the property not to pay rents to the firm, the plaintiff would be entitled to the grant of permanent injunction; *Broadway Centre* v. *Gopaldas Bagri*, AIR 2002 Cal 78 (84): 2002 CWN 605: 2002 (2) CCC 472: 2002 (2) ICC 201.

It may be noted that the interim relief can be granted only in aid of as ancillary to the main relief. Thus the main relief cannot be granted, the temporary relief of the same nature also cannot be granted; *Cotton Corporation of India Ltd.* v. *United Industrial Bank Ltd.*, AIR 1983 SC 1272: (1983) 4 SCC 625.

Thus for example, in respect of an agreement for transmission of signals of television channels by defendant through cable network on monthly subscription basis, there was default by cable network in payment of monthly subscription and the agreed contract period was over and the defendant discontinued transmission, interim order directing defendant to transmit would not be justified because the balance of convenience does not lie in favour of cable network and that the respondent was the chronic defaulter the respondent was not entitled to any relief, interim order directing defendant to transmit signals of T.V. channels would be liable to set aside; *Star India Private Limited* v. *Indus Ind Media & Communications Limited*, AIR 2003 AP 473 (476).

But where the agreement between parties authorised respondent to sell property after dividing it into plots and realise profits and there was no material to show that understanding between the parties that the money was advanced to do business only by dividing the suit properties into plots and selling them and that selling otherwise would amount to breach of agreement, in such circumstances mandatory injunction cannot be issued directing respondent to divide the suit property into plots and then sell it; *S.K. Parthasarathy Naidu* v. *K. Rama Naidu*, AIR 2001 Mad 399 (404): (2001) 2 MLJ 779.

Similarly, where offer for acquisition of shares was to be terminated if no definite agreement was executed by specified date, application for mandatory injunction directing defendant company would be liable to be dismissed because it was merely in the realm of offer and in case of breach, if any, on the part of the defendant could be adequality compensated in terms of money; *Goyal MG Gases Ltd.* v. *Punjab Wireless Systems Ltd.*, AIR 2002 Del 159 (164-165): 2002 (2) Civ LJ 444: 2002 (1) Comp LJ 79: 2001 (94) DLT 697.

Where there was concurrent finding of fact that the plaintiff failed to prove his ownership, he would not be entitled to permanent and mandatory injunction; *Brij Mohan* v. *Parsha,* AIR 2009 (NOC) 2997 (P&H).

Where the suit-land was owned by the defendant and the plaintiff was in unauthorised possession of it, his suit for permanent injunction restraining the defendant from interfering into his tenancy right was not successful on his failure to show payment of rent or any agreement giving some legitimacy to his possession; *Chandsingh* v. *Gangadhar,* AIR 2007 (NOC) 41 (Utra).

While granting the injunction in respect of an alleged passage, the court has to consider whether it is or not within the suit property or whether there is any easementary right of way to the disputed suit land; *Kishorilal* v. *Madan Gopal,* (2005) 9 SCC 243 (245-246).

Where the defendants encroached on the rastha poramboke and constructed a hut, the plaintiffs being public apart from being the abutting owners of a public road had a right to free ingress and egress from each and every point, relief of mandatory injunction could not be negotiated on the ground of availability of some other pathway and the poverty of the defendants; *Thudimella Lakshminarayana* v. *Thummala Narasaiah Naidu,* AIR 2005 AP 357 (364).

3. Encroachment by Defendant – The plaintiff, an ex-service man was allotted land by the Government. A road was laid by the defendant in the land without any notice to the plaintiff or requisition of land. The plaintiff used to earn Rs. 500 p.a. by cultivation on the said land. There was no evidence produced by the defendant regarding the receipt of the compensation amount by the plaintiff. The order of the Trial Court granting mandatory injunction directing the defendant to restore suit land or pay compensation to the plaintiff was upheld; *M.V.K. Murthy* v. *State of Tamil Nadu,* AIR 2007 (NOC) 60 (Mad).

The plaintiff was lawful owner of the property. The defendants tried to erect their structures abutting to compound wall of plaintiff by encroaching pathway and they could not produce any title-deeds to prove that the property abutting to the compound wall of the plaintiff was their own property. They also failed to prove that the property was not public. The plaintiff was entitled to seek mandatory injunction; *Gujjala Hulagappa* v. *Lakshmidevanma,* AIR 2008 (NOC) 1882 (Kant).

Where the order passed by the Civil Court on an application filed under section 151 of the CPC, there was a clear direction that the plaintiff would pay outstanding dues and the defendant *i.e.,* the petitioner would continue to supply soft drinks but the plaintiff, *i.e.,* the opposite party did not pay anything towards outstanding dues, the petitioner was under no obligation to continue supply of soft drink. The fact that in summer public would like to consume soft drink would be no ground for passing mandatory order to supply soft drink; *Hindustan Coca-Cola Beverages Pvt. Ltd.* v. *Maa Sarala Distributor,* AIR 2005 Ori 167 (169): 2005 (2) CLR 95: 2005 (100) Cut LT 163.

Mere because in a suit for recovery of money, the court-fee is higher, the issue of mandatory injunction is not proper. In the instant case, the mandatory injunction was issued for payment of Rs. 47,185 for which court fee was only Rs. 500 as maximum, was held to be not permissible and unheard in the field of law. If it was permitted, it would give bad precedent to encourage the litigants to by-pass the provisions of the Court-Fees Act, 1870 and only if caught they would deposit the court-fee. The Uttaranchal High Court, therefore, did not permit the decree-holder on his argument to do substantial justice, to deposit the court-fee instead of decreeing the suit on technical ground; *Chief Engineer, Central Zone Telecommunication Civil, Lucknow* v. *Dayal Construction Co.,* AIR 2005 Utr 34 (35).

The plaintiff society had given possession of certain accommodation to the defendant during his employment with the plaintiff. After his retirement, he failed to vacate his accommodation which was given to him as part of his employment. He also trespassed upon a hall. It was held that the defendant after his retirement was not justified to remain in possession. His possession was that of a trespasser and the plaintiff would be entitled to mandatory injunction and the defendant would be liable to pay damages for enjoying the property; *Ram Shankar Shukla (D) by LRs.* v. *Ganesh Sewa Ashram Sanstha,* AIR 2006 All 336: 2006 AIHC 3738: 2006 (5) ALJ 812: 2006 (64) All LR 829: 2006 (3) All WC 3050.

4. Sections 36 to 39 of the Specific Relief Act and Section 9 of the Arbitration and Conciliation Act, 1996 – The grant of relief by way of injunction is general governed by the Specific Relief Act and therefore under section 9 of the Arbitration and Conciliation Act, 1996, the provision of approaching the court for an interim injunction, the relevant provisions of the Specific Relief Act cannot be kept out of consideration. The grant of interim injunction under section 9 has necessarily to be based on the principles governing its grant emanating out of the relevant provisions of the Specific Relief Act and the law bearing on the subject. Section 9 cannot keep out the substantive law relating to interim reliefs; *Adhunik Steels Ltd.* v. *Orissa Manganese & Minerals Pvt. Ltd.,* (2007) 7 SCC 125 (135, 136): AIR 2007 SC 2563: 2007 AIR SCW 4558: (2007) 9 SCALE 126.

Where subsequent purchasers failed to prove that they were *bona fide* purchasers for consideration, they were not entitled to injunction; *Tejbir Singh* v. *Darshan Kumar,* AIR 2009 (NOC) 2993 (P&H).

Where a well jointly belonged to the plaintiff and the defendant both and the defendant deepened the well on one side where the motor pump of the defendant was installed and heaps of muds and stones were left in another side causing obstruction of flow of water in that side where the plaintiff's motor pump was installed, the plaintiff was entitled to mandatory injunction for the removal of the debris; *Lakshmana Konar* v. *Namalwar Konar (deceased by LRs),* AIR 2004 Mad 264 (267): 2004 (2) Civ LJ 838: 2004 (2) Mad LJ 172.

5. Privity of Contract – The plaintiff purchased part of the property belonging to the defendant. The defendant agreed to give his tenant a piece of big land in lieu of right of way to the land sold as there was no other approach way to the land sold and the defendant gifted his piece of land to the tenant for this purpose. Denial of right of way and grant of mandatory injunction on the ground that there was no privity of contract between him and tenant was improper. The contract was for the benefit of third party and easement of necessity occurred; *Prithvi Singh* v. *Banshi Lal,* AIR 2004 Raj 100 (105-106): 2004 (2) Raj LR 679: 2004 (2) Raj LW 1183: 2004 (2) WLC 484.

6. Court not to Act Like an Allotting Authority – Where the property belonged to Calcutta Port Trust and they obtained decree and possession of property after the lessee had gone into liquidation, the grant of mandatory injunction directing the trust to hand-over possession of land to another company which had no connection with the original lessee was without any jurisdiction as the court could not act like an allotting authority; *Board of Trustee of the Port of Calcutta* v. *Pearl Transport Co. Ltd.,* AIR 2004 Cal 122 (125) (DB).

7. Award of Damages instead of Permanent Injunction – The suit for mandatory injunction was filed by the plaintiffs on the ground that the plaintiffs' area had been encroached upon by the defendants by dismantling the wall of the plaintiffs and raising construction on the space on which the wall of the plaintiffs was erected. A decree of perpetual injunction was also prayed to be granted against the defendants for checking them in future to raise any construction on the suit property. The plaintiffs did not file documents of title showing their ownership of that area but it was proved by the evidence of defendants' own witnesses and the pleadings of the defendants in their written statement that there was a wall of the plaintiffs and that was dismantled by the defendants. The total length of encroached area was 14.75 metres. Held—The plaintiffs are entitled for the damages under section 40 of the Act. Because, if the decree under section 39 of the Act is allowed to be executed, it would cause havoc and great loss to the defendants as their entire house would be damaged. On balance of convenience to both the sides, the plaintiffs could be compensated by awarding suitable damages to them; *Gyanchand* v. *Mohanlal,* AIR 2007 MP 258 (260-261): 2007 AIHC 594 (NOC).

A party to a suit during its pendency cannot dispossess the other co-sharer. If a party takes recourse to any contrivance to dispossess another, during pendency of the suit either in violation of the order of injunction or otherwise, the court indisputably will have jurisdiction to restore the parties back to the same position; *Tanusree Basu* v. *Ishani Prasad Basu,* (2008) 4 SCC 791 (798): AIR 2008 SC 1909: 2008 AIR SCW 2152: 2008 (4) SRJ 154: (2008) 4 SCALE 71.

8. Compensation not Adequate Relief – Mandatory injunction can be granted when the court is satisfied that in the facts and circumstances of the case it would not be an adequate relief. For example, in *T. Prasad* v. *P.D. Punnoose,* AIR 1995 Ker 157 (158-159): 1994 (1) Ker LJ 693 the plaintiff filed the suit for injunction against the defendant for restraining him form destroying the boundaries of his property. The evidence showed that by trespass the defendant had, in disregard of the property rights of the plaintiff, not only destroyed the boundary wall of the land of the plaintiff but also that the trespass was continuing. The trial court granted temporary prohibitory injunction. The present appeal was preferred against the said order. The High Court dismissed the appeal and held that in such cases granting of compensation would not be an adequate relief and hence the granting of injunction was valid and correct.

The exercise of the power to grant mandatory injunction must be attended with the greatest possible caution and is strictly confined to cases where the remedy of damage is inadequate for the purposes of justice and the restoring of things to their former condition is the only remedy which will meet the requirements of the case. The court will not interfere except in cases where there are extreme serious damages caused which cannot be compensated. These observations were made by the Kerala High Court in *C. Kunhammad* v. *C.H. Ahmad Haji,* AIR 2001 Ker 101 (103): (2000) 2 Ker LJ 915.

40. Damages in lieu of, or in addition to, injunction.—(1) The plaintiff in a suit for perpetual injunction under section 38, or mandatory injunction under section 39, may claim damages either in addition to, or in substitution for, such injunction and the court may, if it thinks fit, award such damages.

(2) No relief for damages shall be granted under this section unless the plaintiff has claimed such relief in his plaint:

Provided that where no such damages have been claimed in the plaint, the court shall, at any stage of the proceedings, allow the plaintiff to amend the plaint on such terms as may be just for including such claim.

(3) The dismissal of a suit to prevent the breach of an obligation existing in favour of the plaintiff shall bar his right to sue for damages for such breach.

SYNOPSIS

1. Damages in Lieu of Injunction
2. Damages in Addition to Injunction
3. Relief of Damages Only when Claimed
4. Amendment of Plaint
5. Dismissal of a Suit a Bar for Subsequent Suit

COMMENTS

1. Damages in Lieu of Injunction – Sub-section (1) of section 40 makes it clear that in a suit for perpetual and mandatory injunction, the plaintiff is entitled to claim damages in addition to perpetual or mandatory injunction. For example, in *K.B. Machaish* v. *Ajjittira S. Mandanna,* AIR 1997 Kant 194: 1997 (1) Kant LJ 438: 1997 (2) LJR 516 the plaintiff sued the defendant for declaration and injunction stating that the plaintiff is entitled to carry on the management of Sri Rama Touring Talkies upto April, 1979 and the defendant be restrained from interfering with his possession and management. Alternatively he claimed compensation of Rs. 10,000. After the suit was filed the defendant got the licence of Touring Talkies cancelled. In these circumstances the trial court instead of granting a decree of declaration and injunction granted a decree of the payment of Rs. 10,000 in favour of the plaintiff. The appeal of the defendant against the said order was dismissed by the High Court by the Civil Judge. In appeal against the said order of the Civil Judge, the High Court affirmed the decision of the Appellate Court and dismissed the appeal; *K.B. Machaish* v. *Ajjittira S. Mandanna,* AIR 1997 Kant 194 (195): 1997 (1) Kant LJ 438: 1997 (2) LJR 516.

It is settled law that if nuisance is a public one then the plaintiff must prove damages. Whereas if it is a private nuisance, although it is said that it should be proved, the will often presume it. However, probably if substantial will ensue, it must be shown by the plaintiff. The character of the acts themselves which produce the damage and the circumstances in which these acts are done must regulate the degree certainty and particularly with which the damage ought to be proved. As much certainty and particularity must be insisted upon the proof of damages as is reasonable having regard to the circumstances and to the nature of acts themselves by which damage is done. To insist upon loss would be to release old and intelligence principle. To insist upon more would be vainest pledantry. This was held by the Karnataka High Court in *S. Narayana Rao* v. *R. Narasinga Rao (deceased by LRs,* AIR 1995 Kant 11 (17): 1995 (1) CCC 270: 1994 (2) Cur CC 634: 1994 (2) Kant LJ 650.

In this case, a suit for permanent injunction restraining the defendants from obstructing free flow of light and air enjoyed by the plaintiff was filed by the plaintiff. There was open space belonging to Municipality but servient owners neither resisted plaintiff's claim for light and air nor were party to the suit. There was concurrent findings of facts in favour of the plaintiff after appraisal of evidence and absence of impleading Municipality would not be fatal to suit. Applying the above principles, the Karnataka High Court held that in the instant case the injury is one actionable *per se* and as such damage could be presumed. The High Court, therefore, dismissed the appeal; *S. Narayana Rao* v. *R. Narasinga Rao (deceased by LRs),* AIR 1995 Kant 11 (17-18): 1995 (1) CCC 270: 1994 (2) Cur CC 634: 1994 (2) Kant LJ 650.

The contract of personal service cannot be enforced even if the order of termination of employee in declared to be arbitrary, illegal and *null* and *void*. The employee cannot be reinstated nor he can be declared deemed to be in service so as to impose him on the unwilling employer. The natural consequence of declaration of termination as *null* and *void* would be for damages; *Goetze (India) Ltd., Bangalore* v. *H.R. Thimmnappa Gowda,* 2007 (4) Kant LJ 654 (672) (DB).

The relief of interlocutory injunction is granted to mitigate the risk or injustice to the petitioner during the period before the uncertainty can be resolved. The object of interlocutory injunction is to protect the plaintiff against injury by violation of his right for which he could not be adequately compensated in damages recoverable in the action if the uncertainty is resolved in his favour in the trial. The need for such protection has, however, to be weighed against the corresponding need to the defendant to be protected against injury resulting from his having been prevented from exercising his own legal rights or which he could not be adequately compensated; *Gujarat Bottling Co. Ltd.* v. *Coca Cola Company,* AIR 1995 SC 2372: 1995 AIR SCW 3485: 1997 SCC (Cri) 651: JT 1995 (6) SC 3.

2. Damages in Addition to Injunction – The plaintiff in a suit for perpetual injunction or mandatory injunction may claim damages in addition to such injunction and the court may award damages. For example, where the proposed building as per plans will obstruct the light enjoyed by a neighbour, the court may award damages because the construction of the building has yet not commenced; *Leeds Industrial Co-operative Society* v. *Slack,* 1924 AC 851.

3. Relief of Damages Only when Claimed – The grant of relief of damages is not automatic. The plaintiff will get damages in lieu of, or in addition to, injunction only when he has claimed it in the plaint. But proviso to sub-section (2) makes it clear that where no such damages have been claimed in the plaint, the court shall, at any stage of the proceedings, allow the plaintiff to amend the plaint on such terms including such claim. The word 'shall' makes it clear that if the plaintiff makes a prayer for amendment of the plaint so as to claim such damages, the court cannot refuse the prayer on the ground of delay, *mala fide* or being time barred and has to allow it; *Jagdish* v. *Har Sarup,* AIR 1978 Del 233: 80 PLR (D) 192.

Relief for damages by way of amendment can be sought at any stage by virtue of provisions of section 40(2). There is no conflict between section 40 and Order VI, rule 17 of the CPC. Right under the Specific Relief Act cannot be subjugated to generality of the Code of Civil Procedure; *Sunil* v. *Sudha Devi,* AIR 2007 (NOC) 2341 (HP).

4. Amendment of Plaint – Where the plaintiff sought the relief of injunction and damages and a claim of tentative damages of Rs. 1,00,000 but in relief para, he stated "any other sum that may be ascertained", clearly indicated the mind of the plaintiff to claim more damages in future and thereafter the plaintiff specified the damages of Rs. 50,00,000 and was ready to pay court-fee on the same, no new case was introduced and therefore it was held that the amendment must be permitted by the court and the point of limitation was immaterial; *Hi Sheet Industries* v. *Litelon Ltd.,* AIR 2007 Mad 78 (89, 91): 2007 AIHC 1281: 2007 (1) Mad LJ 320: 2007 (1) Mad LW 32 (FB).

5. Dismissal of a Suit a Bar for Subsequent Suit – Where the plaintiff's suit for perpetual and mandatory injunction against the order of termination of services was dismissed, the subsequent suit for damages for breach of contract was hit by the provisions Order II, rule 2 of the CPC as well as constructive *res judicata; Sandeep Batra* v. *G.E. Capital Services India,* AIR 2008 (NOC) 896 (Del).

41. Injunction when refused.—An injunction cannot be granted—

(a) to restrain any person from prosecuting a judicial proceeding pending at the institution of the suit in which the injunction is sought, unless such restraint is necessary to prevent a multiplicity of proceedings;

(b) to restrain any person from instituting or prosecuting any proceeding in a court not subordinate to that from which the injunction is sought;

(c) to restrain any person from applying to any legislative body;

(d) to restrain any person from instituting or prosecuting any proceeding in a criminal matter;

(e) to prevent the breach of a contract the performance of which would not be specifically enforced;

(f) to prevent, on the ground of nuisance, an act of which it is not reasonably clear that it will be a nuisance;

(g) to prevent a continuing breach in which the plaintiff has acquiesced;

(h) when equally efficacious relief can certainly be obtained by any other usual mode of proceeding except in case of breach of trust;

(i) when the conduct of the plaintiff or his agents has been such as to disentitle him to the assistance of the court;

(j) when the plaintiff has no personal interest in the matter.

SYNOPSIS

COMMENTS

1. Contract of Employment – Law on – A contract of employment cannot ordinarily be enforced by or against an employer. The remedy is to sue for damages. The grant of specific performance is purely discretionary and must be refused when not warranted by the ends of justice. Such relief can be granted only on sound legal principles. In the absence of any statutory requirement, Courts do not ordinarily force an employer to recruit or retain in service an employee not required by the employer. There are, of course, certain exceptions to this rule, such as in the case of a public servant dismissed from service in contravention of article 311 of the Constitution; reinstatement of a dismissed worker under the Industrial Law; statutory body acting in breach of statutory obligations, and the like; *Nandganj Sihori Sugar Co. Ltd., Rae Bareli* v. *Badri Nath Dixit*, AIR 1991 SC 1525: JT 1991 (2) SC 338: 1991 (1) SCALE 794: 1991 (3) SCC 54: 1991 (2) SCR 468 **[Hon'ble Judges:** K. Jagannatha Shetty, T. Kochu Thommen, Yogeshwar Dayal] [*S.R. Tewari* v. *District Board, Agra*, AIR 1964 SC 1680; *Uttar Pradesh State Warehousing Corporation* v. *C.K. Tyagi*, (1970) 2 SCR 250: AIR 1970 SC 1244; *Executive Committee of Vaish Degree College, Shamli* v. *Lakshmi Narain*, (1976) 2 SCR 1006: AIR 1976 SC 888; see *Halsbury's Laws of England*, 4th Edn., Vol. 44, paras 405 to 420].

2. Equally Efficacious Relief – Law on – Section 41(h) of the Specific Relief Act, 1963, which lays down that an injunction, which is a discretionary equitable relief, cannot be granted when an equally efficacious relief is obtainable in any other usual mode or proceeding except in cases of breach of trust; *Municipal Corporation of Delhi* v. *Suresh Chandra Jaipuria*, AIR 1976 SC 2621: 1976 (4) SCC 719: 1977 (2) SCR 10.

3. Injunction Restraining *Karta* – Law on – The provisions of section 38 have to be read along with section 41. Section 41 provides that an injunction cannot be granted in the cases falling under clauses (a) to (j). Clause (h) thereunder provides that an injunction cannot be granted when a party could obtain an efficacious relief by any other usual mode of proceeding (except in case of breach of trust). The coparcener has adequate remedy to impeach the alienation made by the *karta*. He cannot, therefore, move the Court for an injunction restraining the *karta* from alienating the coparcenary property; *Sunil Kumar* v. *Ram Parkash*, AIR 1988 SC 576: JT 1988 (1) SC 387: 1988 (1) SCALE 80: 1988 (2) SCC 77.

4. Perpetual Injunction – Law on – Part III of the Act bears the heading 'Preventive Relief' and fasciculus of sections therein included provide for injunctions generally. Section 36 provides that preventive relief is granted at the discretion of the Court by injunction, temporary or perpetual. Section 37 specifies the nature, and character of temporary and perpetual injunctions. Temporary injunctions are such as are to continue until a specified time, or until the further order of the Court, and they may be granted at any stage of a suit, and are regulated by the Code of Civil Procedure, 1908. Permanent injunctions can only be granted by the decree made at the hearing and upon merits of the suit and thereby, defendant in the suit is perpetually enjoined from assertion of a right or from commission of an act, which would be contrary to the rights of the plaintiffs. Section 38 sets out situations in which the Court can grant a perpetual injunction to the plaintiff to prevent the breach of an obligation existing in its favour, whether expressly or by implication. Section 38 is thus an enabling section which confers power on the Court to grant perpetual injunction in situations and circumstances therein enumerated. Section 41 caters to the opposite situation. It provides that an injunction cannot be granted in the situation and circumstances therein set out; *Cotton Corporation of India Limited* v. *United Industrial Bank Limited,* AIR 1983 SC 1272: 1984 (55) Comp Cas 423: 1983 (2) SCALE 324: 1983 (4) SCC 625.

5. Temporary Injunction during Pendency of Suit – Law on – The grant of temporary injunction during the pendency of the suit is governed primarily by the provisions of Order XXXIX, rules 1 and 2, Civil P.C. Rule 1 provides that where in any suit it is proved by facts or otherwise that any property in dispute is in danger of being wasted, damaged or alienated or that the defendant has threatened or intends to remove or dispose of his property with a view to defraud the creditors or that the defendant has threatened to dispossess the plaintiff or otherwise cause injury to him in relation to the property in dispute, the court may by order grant temporary injunction restraining such act. Rule 2 provides that in any suit for a permanent injunction the plaintiff may apply to the Court for a temporary injunction to restrain the defendant from committing a breach of contract or injury complained of arising our of a contract or relating to any property or right. A bare perusal of these two rules would show that no limitation as envisaged in the various clauses of section 41 of the Act has been placed on the discretion of the court in the matter of grant of temporary injunction; *Ram Gopal Banarsi Dass* v. *Satish Kumar,* AIR 1986 P&H 52: 1985 (2) Cur LJ 630: 1986 (1) RCR (Rent) 236: 1985 RRR 25 **[Hon'ble Judges:** Pram Chand Jain, S.P. Goyal, I.S. Tiwana].

6. Injunction – Law on – The Legislature manifestly expressed its mind by enacting section 41(b) in such clear and unambiguous language that an injunction cannot be granted to restrain any person, the language takes care of injunction acting *in personam,* from instituting or prosecuting any proceeding in a court not subordinate to that from which injunction is sought. Section 41(b) denies to the court the jurisdiction to grant an injunction restraining any person from instituting or prosecuting any proceeding in a court which is not subordinate to the court from which the injunction is sought. In other words, the court can still grant an injunction restraining a person from instituting or prosecuting any proceeding in a court which is subordinate to the court from which the injunction is sought. As a necessary corollary, it would follow that the court is precluded from granting an injunction restraining any person from instituting or prosecuting any proceeding in a court which is not subordinate to it. This change in language deliberately adopted by the Legislature after taking note of judicial vacillation has to be given full effect; *Export Credit Guarantee Corporation of India Ltd.* v. *Annamma Philips,* AIR 2011 Bom 18: 2010 (6) All MR 50: 2010 (5) BCR 823: 2010 (112) BLR 4118: 2010 (5) Mh LJ 659.

7. Clause (a): Restrain Prosecuting Pending Judicial Proceedings – An injunction cannot be granted to restrain any person from prosecuting a judicial proceeding pending at the institution of the suit in which the injunction is sought, unless such restraint is necessary to prevent a multiplicity of proceedings. This provision applies where the suit has already been filed and is pending and not one which is threatened; *Maliaperumal Iyengar* v. *Nachiapppa Chetty,* (1895) 5 Mad LJ 294.

But this provision will not apply where the restraint is necessary to prevent a multiplicity of proceedings; *Radha Madhab Jiu Thakur* v. *Rajendra Prasad Bose*, AIR 1933 Pat 250.

Where the District Board started prosecution against the plaintiff for non-compliance of its order to stop working his klin, injunction to restrain the board from prosecuting cannot be granted; *Gauri Shanker* v. *District Board of Farrukhabad*, AIR 1947 All 81: 1946 ALJ 361: 231 IC 78.

8. Balance of Convenience – For an injunction to enforce negative covenant in contract, balance of convenience is material; *Farinni* v. *Dream Food Products*, AIR 2008 (NOC) 1399 (Cal).

9. Clause (b): Proceeding in a Court not Subordinate – Injunction cannot be granted to restrain any person from instituting or prosecuting any proceeding in a court not subordinate to that form which the injunction is sought. As compared to clause (a), clause (b) applies to proceedings pending as well as those which have been threatened. According to section 41(b) an injunction cannot be granted to restrain any person from instituting or prosecuting any proceeding in a court not subordinate to that from which the injunction is sought, but this provision must not be stretched to the extent of rendering a court helpless in preventing abuses of its own proceedings. Thus the interdict contained in section 41(b) is not applicable when injunction is to be issued in respect of the proceedings pending in the same court; *Santha w/o Sahadevan* v. *Vasu s/o Chami, Muthalamada*, AIR 1996 Ker 188 (190-191): 1995 (2) CCC 352: ILR (1995) 3 Ker 475: 1995 (2) Ker LT 235.

The expression 'injunction' in section 41(b) is not qualified by an adjective and it therefore it would comprehend both interim and perpetual injunction. An interim relief can be granted only in aid of, and as ancillary to the main relief, which may be available to the party on final determination of his rights in a suit or proceedings; *Cotton Corporation of India Ltd.* v. *United Industrial Bank Ltd.*, AIR 1983 SC 1272: (1983) 4 SCC 625.

It has been held the Debts Recovery Tribunal is not court within the scope of section 41(b) of Specific Relief Act, 1963. This Tribunal is not subordinate to the High Court. Subordination to Article 226 or Article 227 does not make it a court within the meaning section 41(b); *State Bank of India* v. *Madhumita Construction (Pvt.) Ltd.*, AIR 2003 Cal 7 (18-19): (2003) 1 CHN 222.

Section 41 of the Specific Relief Act does not operate on the jurisdiction of the court but it relates to the exercise of that jurisdiction. Grant of relief of injunction is discretion of the court and section 41 lays down the procedure of grant of injunction. Occasion for a prospective purchaser in possession to institute a suit for perpetual injunction for protecting his possession may arise because of equity in his favour even when the cause of action for instituting suit for specific performance has not arisen nor where it is barred by the law of limitation; *Sadashiv Chander Bhamgare* v. *Eknath Pandharinath Nangude*, AIR 2004 Bom 378 (386-387): 2004 (4) Bom CR 564: 2004 (4) Bom LR 217: 2004 (3) Mah LJ 1131 (FB).

Applicability of section 41(b) is relevant before the Trial Court when any relief is claimed in a suit for injunction for restraining any person from executing or prosecuting any proceeding in a court not subordinate to the court from which the injunction is sought; *Jitendra Kumar* v. *Krishna Dutt Sharma*, AIR 2006 All 257 (258): 2006 (4) ALJ 231: 2006 (63) All LR 721: 2006 (4) All WC 3379.

The plaintiff has to show that by refusal of injunction more prejudice will be caused to him than the prejudice caused to the defendant by grant of injunction.

Any person is entitled to adopt proceedings in a court or before a tribunal or authority to enforce his rights or seek redressal of his grievances. An order to restrain him from instituting or prosecuting legal proceedings already instituted is an exception to this rule. Curtailment of the right is a serious matter. The *onus* must necessarily be on the party seeking reliefs under section 41 (b) restraining a party from instituting/prosecuting legal remedies. The plaintiff must establish that the grant of injunction under section 41(b) will cause less prejudice to the defendant than the prejudice that may be caused to the plaintiff by the refusal of such an injunction; *Export Credit Guarantee Corporation of India Ltd.* v. *Annamma Phillip,* AIR 2007 (NOC) 112 (Bom): 2006 (6) AIR Bom R 656.

10. Clause (d): Instituting or Prosecuting a Proceeding in a Criminal Matter – An injunction cannot be granted to restrain any person from instituting or prosecuting any proceeding in a criminal matter. For example, where the District Board directed the plaintiff not to work its kiln and for non-compliance of its order started criminal proceedings, such criminal proceeding cannot be restrained by an injunction at the instance of the plaintiff; *Gauri Shanker* v. *District Board of Farrukhabad,* AIR 1947 All 81: 1946 ALJ 361: 231 IC 78.

During pendency of proceeding under section 138 of the Negotiable Instruments Act, the accused instituted civil suit against the complainant for return of blank cheques allegedly deposited with complainant. Since both the proceedings under section 138 of Negotiable Instruments Act and civil suit were based on independent cause of action, it was held that the complaint under section 138 was not liable to be stayed; *Anuj Trading Co.* v. *Electrolux Kelvinator Ltd.,* AIR 2007 (NOC) 1681 (Del): (2007) 2 Bank Cas 107.

The plaintiff did not deny that the cheques issued by it to the defendant if presented were likely to be dishonoured, the court could not grant a temporary injunction as the suit would be *prima facie* barred in terms of section 41(d) of the NI Act; *Ratna Commercial Enterprises Ltd.* v. *Vasutech Ltd.,* AIR 2008 Del 99 (107): 2008 AIHC 508 (NOC): 2008 (5) Kant (NOC) 822 (DB).

Where the relief was sought restraining the defendants from presenting cheques in their favour for encashment, it was held to be barred by the provisions of section 41(b) and (d) as it would amount to restraining the defendants to institute civil or criminal proceeding against plaintiff on account of non-encashment of cheques which would amount to hampering access to justice; *Vasu Tech Ltd.* v. *Ratna Commercial Enterprises Ltd.,* AIR 2008 Del 122 (126): 2008 AIHC 616 (NOC): 2008 (5) ALJ (NOC) 995.

11. Clause (e): Prevent a Breach of Contract Specifically Unenforceable – Section 41 read in juxtaposition with section 14 makes it clear that a contract cannot be specifically enforced where for its non-performance compensation in money is an adequate relief and the contract in its nature is determinable and no injunction can be granted; *Managing Director, Century Textile Industries Ltd.* v. *Manju Gupta,* AIR 2009 MP 124: 2009 AIHC 589 (NOC): 2009 (3) Civ LJ 836: 2009 (2) MPLJ 70 (DB).

Where the plaintiff who was refused to be granted dealership alleged in the plaint itself that he had suffered loss of Rs. 1 lakh, the compensation being ascertainable, the mandatory injunction was held to be not grantable; *I.B.P. Co. Ltd.* v. *Ramashish Prasad Singh,* AIR 2006 Pat 91 (95): 2006 AIHC 2439: 2006 (1) BLJR 132: 2006 (1) Pat LJR 513.

A memorandum of understanding was signed between the plaintiff and the defendant 1 whereby the plaintiff was to market the product of defendant 1. It was alleged that the defendant 1 entered into an agreement with the defendant 2 which was in breach of memorandum of understanding between the plaintiff and the defendant 2. It was a disputed point as to whether the memorandum of understanding was enforceable in absence of a formal agreement between the parties. Held—Even if it is held that the memorandum of understanding was a complete agreement between the parties, the plaintiff was not entitled to grant of injunction for restraining the defendant 1 from marketing its product through the third party. He could be compensated in terms of money; *Cogent Silver Fibre Pte. Ltd.* v. *Noble Fibre Technologies Inc.,* AIR 2006 Del 292 (297-300): 2007 AIHC 19 (NOC): 2006 (3) CCC 673: 2006 (3) Cur CC 55.

For example, in a suit for perpetual injunction for restraining the defendant from interfering with suit premises, documentary evidence showed that the defendant was the chief tenant and plaintiffs were sub-tenants and there was no clear allegation against chief tenant showing interference with the possession of sub-tenants, it was held that mere demand of rent by chief tenant does not amount to interference in possession and as such injunction cannot be granted; *A.B. Hassan* v. *Sundari,* AIR 2002 Mad 342 (345-346): 2002 (3) Civ LJ 922: 2002 (2) Mad LJ 305: 2002 (3) Mad LW 798.

The Madras High Court also held that the court will not grant injunction where it appears, as in the present case, that any injunction, which may be granted would inflict more injury on the defendant than any advantage which the plaintiff would derive from it. In this case, the allegation made against the defendant is not reasonably clear that would cause injury to the plaintiffs. The first appellate court, therefore rightly refused the injunction sought for by the plaintiffs; *A.B. Hassan* v. *Sundari,* AIR 2002 Mad 342: 2002 (3) Civ LJ 922: 2002 (2) Mad LJ 305: 2002 (3) Mad LW 798.

Similarly, where the plaintiff was appointed as franchisee by the defendant or non-exclusive basis, the defendant reserving right to appoint any number of franchisees in that area as it deemed proper, and the agreement being determinable by serving 90 days, notice, such an agreement would not be specifically enforceable in view of section 41(e), injunction restraining defendant from appointing other franchisee cannot be granted; *Mittal Services* v. *Escotel Mobile Communications Ltd.,* AIR 2003 Del 410 (413): 203 CLC 1083.

There was an agreement between the Indian Oil Corporation and plaintiff for supply of kerosene. The plaintiff was held entitled for supplies subject to policy framed by the Corporation. The suit for injunction against the Corporation was maintainable and not barred by the provisions of section 41 for enforcement of contractual agreement between the parties; *Indian Oil Corpn. Ltd.* v. *Munesh Kumar,* AIR 2007 (NOC) 2600 (Uttr).

If the goods have already been sold, relief of permanent injunction cannot be granted. The plaintiff would be entitled to claim damages on the proof that he had suffered damages due to deficiency or breach on the part of the defendant; *Arti Steels Ltd.* v. *American President Lines Ltd.,* AIR 2007 (DOC) 189 P&H: (2007-1) 145 PLR 516.

Where the lease of fishery of plaintiff was cancelled by the authority, no injunction could be granted to allow the plaintiff to continue with his fishery right; *Bala Devi (Gram Pradhan)* v. *State of Uttar Pradesh,* AIR 2009 (NOC) 1363 (All).

12. No Injunction against a Foreign Court – The marriage was performed in Dehradun and the husband and wife were residing at Panchkula but the wife went abroad without consent of her husband. Thereafter, she returned but again left her matrimonial home and she filed a complaint for divorce in the Superior Court of New Jersey Chancery Division-Family Part Passaic County, *i.e.,* in a Foreign Court. The husband filed a suit for mandatory injunction/prohibitory injunction restraining the defendant wife from continuing her complaint or filing any other suit in any other foreign court in contravention of the provisions of the Hindu Marriage Act, 1955. Held—The defendant is not amenable to the jurisdiction of the court at Panchkula. Even if the injunction is declined, it cannot be said that the ends of justice will be defeated. The effect of decree for divorce if granted needs to be examined in terms of section 13 of the Code of Civil Procedure. The Foreign Court is yet to pass an order on the objections filed. The principles of comity *i.e.,* respect for the court in which commencement of continuation of action proceedings is sought, has to be borne in mind. The court also no jurisdiction to grant injunction restraining a person to institute proceeding in a court not subordinate to it. The Foreign Court cannot be treated as a court subordinate to Panchkula Court; *Rakesh Kumar* v. *Ashima Kumar,* AIR 2007 P&H 63 (65-66): 2007 AIHC 307 (NOC): 2007 (2) AIR Jhar (NOC) 663: 2007 (1) Punj LR 806.

The petitioner had voluntarily accepted the terms of the tender to supply the chairs of the make 'Godrej' of various models and the petitioner had quoted rates of 'Godrej'. The petitioner did not supply the chairs and therefore rescission of the agreement could not be termed to be illegal. The petitioner was not entitled for directions to the respondents to recall the tender and direct the respondents to issue fresh tender and allow the petitioner to participate in the same. It was difficult to infer that the forfeiture of EMD of the petitioner for not submitting the performance guarantee was not based on reasons. The petitioner was not entitled to reliefs claimed under section 14(1) and 41(e) of the SR Act; *Nawab Consultants For Ideas* v. *Govt. of NCT of Delhi,* 138 (2007) DLT 29 (28) (Del).

Where the transfer of land to a non-agriculturist could be made with the permission of the Government under section 118 of the H.P. Tenancy and Land Reforms Act, 1974, there being no absolute bar on transfer of land to non-agriculturist, the suit for specific performance and injunction of the basis of agreement would not be barred; *Rahul Bhargava* v. *Vinod Kohli,* AIR 2008 (NOC) 1144 (HP).

The families of the plaintiffs had been performing *pooja* as hereditary archakas from long time but no appointment letter was issued at any point of time either to the plaintiffs anecstors or to the plaintiffs. There was also no scheme or statutory relationship between archakas on one side and trustees on the other side. The plaintiffs were entitled to declaration that termination order was void and also relief of injunction as mere declaration was of no consequence; *Ramachandra* v. *Shivarama Narayana Bhal,* AIR 2009 (NOC) 595 Kant: 2008 (6) AIR Kant R 546.

Where the plaintiff after execution of agreement for development of site spent huge sum of money for thirteen years but the defendant committed various defaults and was trying to back out of the agreement so that the agreement could not be given effect to and the balance of convenience was in favour of the plaintiff besides an irreparable injury would be caused to the plaintiff if no injunction was granted, the plaintiff was held entitled to injunction to restrain the defendant from committing breach of such contract or causing the injury complained of unless the defendant gave appropriate security to the amount spent by the plaintiff in furtherance of agreement; *Kalidas Sadhu* v. *Sushil Kumar Agarwal,* AIR 2005 Cal 274 (277): 2005 (2) Cal HN 511 (DB).

13. Clause (f): Prevent an Act which is not Nuisance – The court will also refuse to grant injunction to prevent on the ground of nuisance, an act of which it is not reasonably clear that it will be a nuisance. Thus a mere apprehension of personal discomfort like deprivation of free air and light on account of construction of multistoried building by the defendant would not give rise to the existence of a *prima facie* case for grant of injunction especially when permission for construction was given by the Development Authority and the balance of convenience was also in favour of the defendants as they had invested huge amount and construction was taking place. In such circumstances grant of temporary injunction restraining defendants from construction of building would be illegal; *Ratna Paul* v. *Subhash Ranjan Paul,* AIR 2001 Gau 133 (138-139): (2001) 2 Gau LR 595.

The respondent sought injunction against the tenant of his shop that he was creating nuisance by not following rules for opening and closing time of shop. The suit was dismissed because the court could not monitor the hours prescribed for opening and closing the shop. The court directed the Inspector, Shop and Establishment to see the observance of rules regularly by the tenant; *Kuldeep Chander* v. *Chief Inspector of Shops,* AIR 2004 Del 130: 2004 (1) Cur CC 368: 2004 (109) DLT 454: 2004 (72) DRJ 553.

14. Clause (g): Continuing Breach Acquiesced by Plaintiff – The court will refuse to grant injunction to prevent a continuing breach in which the plaintiff has acquiesced. For example, where appellant, brother of respondent, constructed a house adjacent to that of respondent and respondent actively participated in construction and allowed her to take the support of his wall and never objected to it, the respondent woke up suddenly and started claiming of demolition of the same two years later, order for demolition would be refused by the court. The court would however grant injunction against future construction; *Dhaniya Bai* v. *Jiwan*, AIR 2003 MP 71 (73): (2002) 3 MPLJ 174.

Where the defendant had neither any right nor title in the land in dispute and the defendant had objected in the very beginning in raising construction on the land, the plaintiff could not be said to have acquiesced in the construction, the suit for demolition of construction and possession as decreed by the Trial Court and confirmed by the first appellate court was held to be proper; *Ram Narain* v. *Mirza Mohammad Hasnain*, AIR 2004 (NOC) 12 (All): 2003 All LJ 38.

15. Clause (h): When Equally Efficacious Relief Available – An injunction cannot be granted when equally efficacious relief can certainly be obtained by any other usual mode of proceeding except in case of breach of trust. For example, a coparcener has adequate remedy to impeach the alienation made by the *Karta*. He cannot therefore move the court for an injunction restraining the *karta* from alienating the coparcenary property; *Kailash Chand* v. *Bajrang Lal*, AIR 1997 Raj 205 (208): 1996 (2) Raj LR 622: 1997 (1) Raj LW 550: 1997 (1) WLC 38.

In *Bheemasenacharya Srinivasacharya Gudi* v. *Gadag Veera-Narayana Dev*, AIR 2002 Kant 1: 2001 AIR Kant HCR 2461: ILR (2002) 1 Kant 2377 plaintiffs rendered services of Parupatyagars and Paricharakas of temple as their hereditary right. They filed suit for injunction against the temple trust committee for restraining it from interfering plaintiff in rendering their services. There was no plea on behalf of the plaintiffs that they were not paid their salaries which were withheld by the committee for a particular period. It was held that section 41(h) was not attracted for refusing injunction and paying compensation; *Bheemasenacharya Srinivasacharya Gudi* v. *Gadag Veera-narayana Dev*, AIR 2002 Kant 1 (23): 2001 AIR Kant HCR 2461: ILR (2002) 1 Kant 2377.

But where under an agreement between the parties for development of property, provided for accounting liabilities of parties before completion of construction, property was delivered to the plaintiff and the power of attorney executed by defendant in favour of the plaintiff to facilitate execution of terms of agreement, dispute having arisen between the parties, the plaintiff sued the defendant for protection of possession on basis of agreement setting out in detail in plaint the outstanding liabilities of the defendant, the suit would be maintainable under the provisions of clause (h) of section 41 and section 14 of the Specific Relief Act as the plaintiff confines the claim only for protection of possessory rights by virtue of the terms of agreement and the same is a distinct relief not relatable to the monetary liabilities under the agreement; *Rocklives Constructions* v. *Trupti K. Patel*, AIR 2003 Kant 73 (75): (2002) 6 Kant LJ 214.

To succeed in a suit for injunction, the plaintiff must prove his possession and interference by the defendant and further injunction being an equitable remedy, he should also show that he is entitled to equity. Further, if an equally efficacious remedy can be obtained, injunction will not be granted in view of section 41(h); *S. Ponnuthai* v. *P. Muthusamy*, AIR 2004 Mad 450 (453, 455): 2004 (2) Mad LJ 530.

The plaintiff-company was running a nursing home. It allowed defendants who were doctors and share-holders of the company and also directors to practise their profession in chambers or cabins of the nursing home. The defendants, despite the termination of their directorships and withdrawal of permission to practise in the nursing-home entered the premises and disrupted the work. They were restrained by prohibitory injunction. It was held that a suit for injunction simpliciter would not lie where an equally efficacious remedy for possession could be obtained but in case of some jural relationship between the parties, the requirement of obtaining first decree of possession would not lie; *Geetanjali Nursing Home (P) Ltd.* v. *Dileep Makhija (Dr.)*, AIR 2004 Del 53 (62): 2005 (127) Comp Cas 659: 2004 (1) Comp LJ 457: 2003 (107) DLT 180.

Where the property was ancestral and co-parcenary and the succession was to be governed by uncodified Hindu Law, the plaintiffs, being agnates within five degrees, could claim right over property by way of partition, the suit for injunction was held to be not maintainable; *Kishan Singh* v. *Sucha Singh,* AIR 2008 (NOC) 925 (P&H).

The plaintiff alleged that the defendant was threatening to interfere with peaceful use of passage existing between adjoining properties. It was established that there was passage which was open and was owned by the State in possession of the Municipal Council. The plea that the passage was not dedicated to the public and therefore nobody had any right to passage was held to be not tenable. The plaintiff was entitled decree of injunction. His right to bring suit was not barred under section 41(h); *Sarabjeet Singh* v. *Chander Prakash,* AIR 2008 (NOC) 818 (HP).

The suit was filed on a dispute relating to cancellation of licence granted by the Municipal Board. The UP Municipalities Act, 1916 provides a complete mechanism for redressal of dispute. It was held that the jurisdiction of Civil Court under section 9 of the CPC stood excluded by necessary implication and the Civil Court was not competent to entertain any suit for mandatory injunction directing the Municipality to cancel the licence; *Chhedilal* v. *Rajaram (deceased),* AIR 2008 (NOC) 334 (All).

The notice for demolition was served to one of the occupiers of building, *i.e.,* the wife of the owner under section 254(2) of the Cantonments Act, 1924. The owner had remedy of appeal under section 274. It was held that the suit for permanent injunction was barred under section 41(h) of the SR Act; *Anil Kumar Jain* v. *Cantonment Board, Meerut Cantt.,* AIR 2007 (NOC) 1949 (All): 2007 (3) ALJ 282.

16. Clause (i): Conduct of Plaintiff – Where the plaintiff claims the land to be his, the defendant is attempting to raise construction on the land claiming the land to be his and the same to have been acquired in such a dispute in which the plaintiff ought to have sought for declaration of his title and consequential injunction, if at all it was in his possession. Filing of a mere suit for perpetual injunction is a conduct of plaintiff to avoid a normal course and conduct disentitles and profits the assistance of the court get the relief under section 41 of the Specific Relief Act, 1963. This was held by the Division Bench of the Allahabad High Court in *Dasnam Naga Sanyasi* v. *Allahabad Development Authority, Allahabad,* AIR 1995 All 418: 1996 All LJ 39: 1995 (1) All CJ 268: 1995 (1) All LR 509.

Where the vendor after leasing the plots for public purpose obtained sanction to layout plan but in contravention of the plan he sold the plots to the appellant, the appellant was not entitled to injunction against interference by Municipality with his possession which was not lawful; *Ammani* v. *Tiruchengode Municipality,* AIR 2004 Mad 333 (336): 2004 (3) CTC 251: 2004 (2) Mad LW 112.

Where the lands in dispute belonged to the State and were public properties and the petitioners were encroachers against whom the orders of eviction were passed by the competent authorities which had become final and the suits filed by the petitioner for claiming perfection of their title over suit land had also been dismissed, the petitioners could seek no injunction against the rightful owners and further no injunction could be granted against the statutory authority from discharging its statutory duties; *Laxmipriya Sahoo* v. *State of Orissa,* AIR 2005 Ori 174 (177): 2006 (3) Civ LJ 92: 2005 (100) Cut LT 378: 2005 (2) Ori LR 512.

Where the possession of plaintiff if any is nothing but as a trespasser or it is an unauthorised occupation, injunction cannot be granted against the true owner of the land; *Shivappa* v. *Administrator, Madev Textile Mills, Hubli,* AIR 2006 Kant 114 (115): 2006 (2) AIR Kant R 4: ILR 2006 Kant 1175: 2006 (1) Kant LJ 569.

Where in a suit for permanent injunction to restrain defendant from entering into suit land, the defendant alleged that she had advanced money to the plaintiff for purchase of some of the properties but the plaintiff got sale-deeds executed in his own name and the defendant being an illiterate lady could not understand the same. There were neither any pleadings nor any evidence to support the defendant regarding the declaration of title and the question was raised for the first time before the High Court, the provisions of section 41(g) and (i) were held to be not applicable; *Rohini Devi* alias *Rajeswari Dasi* v. *Babaji Jagannath Das,* AIR 2006 Ori 141 (143): 2006 (5) AKANT (NOC) 714: 2006 (101) Cut LT 646.

An injunction cannot be granted against the employer to conduct a domestic enquiry when the respondent seeks to enforce a contract for personal service; *Bannari Amma Sugars Ltd.* v. *R. Sakthivel,* (2008) 2 MLJ 646.

Where the plaintiff licensee had not paid licence fee for accommodation and initiated arbitration proceeding and after award of arbitrator there was no reason not to follow the same by the plaintiff, no injunction can be granted to him to restrain his eviction; *Bhagwan Dass Goel* v. *Vice-Chancellor Govind Ballabh Pant University of Agriculture and Technology,* AIR 2008 (NOC) 1402 (Utr).

17. Litigation thought of to Prevent Execution of Decree – Where the sale of immovable property in execution of decree by the defendant was sought to be restrained by the plaintiff seeking perpetual injunction on the ground of an unregistered alleged Will and that too surrounded by suspicions circumstances and the fact showed that the litigation was thought of only with a view to prevent further execution of decree lawfully obtained by the defendant but the defendant was successful in putting property to sale by way of execution and other defendant became successful bidder, the interference was uncalled for; *Kukkala Balakrishna* v. *Vijaya Oil Mills,* AIR 2009 (NOC) 648 (AP).

18. Clause (j): No Personal Interest of Plaintiff – An injunction cannot be granted when the plaintiff has no personal interest in the matter. Under clause (j) of section 41 of the Specific Relief Act, 1963, the interest of right of the plaintiff which is not shown to be in existence, cannot be protected by injunction; *Premji Ratansey Shah* v. *Union of India,* (1994) 5 SCC 547 (550): JT 1994 (6) SC 585: 1995 AIR SCW 2425.

In *Brahmin Nijog* v. *Badu Nijog,* AIR 2003 Ori 64: (2002) 94 Cut LT 755 as per old age custom, members of group of sevaks, namely Brahimn Nijog and Pujapanda Nijog performed puja of deity and were getting share out of offerings made to deity and also getting Dakshina from pilgrims for performing puja. Members of other group of sevaks namely Badu Nijog were only supposed to collect 'Bela' leaves and flowers and offer the same to Brahmin for performing puja. They cannot therefore be said to have no interest in the offerings made to the deity. Therefore, the suit filed by them for injunction against Trust Board and Badu Nijog for restraining them from implementing resolution providing for introducing ticket system is not hit by section 41(j) of the Specific Relief Act because the rights of servants having not been decided by any authorities; *Brahmin Nijog* v. *Badu Nijog,* AIR 2003 Ori 64 (71): (2002) 94 Cut LT 755.

Under section 307(5) of the M.P. Municipal Corporation Act, 1956 not only the Corporation but any other person can apply to the District Court for an injunction if a building does not comply with the provisions of the M.P. Municipal Corporation Act and bye-laws made thereunder. The remedy under section 307(5) of the said Act is independent of and different from the remedies under the Specific Relief Act. The remedies under the Specific Relief Act, as is clear from section 4, are provided for the individual civil rights. Section 41(j) of the Specific Relief Act, therefore, does not apply to the rights conferred on the Corporation or other persons; *Dilip Kaushal* v. *State of Madhya Pradesh,* AIR 2008 MP 324 (327): 2008 (3) Jab LJ 171: 2008 (4) MPHT 273: 2008 (3) MPLJ 591.

19. Injunction Restraining FIR – In case of *Sangram Singh* v. *State of Uttar Pradesh,* AIR 2010 All 65 it was held that injunction could not be issued restraining any person from lodging F.I.R.

42. Injunction to perform negative agreement.—Notwithstanding anything contained in clause (e) of section 41, where a contract comprises an affirmative agreement to do a certain act, coupled with a negative agreement, express or implied, not to do a certain act, the circumstances that the court is unable to compel specific performance of the affirmative agreement shall not preclude it from granting an injunction to perform the negative agreement:

Provided that the plaintiff has not failed to perform the contract so far as it is binding on him.

COMMENTS

Court-Fees – Law on – Under the proviso to section 42 of the old Specific Relief Act, a suit for a declaration is not maintainable if the plaintiff being able to seek further relief than a mere declaration of title omits to do so and under section 7(iv)(c) of the Court-fees Act 'to obtain a declaratory decree or order where consequential relief is prayed' court-fees are payable on the amount at which the plaintiff values the relief sought. It is also settled law that for the purpose of determining whether the suit is really one for a declaration simpliciter or for a declaration with consequential relief, the plaint has to be read as a whole. Any camouflage attempt in words to disguise a specific relief claimed in the garb of a suit for a declaration without a consequential relief cannot help the plaintiff; *Baldeo Singh Raghuraj Singh* v. *Gopal Singh Raghuraj Singh*, 1967 Jab LJ 350: ILR 1969 MP 264: AIR 1967 MP 221.

43. Amendment of Act 10 of 1940.—[*Rep. by the Repealing and Amending Act, 1974 (56 of 1974), sec. 2, Sch. I (w.e.f. 20-12-1974).*]

44. Repeal.—[*Rep. by the Repealing and Amending Act, 1974 (56 of 1974), sec. 2, Sch. I (w.e.f. 20-12-1974).*]

MODEL SPECIMEN

SPECIFIC PERFORMANCE OF CONTRACT

(Section 10, the Specific Relief Act, 1963)

1. The (name of the owner) the sole owner of the properties described in full in the schedule below entered into an agreement on.......for the sale of the said land and house to the plaintiff for a sum of Rs.....and in pursuance thereof executed a deed of agreement on the same day which is annexed herewith as a part of the plaint.

2. That out of the consideration (name of the owner) the defendant received a sum of Rs..........on the date of agreement and a further sum of Rs....on ....for which he granted a receipt in favour of the plaintiff which is also filed herewith. This balance of Rs.......was to be given to be the defendant on the execution of the sale deed.

3. That in pursuance of the agreement, the defendant purchased the stamp paper and handed it over to the plaintiff to prepare the sale deed which the plaintiff has got drawn up accordingly.

4. That inspite of repeated demands the defendant has not executed the sale deed and has been putting off the matter on some pretext or other. At last the plaintiff had to serve a lawyer's notice calling upon the defendant to execute the sale deed but inspite of the receipt thereof on.........the defendant has not executed the sale deed.

5. That the plaintiff is ready and willing to do his part of the contract and hereby offers the balance sum of the consideration to be paid to the defendant immediately the court so orders.

6. That in the circumstances unless the defendant be directed through court to perform his part of the contract, the plaintiff has no other remedy.

7. That the cause of action for the suit arose on the day of the agreement and on.........when the plaintiff gave the lawyer's notice to the defendant within the jurisdiction of this court.

The suit is valued at Rs......., Court fee payable on the consideration amount is Rs...... under section 7(x)(a) of the Court Fees Act, 1870, is affixed hereto.

Reliefs Sought

(i) Let a decree be passed against the defendant calling upon him to specifically perform the agreement dt.........by executing and registering a sale deed in favour of the plaintiff conveying the schedule land and house in favour of the plaintiff and the putting the plaintiff in possession thereof and if the defendant does not perform the same within a specified date fixed by the court the same be does through Court.

(ii) Let the costs of the suit or such other relief/reliefs as in the circumstances be deemed just and proper be awarded to the plaintiff.

•••